*To those students at
Perkins School of Theology
whose commitment to their discipleship
led them to watch over one another in love
and thereby discover the open secret
of their Methodist heritage.*

THE EARLY METHODIST CLASS MEETING

ITS ORIGINS AND SIGNIFICANCE

David Lowes Watson

DISCIPLESHIP RESOURCES   NASHVILLE

Cover design adapted from class and band tickets in the
private collection of Dr. Frank Baker.

ISBN 0-8817-107-5
Library of Congress Card Catalog Number: 85-71073

CONTENTS

FOREWORD

The full story of the class and band meetings in early Methodism has never been told before—despite the fact that stereotypes about them are firmly fixed in Methodist tribal memories, and in church history generally. In their heyday, such a story did not need much telling; it was a matter of common awareness. Nor was it likely that the story would have been told by those who were letting the tradition slide; they were too intent upon their own innovations. Now, however, with the great era of Methodist expansionism over—with our entry, willy-nilly, into a "postliberal age"—the time ripens for recalling our origins, not for nostalgia's sake but with a view to the transvaluation of the perennial.

To what extent, on the one hand, was the class meeting format an expedient device, suited to its own time but finally outpaced by progress? And, on the other hand, in what sense was it the practical implementation of a distinctive view of the Christian order of salvation—of the need for intimate Christian fellowship in the mysterious process of our "growth in grace and in the knowledge of our Lord Jesus Christ." We know a great deal about the spiritual heroism of singular individuals, and a great deal about the anomalies of institutional, mass Christianity. But we are less familiar with small-group Christianity and its linkage-functions between conversion and nurture, on the one hand, and our *koinonia* in the Body of Christ, on the other.

This linkage is all the more important because of the rise and spread, in what Paul Gross has labeled "our psychological society," of humanistic encounter groups in great abundance and variety—all aimed more at self-help than social transformation. The churches have their coterie-theologies and interest groups galore, but not many of them are covenanted to Christian mutuality in prayer, to the "searching of the scriptures," to the moral reinforcement of their members, to on-site works of love and mercy. Memories of the class meeting tradition linger on, but they stand in need of the sort of refurbishment and reinterpretation that Dr. Watson has now provided us.

One of this volume's special merits is the way in which it tells the class meeting story in loving and circumstantial detail. The records, scattered as they are, have been ransacked and winnowed. Moreover, in addition to all the familiar references, Watson has come up with primary source material that most of us never knew existed. From this treasure trove of data he has constructed a credible narrative of how the class meetings came to be so distinctive a feature of early Methodism—how and why they worked and what their impact was on their environing society. He has also considered their distinctive self-understanding of the universal church and of themselves as "little churches" within it. This, not incidentally, goes a long way toward explaining the difference between the Methodist movement ("the connection") and other revivals at the same time that flourished and then faded.

But, not content with a historical perspective alone, Dr. Watson has gone on to probe the analogs between early class meetings and contemporary group theories; the result is a rich treasure of striking suggestions about possible correlations between the eighteenth century situation and our own. Besides all this, as pastor and seminary professor, he has been experimenting with updated versions of the older forms for long enough to have formulated some truly practical proposals. In the course of this he has discovered how eager church folks are, and even seminarians, for more orderly and intentional patterns for further experiences of "life in the Spirit."

What he has thus learned, he is now prepared to teach—on two levels at once. On the level of program and praxis he has already published a handbook for Covenant Discipleship Groups in local congregations and communities. Its title, *Accountable Discipleship*, implies the unoriginal but sadly neglected thesis that solitary discipleship, or what is so-called, is actually a misnomer; but also that mass evangelism tends to be shallow rooted. Something more is urgently needed—namely, Christian comradeship, on a human scale and with firm commitments. Christian living requires spiritual direction, and this is provided more adequately by groups of covenanted Christians who make themselves accountable to each other than by single individuals to others. In Watson's handbook, there are abundant practical directives for the oversight of such groups within the sacramental life of the church at large. In this way, it manages to overcome the false distinction between evangelism (outreach and in-gathering) and nurture (growth and fruitage).

Here, in *The Early Methodist Class Meeting*, we have the needed background filled in, with an extensive historical review, an insightful theological appraisal, plus an interesting analysis of contemporary socio-psychological theory. The focus is on the ecclesiological import of the interrelationships between the intimate church (*ecclesiola*) and the general church (*ecclesia*)—without supersessions on either side. The historical research is rigorous and comprehensive, and the narrative skills impressive. I learned a lot from it (especially from the appendices!) and found several familiar questions recast in a new perspective.

But more: There is a demonstration here of the consonance of the Wesleyan doctrines of justification and sanctification with the dynamisms of group experience which strikes me as an important contribution to a richer understanding of Wesleyan theology in general. The result is a fresh interpretation of the idea of Christian intimacy as a resource for church renewal. Dr. Watson is not talking simplistically about more revivals of ancient ways; his concern is for their adaptation and further development. The class meeting was more than another experiment in "Christian togetherness." It was, in fact, a *schola animarium*—a "school for growing souls." It was also an agency in the permanent Christian revolution on behalf of God's kingdom, God's righteousness—here on earth as in heaven. *The Early Methodist Class Meeting* provides ample grist for further reflection on these questions, for further study, and further practical action.

The book afforded me yet another level of personal satisfaction: It is a splendid instance of a working partnership of authentic zeal in evangelism with rigorous standards of scholarship. It is well-known that in the academic establishment (including its Methodist wing!) evangelism has not been widely accepted as a scholarly discipline in its own right—and there is enough negative evidence to explain such an unfortunate prejudice without justifying it. Here, however, is a book by an evangelist about evangelism that meets all the public norms of theological scholarship—rigor, competence, cogency, originality. Its "data base" is comprehensive, both evidence and argument are extensive and careful, the bibliographies are exemplary, and the conclusions persuasive. Thus it is a fruitful marriage of "knowledge and vital piety." It is also a quiet reproof to biased critics.

Western Christianity, in the past two centuries, has been dominated by expansive moods and patterns. We are witnesses to a sharp deflation of this optimism. Langdon Gilkey has spoken presciently of the need for "theology of culture in decline"; George Lindbeck has invited us to reappraise "the nature of doctrine in a postliberal age." Mainline churches, hobbled with their top-heavy structures and outmoded management theories, struggle unsuccessfully with seepages in membership and morale. Even so, the Christian future does not lie on the other side, with the electronic church or with the neo-fundamentalists.

What is required is spiritual refreshment and commitment, sustained by the disciplines of prayer and grace. This can be provided by various sorts of Christian covenant fellowship that can hold the faithful to account and aid their maturation toward "the fullness of faith." Individuals may attempt this on their own but rarely to any great effect, save for the occasional saint. Small congregations (and "sects") sometimes set themselves above the anomalies of being "mixed companies," but they seldom stay the course. The positive alternative to such extremes would seem to be a networking of small groups, taprooted in the church, consciously dependent upon the means of grace which only the church catholic can supply—yet also free to develop appropriate patterns of spiritual discipline and service, and courage for Christian prophecy in society. This would be something rather different from pietistic anti-ecclesiasticism and equally different from the Troeltschian dichotomy of "church" and "sect."

No "new" evangelistic formulary is a panacea, and none will supersede our need for the liturgical and sacramental riches of the church universal. Watson's proposals about a repristination of the older class meeting are more demanding than most nominal Christians will welcome. They are aimed at the unconverted, out of the church and within. This is evangelism in a new key and it holds the promise of a future that will conserve our heritage by reviving its genius. Such a review and "prescription" should, therefore, be read with care, its references checked, its conclusion pondered. The harvest of any such effort is bound to be fruitful.

ALBERT C. OUTLER

PREFACE

There is comparatively little in the earliest Methodist literature about the class meeting. Even though Wesley makes many references to the importance of attending it, especially in his correspondence, his descriptions of how it actually functioned are quite terse, and other eighteenth-century references are few and far between. Moreover, when detailed accounts do emerge with more frequency in the nineteenth century, they tend to be written with the implicit hope of revitalizing what had already become a moribund dimension of Methodist life and practice.

There is a good reason for this paucity of early literature: the class meeting was a means to an end rather than an end in itself. It was taken for granted by the early Methodists that its purpose was well known and its dynamic understood. What we have in the contemporary accounts of Wesley and others, therefore, is not so much a description of how the classes functioned as an explanation of why they met each week, and what they were intended to accomplish. In a word, they were points of accountability for faithful Christian living in the world. And as long as they continued to serve this purpose, it was more important to affirm their objective than assess their method.

This is why studies of the class meeting through the perspectives of small group dynamics—interpersonal relationships, faith development, pastoral oversight, spiritual nurture, etc.—can easily miss the point. All of these perspectives were present, of course, and significantly so; but none of them was the immediate concern of Wesley and his preachers. What mattered to them was that people who had met the challenge of Christian discipleship in their lives, whatever the stage of their spiritual pilgrimage, should have a means of mutual support. The class meeting was the essential referent for early Methodist commitment, which is why the following study is first a theological investigation, and only then a historical and sociological survey.

Much of the material in these pages was originally researched for a Duke University Ph.D. dissertation in 1975-78. That it only now comes to print is to some extent an indication of the practical imperatives of the class meeting, since much of my time has subsequently been devoted to applying its principles in the contemporary church—something which proved to be more of a priority than preparing the research for publication. And if one might be so bold as to make the comparison, the outcome is a great deal more Wesleyan than once it might have been, in that the years of application have resulted in an adaptation of the class meeting for the contemporary church: Covenant Discipleship Groups. Practical guidelines for establishing and maintaining these groups can be found in a companion volume, *Accountable Discipleship*, published by Discipleship Resources as a handbook for use in local congregations. The purpose of what follows in this volume is to make available to the interested reader a more detailed theological and historical analysis, including some materials from eighteenth and nineteenth century Methodism which are not readily accessible. It is intended for use with the handbook as an introduction to further dimensions of the Methodist heritage.

I owe much to those whose scholarship has guided me into these paths, and whose example continues to stimulate further investigations. Frank Baker, who supervised the original doctoral study, has been unfailingly generous, courteous, supportive, and exacting—qualities rarely found in quite that combination. He has graciously allowed a number of items from his personal collection of early Methodist documents to be photographed and included in the appendices, thereby greatly enhancing the volume. Robert E. Cushman, who exemplifies the highest accomplishments of ecclesial learning, opened up for me the great wealth of the Anglican tradition, so pivotal for an understanding of Wesley, yet so difficult for a product of British Methodism like myself to acquire in England. Frederick Herzog, whose considerable theological craftsmanship is always held accountable to the imperatives of Christian discipleship, has been a constant safeguard against allowing my fascination with the class meeting to become an end in itself. And most recently I am deeply indebted to Albert C. Outler. His guidance and friendship have been a high privilege of my years in Dallas, and his insights have occasioned many improvements to the manuscript. He has a legendary reputation in the church, and this is altogether warranted. But I can further testify that his awesome scholarship is wholly dedicated to serving the Christ whom he knows and loves.

At the General Board of Discipleship, I have been greatly helped by the General Secretary, Ezra Earl Jones, who encouraged me to pursue the two-fold approach of academic research into the early class meeting and its application to contemporary Christian living. That Covenant Discipleship Groups are emerging as a connectional program of The United Methodist Church is in large measure due to his vision. In preparing the book for publication, I have received warm collegiality from the staff at Discipleship Resources: from Chester E. Custer, who shepherded the publication of this volume and the companion *Account-able Discipleship;* from George E. Koehler, who has given wise editorial direction; from J. Lee Bonnet, whose production skills have shaped the book with sensitivity; and from Mary Pugh, whose expertise in connectional resourcing has honed the whole enterprise.

I am grateful to Jerry D. Campbell, Roger L. Loyd, and the staff of the Bridwell Library, Southern Methodist University, for their assistance with further research; to my colleagues at the Perkins School of Theology for their support in a community of learning; to the Perkins and Divinity School Libraries at Duke University for permission to reproduce excerpts from their copies of Josiah Woodward's *Account of the Religious Societies* and the pamphlet *A Description of Class Meetings;* to Lawrence O. Kline, Head of the Monographic Cataloging Department at the Perkins Library, for generously arranging the reproduction of items from the Baker Collection; and to D.W. Riley, Keeper of Printed Books at The John Rylands Library, University of Manchester, for his assistance with research in the Methodist Archives. I owe a special word of thanks to my good friend in the faith, Judge Merrill Hartman. The entire manuscript was prepared on his word processor, without which the whole undertaking would have been much more laborious.

My wife Gayle, my daughter Dessa, and my son Timothy have watched this project form and develop over the years. They know better than most how much it has been a work of grace. But they may not know, because I usually fail to tell them, that they are my most important means of grace.

Perkins School of Theology
Dallas, Texas
May 1984

Introduction

WESLEY AND THE CHRISTIAN TRADITION

Earliest Origins: Primitive Christian House Groups

Strictly speaking, the title of this study takes us back to the first century A.D. and the taproot of the Christian tradition. To examine the New Testament in its context with the insights of social historiography makes clear that the pattern of the primitive *ekklesía* was precisely the sort of small group fellowship which provided the basis of early Methodism. In his seminal book, *The First Urban Christians*, Wayne A. Meeks observes that the basic cell of the Christian movement was the individual household-based group, the nucleus of which was often an existing household.[1] The letters of Paul make clear that these groups "enjoyed an unusual degree of intimacy, high levels of interaction among members, and a very strong sense of internal cohesion and of distinction both from outsiders and from 'the world.'" Moreover, the "intimate, close-knit life of the local groups was seen to be simultaneously part of a much larger, indeed ultimately worldwide, movement or entity."[2] Once again the pedigree of early Methodism emerges with force and clarity.

The lineage of these household groups, from the first-century Roman Empire to the present day, is a component of the Christian tradition which has yet to receive full recognition, not least because it necessitates the detailed re-interpretation of a wealth of data which have hitherto been viewed as peripheral to ecclesial history. It is a task which requires urgent attention, however, because substantial initiatives for this re-interpretation have already been taken by social historians.[3] And if the groups are not to be viewed as mere social phenomena, they must be grounded firmly in the tradition.[4] Such at least is the purpose of this study, in which an attempt is made to view the early class meeting, not only as small-group fellowship through the experiences of those who belonged to Methodist Societies, but also as *ecclesiola in ecclesia* through the theology and churchmanship of John Wesley as he stood in the Christian tradition.

1

Traditioning the Faith

As with all traditioning, this merits a word of caution. Historiographers have long been telling us that we cannot use the past to buttress contemporary preconceptions, and Methodism has certainly had its share of this abuse. Yet on the further premise that the Christian tradition has much to offer us if we will take our forebears *just as they were*, and accept the integrity of their witness in its own context, the early Methodist class meeting merits careful examination. Quite apart from the fact that this happens to be good historiography, it provides an important link between the two dimensions of traditioning the Christian faith: the handing *on* of the gospel within the ecclesial community, and the handing *over* of the gospel to the world. Christians who take their witness seriously are always sensitive to the particular factors which govern their social, cultural, economic, intellectual, and religious context, and thereby understand more perceptively what it means to be a Christian in different contexts. This is to do no more than to take seriously what Christians in times past perceived to be their responsible witness to the world, and accept the integrity of their conclusions with the same charity and understanding we might expect from future generations who study our own contemporary witness.[5]

Methodist Discipleship

Methodism was forged in the grist and grind of eighteenth-century England, and its folklore is rich in the experiences of ordinary people endeavoring to live as Christians in the world. They took their commitment with sufficient seriousness to want to sustain one another in their discipleship, and they found that the most effective way to do this was to meet together once a week in order to be accountable to one another. These weekly *class meetings*, a subdivision of the Methodist societies, were regarded by Wesley as the "sinews" of the movement.[6] Not only did they have a specific format; they were grounded in solid theological principles which, as with all of Wesley's theology, were couched in the language of ordinary people with a view to their application in practical discipleship. This gave the class meeting validity as well as authenticity, and ensured that the weekly gatherings were not only a point of mutual accountability, but were also a deep traditioning of the gospel.

Wesley as Church Leader

To a large degree, this was due to the leadership of Wesley himself, who placed the connection of Methodist societies under his pastoral supervision, and exercised this responsibility with meticulous care. Through his *episkopé*, they were led into an understanding of discipleship which evinced both the structure and the spirit of faithful Christian witness. His upbringing had instilled in him the importance of the Christian tradition, not least because this had been the apologetic touchstone of the English Reformation and the church which it spawned. His encounter with Moravian Pietism, together with the Puritan heritage of English Nonconformity, subsequently gave him the necessary complement of the continental Reformation: a rich doctrine of justification by faith.

Wesley as Theologian

We can follow these developments in Wesley's theology and churchmanship in some detail, because there are few past leaders of the church who have left more complete records of their life and work. His journal presents us, with relatively few gaps, an almost daily account of his activities, his thought, and his reactions to the world in which he lived.[7] His letters supplement this record with the richness of eighteenth-century dialogue, providing the informalities which enable us to assess his limitations as well as his strengths.[8] His own published writings and his editing of many earlier and contemporary works further make it possible to follow the Methodist movement as an embryonic church.[9] Yet Wesley has been underestimated in the history of the church, and comparatively underwritten, not least because we do know so much about the man himself and what he did. The impact of his leadership and the almost superhuman dimensions of his daily routine have frequently led to the neglect of his theology, and his mission as an evangelist has rendered him academically suspect to those willing to settle for a superficial reading of his work. As the late Tom Dring put it:

> He has been called an evangelist; and evangelists are a mixed crowd. We have had many evangelists not at all like him; we have had none quite like him. Wesley was much more than an evangelist . . . he was interested in everything and yet quite

detached. . . . To combine detachment with love seems an almost impossible task, and yet Wesley accomplished it.[10]

He was not, Albert Outler has observed, "a theologian's theologian. His chief intellectual interest, and achievement, was in what one could call a folk theology: the Christian message in its fullness and integrity, in 'plain words for plain people' "[11]

This concern to make theology relevant to Christian living, and to present the Christian message to as many as possible, has left us without a detailed Wesleyan systematic. It therefore becomes important to read him in his own context and within the Christian tradition as a whole.[12] To do so is to find, in the relationship he maintained between the Methodist societies and the Church of England, nothing less than the essential tension of the Christian faith: mission and order, scripture and tradition, prophetic and priestly ministry. Just as important are his distinctive doctrines of justification and sanctification, in which he brought together the fundamental theological issues of the sovereignty of God and the freedom of the human will.

The Praxis of Wesley's Ministry

If it is important to read Wesley in the context of the tradition he received and handed on, it is just as important to acknowledge that his churchmanship and his theology were profoundly affected by his ministry. It is this which arguably makes him the most significant ecclesial leader in Protestantism, in that he constantly took into account the reaction of the people of eighteenth-century England to the message he and his preachers proclaimed. A careful reading of the minutes of early Methodist conferences clearly indicates not only that the content and form of early Methodist preaching occasioned questions of doctrine and practice, but that the responses and experiences of the society members were integral to the formulation of his developing thought and polity.[13]

In other words, Wesley took seriously the manifestations of the gospel among ordinary people, granted them full integrity, and correlated them with the criteria of the faith already established in the Church of England. Thus, while the class meeting gives us an important insight into Wesley's view of the church, his ecclesiology is just as helpful for an understanding of how the classes functioned. Methodist polity was not unique as an ecclesial or social structure, but it was effective in the context of the eighteenth-century revival, and was adopted primarily because it proved effective in practice. Indeed, as Wesley himself observed, the class meeting was conceived at Bristol while the society was occupied with quite another matter—a building debt, as it happened.[14] Yet it was quickly adopted as a feature of the movement once it proved its usefulness. It was typical of a pragmatism which Wesley often described as the use of "prudential means of grace," the practical measures he took to meet the exigencies of a given situation for which there might not be a precedent, but against which no scriptural or doctrinal objections could be made.[15] Frank Baker's assessment is succinct and apposite:

> Each situation was approached with a prayerful heart and an open mind, unswayed by prejudice, by an undue regard for precedents, or by any inflexible convictions about the pattern of Methodist polity. The eventual expedient might be derived from an ecclesiastical practice ancient or modern, from church or sect; it might equally well come from the committee-room or the law court, from Parliament or prayer meeting. It might be the result of "pure chance." Wesley was not concerned about the source, so long as the projected method of furthering the purpose of God in Methodism met his own peculiar brand of churchmanship—and *worked.*[16]

The Purpose of the Church

This predominantly practical churchmanship points to the focal point of his ecclesiology: an overwhelming concern for the *purpose* of the church. There was no question that Wesley saw this to be first and foremost a reaching out to people with the gospel. He was convinced that Methodists had been called by God to take the good news of salvation in Christ the length and breadth of the land, and that all other questions of order and doctrine were ultimately of secondary importance. It is this which explains his concern for the essentials of the faith, and his disdain for the strife occasioned by "mere opinions."[17] And it is this which broadened his vision of the church from details of episcopal order and succession—on which he was frequently taken to task by Anglican clerics—to the order of God's salvation in the world. To understand him in this regard is to resolve the question of his inconsistency on separation from the Church of England, and to be directed to his ecclesiological tension of authority and commission, of structure and spirit, of tradition and divine imperative, all subjected to the larger work of proclaiming Christ abroad.[18]

Wesley's Protestant Heritage

Fundamental to the whole of Wesley's theology and churchmanship was his English Protestant heritage. As an Anglican he affirmed the integrity and authority of the visible and universal church, of which the Church of England was a particular manifestation.[19] He also inherited the Puritan concept of the gathered church, the *coetus electorum*, an ecclesiology which rejected the traditional authority of the church, and based its tenets on scripture alone.[20] The Wesleyan emphasis was that both concepts must be held in tension. He acknowledged the validity of a gathered community, elected by God for a purpose; but he did not thereby regard as invalid the wider concept of an inclusive and visible church, reaching out to all, firmly in and of the world, a means of God's prevenient grace.[21] The reality of *ecclesiolae*, little churches, of which his societies were a self-evident manifestation, was something he affirmed from his earliest years, and found to be authenticated by the fruits of the Spirit among the people to whom he ministered. Yet he grounded his societies in the Anglican tradition, the mainstream of English Protestantism; and as long as he lived, he regarded them as valid only insofar as they were firmly part of the larger church— *ecclesiolae in ecclesia.*[22] It is precisely this presupposition of Wesley, that Methodism was grounded in the Anglican tradition, which is the key to an understanding of the Methodist societies and classes. He never perceived them as anything other than integral to the visible Church of England.[23]

The Tension of Wesley's Churchmanship

This is why, in spite of the organizing genius which Wesley brought to the movement, it is a mistake to infer that Methodism was planned; it just happened. To use Frank Baker's words again, "Wesley had not the slightest intention of founding a new denomination. His avowed purpose was not 'to form the plan of a new church,' but to reform the old one."[24] And this remained his purpose to the end of his ministry. In 1784 he ordained elders for America, and the following year for Scotland, but he still resisted separation of the English societies from the

Church of England, even though the practical steps he took to ensure their future were quite clearly "setting up Methodism as a separate institution."[25] As late as December 1789, he felt it important to argue the point:

> When the people joined together, simply to help each other to heaven, increased by hundreds and thousands, still they had no more thought of leaving the Church than of leaving the kingdom. Nay, I continually and earnestly cautioned them against it; reminding them that we were a part of the Church of England, whom God had raised up, not only to save our own souls, but to enliven our neighbours, those of the Church in particular. And at the first meeting of all our Preachers in Conference, in June, 1744, I exhorted them to keep to the Church; observing, that this was our peculiar glory,—not to form any new sect, but, abiding in our own Church, to do to all men all the good we possibly could.[26]

This resolve proved to be a source of tension within the Methodist societies, not least because of the precedents of English Nonconformity, and the influence of Dissenters on the membership.[27] But the basis of Methodism's distinctive polity had deep ecclesiological foundations. In the priorities of order and mission which Wesley constantly sought to maintain lay the tensions of prophetic and priestly ministry which have always given the church its true identity in the world. As Colin Williams has observed, Wesley struggled to an amazing degree with these tensions because he believed that the unity and continuity of the church were vital to its mission no less than the true preaching of the Word.[28]

To understand the extent to which this ecclesiological struggle engaged Wesley throughout his leadership of early Methodism, it will be important to examine its two polarities in some detail: the Anglicanism of his upbringing and education; and the Puritanism he imbibed as his ministry took him into every corner of a nation which, less than a hundred years earlier, had been religiously divided to the point of Civil War.

Chapter One

WESLEY'S UNDERSTANDING OF THE CHURCH

1. THE ANGLICAN TRADITION

The Visible Church of England

Wesley's concept of the church underwent a number of changes during the course of his life's work, but the underlying principle was always that of the 19th Article of the Church of England:

> 1. The visible Church of Christ is a congregation of faithful men, in the which the pure word of God is preached and the sacraments be duly ministered according to Christ's ordinance in all those things that of necessity are requisite to the same.
> 2. As the Church of Jerusalem, Alexandria, and Antioch have erred; so also the Church of Rome hath erred, not only in their living and manner of ceremonies, but also in matters of faith.[1]

Wesley followed this definition closely in his sermons and his polemical writings, using the first part of the article often, both as defense and attack against his detractors.[2] He also seems to have accepted the reasoning of the second part of the Article, less frequently cited than the first, but significant both in its original purpose and function. At the time of its composition in 1552, it was probably intended, not only to refute the claim of Rome to be the only church, but also to exclude the Reformers' definition of the true church as invisible. Wesley's ecclesiology was Anglican, therefore, on two counts: that the church universal consisted of different parts, with no one church having pre-eminence over the others; and further, that its unity was visible, a definition which implied that it was inclusive rather than selective. He did not wish to press the terminology of the first part of the Article to the point of excluding from the larger church "all those congregations in which any unscriptural doctrines, which cannot be affirmed to be 'the pure word of

9

God,' are sometimes, yea, frequently preached; neither all those congregations, in which the sacraments are not 'duly administered.' "³

His interpretation of the 19th Article, as with much else which he
affirmed in the Anglican tradition, was in fact quite pragmatic. He
regarded the Church of England as the particular visible order of
the church, "that part, those members, of the Universal Church who are
inhabitants of England, in whom 'there is one Spirit, one hope, one
Lord, one faith'; which have 'one baptism,' and 'one Lord and Father of
all.' "⁴ And he was firmly committed to this church. He tempered his
loyalty with the passing years, and many of his ecclesial relationships
proved difficult and tense. But he constantly expressed a genuine
affection for the Church of England, and persistently defended it as the
most scriptural national church in the world, next only to the primitive
church itself.⁵ At the 1755 Conference, in many ways the most critical in
terms of the pressures within Methodism to separate, he presented an
impassioned appeal against such a move:

> If we continue in the Church, not by chance, or for want of
> thought, but upon solid and well-weighed reasons, then we should
> never speak contemptuously of the Church, or anything pertaining
> to it. In some sense it is the mother of us all, who have been
> brought up therein. We ought never to make her blemishes matter
> of diversion, but rather of solemn sorrow before God. We ought
> never to talk ludicrously of them; no, not at all, with clear necessity.
> Rather, we should conceal them, as far as ever we can, without
> bringing guilt upon our own conscience. . . . It is expedient, in the
> highest degree, that we should be tender of the Church to which
> we belong.⁶

Not that this allegiance to the Church of England was mere sentiment.
In exhortation, instruction, or disputation, Wesley was at pains to dem-
onstrate his firm adherence to its discipline. To those who objected that
he did not observe its laws, but rather undermined them, he retorted
that in every parish where he had served, the rubrics had been observed
with a "scrupulous exactness, not for wrath, but for conscience' sake."⁷
The real question, as he pointedly argued, was not whether *he* ought to
obey the rubrics of the church, but whether, in fact, the rubrics were
being observed at all, and by whom. His reasoning was forceful: that he
was keeping the discipline of the Church of England more strictly than
his critics. Indeed, late in life he conceded that in his youth he had been
not only a member of the Church of England, "but a bigot to it,

believing none but the members of it to be in a state of salvation." He began to "abate of this violence in 1729," but was still "as zealous as ever," observing every point of church discipline and teaching all his pupils to do likewise.[8]

The Anglican Theological Method

The source of Wesley's ecclesiology was the Anglican theological method in which he had been schooled, whereby all matters of faith and practice were subjected to the three-fold criteria of scripture, tradition, and reason. Thus he invariably took scripture as the bedrock of his churchmanship, in accordance with the 6th Article of the Church of England:

> Holy Scripture containeth all things necessary to salvation; so that whatsoever is not read therein, nor may be proved thereby, is not to be required of any man, that it should be believed as an article of the faith, or be thought requisite necessary to salvation.[9]

He regarded the rule of scripture as the difference between two ranks of Christian—the higher and the lower—and in his many discussions of the nature of church government, scripture was always the final authority.[10]

Next to scripture, he affirmed the authority of the primitive church, so much so that he later acknowledged his esteem of the early church fathers to have been too high during his early years as a scholar. On his return voyage from Georgia, he noted in his journal that he had "bent the bow too far" by making antiquity a coordinate rather than a subordinate rule with scripture; and further, that he had extended "antiquity too far, even to the middle or end of the fourth century, . . . believing more practices to have been universal in the ancient Church than ever were so. . . ."[11] Although the early church fathers never assumed as predominant a position in his thought as they had during these early years at Oxford, and while he limited their authority to that of the ante-Nicene period, Wesley nonetheless continued to regard them as an important secondary norm.[12] In 1749, for example, he delayed a journey to Rotterdam for twenty days in order to dispute with Dr. Conyers Middleton as to the fathers' place in Christian tradition.[13] And in the preface to his abridgement of the Epistles of Clement of Rome,

Ignatius, and Polycarp, he made clear his high regard for their contribution to the life of the church:

> The authors of the following collection were contemporaries of the holy Apostles. . . . We cannot therefore doubt . . . of what they deliver to us as the Gospel of Christ; but ought to receive it, though not with equal veneration, yet with only little less regard than we do the sacred writings of those who were their masters and instructors.[14]

Wesley further affirmed the Anglican theological method in holding reason to be an interpretative principle, both for the scriptures, and for faith itself. He trusted that in all people there was an active reasonableness which could be convinced by rational argument.[15] His caution in testing every innovation by logic, and his resistance to the very enthusiasm of which he was so frequently accused, prevented Methodism's emphasis upon personal experience from degenerating into mere emotionalism.[16] We find this most clearly evidenced in his *Appeals to Men of Reason and Religion*:

> Is it not reasonable then to love God? . . . seeing he is the parent of all good. . . . Is it not reasonable also to love our neighbour: every man whom God hath made? . . . Is it not reasonable, then, that "as we have opportunity" we should "do good unto all men": not only friends, but enemies . . . ? If therefore you allow that it is reasonable to love God, to love mankind, and to do good to all men, you cannot but allow that religion which we preach and live to be agreeable to the highest reason. . . . We join with you then in desiring a religion founded on reason, and every way agreeable thereto. But one question still remains to be asked: "What do you mean by reason?" I suppose you mean the eternal reason, or the nature of things: the nature of God and the nature of man, with the relations necessarily subsisting between them. Why, this is the very religion *we* preach: a religion evidently founded on, and every way agreeable to, eternal reason, to the essential nature of things.[17]

Wesley's purpose in these polemical "Appeals" was not so much to answer the many ill-informed and hostile attacks which Methodism occasioned,[18] but to address the more respected representatives of the Hanoverian church. The eighteenth century was the flowering of the Age of Reason, and in the early part of the century the prestige of

English thought stood high. Isaac Newton was unfolding an orderly universe, a creation guided by a purpose and system which human intelligence could grasp; and John Locke was pointing to a concept of the human mind which assumed that Christianity could and should be attractive to the light of reason. The overriding concern of the age was for a rational Christianity, and this governed much of the theological discourse of the period: in Latitudinarianism, for example, which tried to assimilate the new intellectualism; and in Deism, which went so far as to concede the very tenets of the faith to reason.[19]

The Polemics of Separation

Wesley clearly emerges in the *Appeals* as a product of this climate. As we shall note in the following chapter, he was not slow to engage his critics on the issues of faith and reason; but he was also ready to answer those who accused him of separatist tendencies. " 'Leave the Church'! What can you mean?" he taunted. "Do we leave so much as the *church walls*? Your own eyes tell you we do not. Do we leave the *ordinances* of the Church. You daily see and know the contrary. . . . In truth, I cannot conceive what you mean. I doubt you cannot conceive yourself. . . . And no marvel, for it is a true observation: *Nonsense is never to be understood.*"[20] A rational appraisal of the Methodist societies, he argued, could not but reveal a marked difference from Quakers, Baptists, Independents, or Presbyterians. "They avowedly separate from the church: we utterly disavow any such design. They severely, and almost continually inveighed against the doctrines and discipline of the church they left: we approve both the doctrines and discipline of our church, and inveigh only against ungodliness and unrighteousness."[21]

The real dissenters, Wesley claimed, were those who failed to abide by the 19th Article of the Church of England. Since this clearly stated that the Church of England was a body of faithful people among whom the Word of God was preached and the sacraments duly administered, the worst dissenters from the church were in reality the "unholy men of all kinds," the "swearers, Sabbath-breakers, drunkards," those who were "unsound in the faith" and who denied the truth of the scriptures. These dissenters "of a very high kind" struck at the foundation of the church, because, if their principles were to prevail, "there could be no true Church upon the earth."[22]

To refute the charge of schism leveled against the Methodist movement, Wesley did not hesitate to press the argument to the very identity of the Church of England:

> I ask once more, "What do you mean by schism?" "Schism! Schism! Why, it is separating from the Church." Ay, so it is. And yet *every* separating from the church to which we once belonged is not schism. Else you will make all the English to be schismatics in separating from the Church of Rome. "But we had just cause." So doubtless we had; whereas schism is a *causeless* separation from the church of Christ. So far so good. But you have many steps to take before you can make good that conclusion, that a separation from a *particular national* church, such as the Church of England is, whether with sufficient cause or without, comes under the scriptural notion of schism.[23]

Wesley argued strongly for the legitimacy of the Methodist societies according to Anglican faith and practice. He pointed out that the members had consulted on the most probable means of meeting together in fellowship, following only common sense and scripture; though "they generally found, in looking back, something in Christian antiquity likewise, very nearly parallel thereto."[24] Moreover, since the purpose of the societies was to encourage members to strengthen each other by talking and praying together as often as possible, there could surely be no objection. Such practices were "grounded on the plainest reason, and on so many scriptures both of the Old Testament and New, that it would be tedious to recite them."[25]

The Anglican tradition had early made a distinction between essential and non-essential church discipline in the 34th Article of the Church of England, and it was this which gave Wesley his strongest argument for the various "prudential means" which he adopted for Methodist polity. Precisely because the societies functioned in the area of non-essentials, Wesley felt free to adopt whichever measures fostered the discipleship of their members. The lack of a specific scriptural authority did not invalidate such expedients, as he noted in one of his *apologiae* for the class meeting:

> That with regard to these little prudential helps we are continually changing one thing after another, is not a weakness or fault, as you imagine, but a peculiar advantage which we enjoy. By this means we declare them all to be merely prudential, not essential, not of divine institution. . . . You seem not to have observed, that the

Scripture, in most points, gives only general rules; and leaves the particular circumstances to be adjusted by the common sense of mankind. . . . But it is common prudence which is to make the application of this in a thousand particular cases.[26]

The Dangers of Schism

It was Wesley's concern at the outset, however, to ensure that the societies did not acquire the nature of a *gathered* church. In the various sets of rules which constituted Methodist polity, the emphasis was on discipleship, not doctrine (see Appendices "E" and "F"). Even so, the very necessity of discipline created an inherent separatist tendency in the movement. Wesley himself could not avoid referring to the "gathering" of Methodists, albeit stressing their non-separation;[27] and in his *Letter to a Roman Catholic* he readily defined the church as "gathered" by Christ unto himself.[28] Likewise in the second edition of *An Earnest Appeal,* he introduced a poem which, in several telling stanzas, revealed the inevitable tension of Methodist ecclesial identity:

1. Happy the souls who first believed,
   To Jesus and each other cleaved,
   Joined by the unction from above
   In mystic fellowship of love.

   . . . .

16. The few that truly call thee Lord
    And wait thy sanctifying word,
    And thee their utmost Saviour own,
    Unite, and perfect them in one.

17. Gather them in on every side,
    And in thy tabernacle hide;
    Give them a resting-place to find
    A cover from the storm and wind.

    . . . .

19. Thither collect thy little flock,
    Under the shadow of their Rock;
    The holy seed, the royal race,
    The standing monuments of thy grace.[29]

Wesley was aware of this tension. He knew that a disciplined fellowship would quickly foster its own ecclesial self-awareness, with a resultant tendency to self-sufficiency. He took pains, therefore, to warn the members of the societies against the ill effects of fragmented religious order. "The thing which I was greatly afraid of all this time," he noted in *A Plain Account of the People Called Methodists*, "was a narrowness of spirit, a party zeal, a being straitened in our own bowels; that miserable bigotry which makes so many unready to believe that there is any work of God but among themselves."[30] In *A Farther Appeal to Men of Reason and Religion* he traced what he regarded as the symptoms of separation through Protestant history, arguing that, once a breach had occurred, the preoccupation of the separated group had become the defining of its own structure in doctrine and practice to the detriment of the real work of the church. Indeed, the stumbling block of the Reformation was the rejection by Luther and Calvin of so many doctrines and practices of the church which others counted most sacred, and their continual invective against the church. The Quakers had at first professed their calling from God to reform the land, but then expended their strength in disputes over mere opinions. The Baptists "immediately commenced a warm dispute, not concerning the vitals of Christianity, but concerning the manner and time of administering one of the external ordinances of it." The Presbyterians and Independents likewise spent much of their time and strength in opinions which were at best circumstantial. And for reasons such as these, said Wesley with heavy irony, they had separated from the church.[31]

The aims of separation, he maintained, were invariably thwarted by the means. "The experiment has been so frequently tried already, and the success has never answered the expectation."[32] Those whom God had raised up to be leaders of the faith since the Reformation had "spread the leaven of true religion far and wide" when they had stayed within the churches to which they belonged, "notwithstanding the wickedness which overflowed both the Teachers and the people therein." But if, "upon any provocation or consideration whatever, they separated, and founded distinct parties, their influence was more and more confined; they grew less and less useful to others, and generally lost the spirit of religion themselves in the spirit of controversy.[33] Should this occur in Methodism, he noted in 1789, the result would be the dwindling of those who separated into "a dry, dull party." And this, he declared, he would do all in his power to prevent as long as he lived.[34]

Wesley's attachment to the Church of England in this regard has been described as almost irrational,[35] but the essence of his argument was forceful: that separation, if avoidable, was a censurable distraction from the priorities of the faith. In his sermon, *On Schism*, he defined such a move as inherently evil, a grievous breach of the law of love, and contrary to the nature of the faith which ought to unite Christians. Schism, being evil in itself, produced evil fruits, opening a door to uncharitable judgments, to anger and resentment, which in turn led to slandering and back-biting. These were not imaginary results, said Wesley, but plain facts, borne out by events in his own experience. The question was not whether separation under constraint was permissible; for clearly, if a church should lead a member against the scriptures or into some other false teaching, then that member should separate. The sin was *unnecessary* division, rendering the separatist justly chargeable with all the consequences, whether he or she foresaw them or not.[36]

Separation Resisted

The tortuous course of Wesley's attempts to avoid such a division between Methodism and the Church of England was plotted between the growing identity of the Methodist societies and the unwillingness of the church to accept them as an integral part of the ecclesial structure. The issue of separation was on the agenda of the first Methodist Conference in 1744, and the minutes of subsequent Conferences indicate continuing efforts to prevent and to educate against it.[37] By no means least among the sources of the tension was the option offered by the 1689 Act of Toleration, whereby it was possible to take out a license as a dissenting minister and to register preaching-houses as legal places of worship. Indeed, in the years following the 1755 Conference, when separation was narrowly averted, Methodist preachers and societies began to do just that. The critical point was reached when it transpired in 1760 that three preachers in Norwich were administering the Lord's Supper also. Due in large part to the vigorous prompting of his brother Charles, Wesley put a stop to this; though the registration of preaching-houses continued, and the issue had merely been shelved until the next crisis of 1784.[38]

The Pragmatism of Church Order: Stillingfleet and King

Although Wesley would never condone separation for English Methodism, he did concede toward the end of his life that it was increasingly inevitable, and in fact had been taking place by degrees for many years.[39] The reason for this was quite simply Wesley's own ecclesiological priority of placing the vision of the church before its function and its spirit before its structure. In the final analysis, therefore, the question of church order was not its rationale but its purpose—a position he came to hold quite early in the development of the Methodist societies, but one which represented, as we have noted, a major shift in his thinking. The change became evident in his correspondence during 1746. "I would inquire, What is the end of all ecclesiastical order? Is it not to bring souls from the power of Satan to God, and to build them up in His fear and love. Order, then, is so far valuable as it answers these ends; and if it answers them not, it is nothing worth."[40]

The change seems to have taken place between 1738 and 1745, due in no small measure to the influence of two works which Wesley read on the subject. One of these was Edward Stillingfleet's *Irenicum*, the argument of which rested on the tension between the authority necessary to maintain order in a society and the freedom of individual judgment. The authority of personal judgment in matters concerning church government, argued Stillingfleet, had to be surrendered in part to the authority of those entrusted with its care and welfare. Otherwise, there could be no unity or peace in a church which was considered a society. On the other hand, the church had no direct power over people's opinions, since that did not properly lie within the cognizance of any ecclesial direction. The purpose of church power was no more than to preserve its own peace and unity—a Latitudinarian argument *par excellence*.[41]

Stillingfleet's propositions, supported by scriptural referents, clearly made a deep impression on Wesley,[42] but the emerging pattern of the Methodist societies seems to have been just as influential in re-shaping his thought. The 1745 Conference reflected this in a description of the origins of church government which gives an important insight into the link between Wesley's pragmatism and his theological method. The question was asked, whether Episcopal, Presbyterian, or Independent church government was most agreeable to reason, and the answer is worth reproducing in detail:

> The plain origin of church-government seems to be this. Christ sends forth a preacher of the gospel. Some who hear him repent and believe the gospel. They then desire him to watch over them, to build them up in the faith, and to guide their souls in the paths of righteousness. Here then is an independent congregation, subject

to no pastor but their own, neither liable to be controlled in things spiritual by any other man or body of men whatsoever.

But soon after some from other parts, who are occasionally present while he speaks in the name of Him that sent him, beseech him to come over and help them also. Knowing it to be the will of God he consents (complies), yet not till he has conferred with the wisest and holiest of his congregation, and with their advice appointed one who has gifts and grace to watch over the flock till his return.

If it please God to raise another flock in the new place, before he leaves them he does the same thing, appointing one whom God has fitted for the work to watch over these souls also. In like manner, in every place where it pleases God to gather a little flock by his word, he appoints one in his absence to take the oversight of the rest, and to assist them of the ability which God giveth. These are Deacons, or servants of the church, and look on their first pastor as their common father. And all these congregations regard him in the same light, and esteem him still as the shepherd of their souls.

These congregations are not strictly independent. They depend on one pastor, though not on each other.

As these congregations increase, and as the Deacons grow in years and grace, they need other subordinate Deacons or helpers; in respect of whom they may be called Presbyters, or Elders, as their father in the Lord may be called the Bishop or Overseer of them all. [43]

Wesley's pragmatic view of church order was further confirmed by his reading of Lord Peter King's *Enquiry* in January 1746. [44] This followed the same line of argument as the *Irenicum*, defining the church as "a Company of Believers who, at one Time, in one Place and the same did associate themselves together," and advocating a pluralism of church government. Consent to non-essential doctrine should not be required, argued King, since breaches of church unity have usually occurred when this has been imposed. [45] Even before reading the *Enquiry*, Wesley had examined this point, and had firmly subordinated ecclesiastical authority to individual conscience. Writing to his brother-in-law in 1745, he had affirmed the commitment of Methodists to obey all the laws of the Church of England, and to obey its bishops—but only insofar as a safe conscience would allow. "Their bare will," he declared, "distinct from those laws, we do not profess to obey at all.[46]

This was made an official position at the 1747 Conference, but with the corollary that independence of conscience was to be kept within a spirit of reasonableness.[47] Wesley was much in agreement with Stillingfleet's latitude in this regard, and viewed disagreement over mere opinions as a fruitless exercise. "I never knew one (or but one) man write controversy with what I thought a right spirit," he observed in one of his many *apologiae* for Methodism. "Every disputant seems to think, as every soldier, that he may hurt his opponent as much as he can."[48] He affirmed the premise of the *Irenicum* that there must be a way to determine and decide all controversies arising in a society which tend to disrupt its peace and unity.[49] But unlike Stillingfleet, whose argument seemed to advocate the *via media* as an end in itself, Wesley claimed more than a freedom from restraint of opinion. He sought freedom *for* a vital and living faith.[50]

Catholic Spirit with a Purpose

He expressed this nowhere more effectively than in his sermon, *Catholic Spirit*, in which he rejected the blandness of a faith too much attuned to reasonableness. A catholic spirit is not a speculative latitudinarianism, an indifference to all opinions; nor is it a practical latitudinarianism, an indifference to church order. Those of a truly catholic spirit are convinced of their own faith, worship, and practice, and yet embrace, "with strong and cordial affection," neighbors and strangers, friends and enemies. Their hearts are enlarged toward all people. They have a catholic, or universal love, and catholic love is a catholic spirit.[51] Orthodoxy or right opinion, he noted elsewhere, was never more than "a slender part of religion, and sometimes no part at all. . . . The religion of a child of God is righteousness, peace, and joy in the Holy Ghost."[52]

It was in reaching out to others, in the working out of faith, that Wesley saw the true purpose of the church. The Anglican *via media* in his day had arrived at a point of stagnation; but for Wesley it had never been a priority *per se*. It had merely been the means of avoiding irrelevancies which might hinder the larger commission of the church. And as Methodists took up this commission, becoming "living witnesses, in and to every party, of that Christianity which we preach,"[53] opinions became less and less important than a knowledge of Christ and an obedience to God's will:

> I am sick of opinions. I am weary to bear them. My soul loathes this frothy food. Give me solid and substantial religion. Give me an humble, gentle lover of God and man . . . laying himself out in the work of faith, the patience of hope, the labour of love.[54]

Tradition was less important than reaching out to the tinners in Cornwall, the keelmen in Newcastle, the colliers in Kingswood and Staffordshire, the drunkards, the swearers, the Sabbath-breakers of Moorfield and the harlots of Drury Lane.[55] The episcopal succession was less important than the apostolic spirit which empowered everyone, clergy or lay, to labor for the good of souls:

> God in Scripture commands me, according to my power, to instruct the ignorant, reform the wicked, confirm the virtuous. Man forbids me to do this in another's parish: that is, in effect, to do it at all; seeing I have now no parish of my own, nor probably ever shall. Whom, then, shall I hear, God or man? . . . I look upon all the world as my parish: thus far I mean, that in whatever part of it I am I judge it meet, right, and my bounden duty to declare, unto all that are willing to hear, the glad tidings of salvation. This is the work which I know God has called me to do; and sure I am that His blessing attends it.[56]

He was well assured that he accomplished far more by preaching three days on his father's tomb at Epworth than he had by preaching three years in his pulpit.[57] For in reaching out to ordinary people with the gospel, he found its spiritual power—and thereby the true identity of the church.

2. THE PURITAN SPIRIT

It is at this point that we can discern Wesley's appropriation of that other strand of the Christian tradition which was so pervasive and so powerful in English ecclesial thought and practice: the Puritan spirit. His views on separation notwithstanding, he could refer to the pastors and teachers of the Reformed churches as the proper successors of those who had delivered through all generations the faith once delivered to the saints. He could likewise refer to the members of these churches as having true communion with the society of true believers because they converted sinners to God—a work that no one could do unless God appointed them to such a task.[58] In short, the Anglican tradition was not the only source of Wesley's churchmanship. It provided him with a firm sense of the authority and identity of the church, but it lacked the discipline and dynamic of a personal religion. Wesley knew better than most that there was indeed a spirit of Anglicanism,[59] but the dialectic of his churchmanship depended also on the Puritan spirit which, in the final analysis, proved just as important.

Wesley's Puritan Heritage

To trace this influence in Wesley's thinking on the church, we must begin with his own family, which had a strong Puritan heritage. Both of his parents came from Nonconformist families before they changed to Anglicanism. His great grandfather, Bartholomew Wesley, was one of the clergy ejected from their livings as a result of the 1662 Act of Uniformity following the demise of the Commonwealth and the Restoration of the monarchy; his grandfather, John Westley, who had been noted for his academic promise at Oxford by the Puritan scholar, John Owen, died at an early age as a result of his imprisonment for preaching to a Nonconformist gathering in 1660; and his mother was the twenty-fifth child of Samuel Annesley, a less famous but still notable contemporary of Owen.[60]

It is difficult to infer how much Wesley was made aware of this heritage during his upbringing. His father, Samuel Wesley, who was ordained into the Church of England from Nonconformity in 1688, seems to have imparted to John the high view of the church which is not uncommon when such a change of identity occurs, to the exclusion of his Nonconformist heritage. Thus John did not discover a family anecdote concerning his grandfather John Westley until 1765. Nor does he seem to have been told of the participation of his grandfather, Samuel Annesley, in the first public ordination held by the Presbyterians after the ejections of 1662.[61] Yet he came to feel strong sympathy for the Puritans who suffered in the preceding century, and this cannot have been without some sense of his own family history.[62]

What is clear, on the other hand, is his familiarity with Puritanism through his reading of its literature—Richard Baxter's *The Saints' Everlasting Rest* in 1730, for example, and Henry Scougal's *The Life of God*

in the Soul of Man in 1732. He subsequently published many other
Puritan works in *A Christian Library*, which gives ample evidence of the
high regard in which he held their leading authors.[63] These writings had
a rich pedigree, not least because Puritanism, as Perry Miller has
described it, was by no means

> a unique phenomenon, peculiar to England of the seventeenth
> century, but . . . one more instance of a recurrent spiritual answer
> to interrogation eternally posed by human existence. . . . Inside
> the shell of its theology and beneath the surface coloring of its
> political theory, Puritanism was yet another manifestation of a piety
> [which] I venture to call . . . Augustinian . . . simply because
> Augustine is the archexemplar of a religious frame of mind of which
> Puritanism is only one instance out of many in fifteen hundred
> years of religious history.[64]

The Puritan frame of mind, according to Miller, was "a reliance on the
moment of aesthetic vision" as opposed to "a dialectical effort to prove
the justice of fact," and Puritan theology was an effort to externalize and
systematize this subjective mood.[65]

The Origins of Puritanism

The name *Puritan* seems to have come into use as early as 1564,
initially as a term of abuse describing those who thought themselves
"more pure than others," and separated themselves from all other
churches and congregations because "they suppose the church which
they have devised to be without all impurity."[66] Contrary to what is
frequently assumed, however, Puritanism was not an import from the
continental Reformation. In what has become a referent for Puritan
scholarship, Leonard Trinterud has shown that it was indigenous to
England, its controlling element being the heritage of medieval English
life and thought. And Jerald Brauer, dating it as a movement from
1570-1680, has ascribed to it four distinguishing marks which further
point to its indigenousness: a deep dissatisfaction with the Anglican
conception of the Reformation and with the Roman Catholic interpretation of the faith; a deep religious experience of dramatic intensity; a zeal
for reform, not only in the church, but in every facet of contemporary
life; and a covenant theology as the primary vehicle for structuring the
experience and understanding of the Christian faith.[67]

Covenant Theology

This last feature was nowhere better articulated than in the writings of one of the earliest English Reformers, William Tyndale. The covenant in Tyndale's theology was conditional rather than absolute, and it incorporated a view of law which had important connotations of reason, conscience, justice, and an ordered social life. God's initiative was paramount in the making of the covenant relationship, and the covenant was furthered and strengthened when the human response was obedience to the laws of God and of the realm—one reason Tyndale's theology was initially well-received.[68]

As Puritanism became systematized, the more radical theology of Calvinism began to take hold, and two dimensions in the handling of the covenant idea emerged: the earlier conditional covenant, stressing the human response to God's initiative; and an absolute covenant, in which God promises *and* fulfills the conditions—a view necessitated by the doctrines of divine sovereignty, human depravity, and predestination.[69] In Christ is the perfect revelation of the whole will of God, bringing salvation to the human race. Application of this is the "making effectual, in certain men, of all those things which Christ has done and does as mediator."[70] It is God who is solely efficient in covenant action, who works in an "effectuall and powerfull way upon the hearts of the elect, and that according to the Lord's decree of election and will of pleasure."[71]

The Inward Witness of the Spirit

It should be noted, however, that Calvinism was not at the root of the conflict between Puritanism and the early English Church. Indeed, until Archbishop William Laud was appointed Archbishop of Canterbury in 1633, giving Arminianism the ascendancy in Anglican thought and practice, the Church of England itself was predominantly Calvinist.[72] The true agenda of Puritanism was rather an experiential yearning for assurance, and in this the central doctrine was that of the indwelling Spirit. It was a doctrine well served by covenant theology, which stressed an experience of forgiveness and faith as a prerequisite for a covenant relationship, and which stipulated communion with God as a means of sustaining it.[73] The dynamic of their assurance was overwhelmingly the love of God. And once this was experienced in the redemptive power of the new birth, the Puritan was "possessed of a spirit that would not let him rest."[74] The belief that everything is to be understood and ordered from the standpoint of the divine "may be the aim of most Christians; but never before or after Puritanism has it been so consciously or self-consciously expressed."[75]

The Puritan sought the illumination of spirit which could come only from God. John Preston put it well:

"If any man love me, and keepe my Commandements, I will shew myselfe to him"; that is, hee shall have an extraordinary manifestation of my selfe, hee shall have such an expression of love and peace and joy, such a thing that no man knowes but himselfe. Beloved, this is the testimony of the Spirit. I confesse, it is a wondrous thing, and if there were not some Christians that did feele it, and know it, you might beleeve there were no such thing, that it were but a fancie or enthusiasme; but, beloved, it is certaine, there are a generation of men, that know what this seale of the Lord is.[76]

Moreover, the Puritan was encouraged and exhorted to seek the indwelling of the Holy Spirit by "pressing" the covenant. Once again the words of John Preston:

Besides all this, know that the Lord is faithful, he cannot denie himselfe, though thou faile on thy part, yet hee continues the same. . . . Labour to know him more . . . labour to get this assurance, for it is this assurance that breedes the love, that seales it up."[77]

The same immediacy could be expected in the reading of scripture. The words of John Owen are, if anything, more vivid:

Let the Sun arise in the firmament, and there is no need of Witnesses to prove and confirme it unto a seeing man that it is day. . . . Let the least child bring a candle into a roome that before was darke, and it would be a madnesse to go about to prove by substantiall Witnesses, men of Gravity and Authority, that Light is brought in. Doth it not evince itselfe, with an Assurance above all that can be obtained by any Testimony whatever?[78]

The Gathered Church

The progression from this spirit of covenant assurance to the principle of ecclesiological separation came early in the Puritan movement, and the grounds can readily be inferred. The elect, being the only true church, could alone discern the sovereignty of God and the headship of Christ over the church, by revelation and through covenant assurance. And since, in Elizabethan England, the whole nation, "however ignorant and however lacking in faith," was presumed to be the church by "a kind of charitable assumption,"[79] it became necessary to distinguish the true church from the rest of the nation.

In keeping with the spirit of Puritanism, the theological principle of separation was preceded by the concept of the church as small communities of believers, living together in the covenant of grace. The gathering of small groups of Christians in mutual fellowship was, of course, no new phenomenon. It had been the form of spiritual movements within the Roman Catholic Church for centuries. But the situation in the sixteenth and seventeenth centuries was different. Protestantism, by rejecting the traditional authority of the *ecclesia*, had created the need for an alternative church order, and there was a genuine fear that the emphasis of Reformation theology on the claims of the individual Christian conscience, "an emphasis which contained at least the elements of religious liberty and toleration,"[80] would lead to ecclesiastical anarchy and social disruption. The claims of Thomas Muntzer to have received direct spiritual inspiration, for example, and the rise of Anabaptism, served only to confirm these fears—especially those of the clergy.[81]

It is noteworthy, therefore, that the ecclesiastical hierarchy of the established Church of England afforded, on the whole, a greater degree of latitude to the Puritan movement than was granted to similar manifestations of the *communio sanctorum* on the continent of Europe.[82] Providing a continuity of tradition and authority, the Elizabethan church gave Puritanism a structure within and against which to develop an ecclesiology of the elect, thereby preventing an excessive fear of threat to the secular order.[83]

Against this relative stability, the development of the Puritan *gathered church* can be seen in two parallel movements: at the structural level of ecclesial hierarchy, and at the level of the individual congregation. These found expression in two main groupings: the Presbyterians, who hoped to take over the religious establishment and run it according to the discipline patterned on Calvin's Geneva; and the Independents, or Congregationalists, who sought to impose stricter limitations on church membership and to gain greater freedom for individual preachers and congregations, if necessary by separation from the church. For it quickly became clear in Elizabethan England that there were those who wanted "reformation without tarying for anie."[84]

The "Classis" Movement and Presbyterianism

The Presbyterian principles were first expressed in the *classis* movement, informal groups of clergy who met at each other's houses for prayer and mutual instruction in the scriptures.[85] As the Presbyterian movement gathered momentum, these became the basis for a church government by assembly, and were systematized by the Cambridge scholars Walter Travers and Thomas Cartwright.[86] In practical terms, it was suggested that episcopacy was not a true form of church government, since Christ was the only true head of the church. A discipline vested in ministers, elders, and synods would be more consonant with scripture.[87]

It was not the intention of the Presbyterians to make a radical change, but to reform the existing system. Indeed, they were only too aware of the schismatic results of Separatism, and felt that some ordered discipline was necessary to stem this trend. Wesley himself put it well:

> "That the irregularities of Mr. Cartwright did more harm than good in the course of a century, than all the labours of his did good," is by no means plain to me. . . . I look upon him, and the body of Puritans of that age, (to whom the German Anabaptists bore small resemblance) to have been both the most learned and pious men that were then in the English nation. Nor did they separate from the Church; but were driven out, whether they would or no. The vengeance of God which fell on the posterity of their persecutors, I think, is no imputation on Mr. Cartwright or them; but a wonderful sense of divine Providence.[88]

But the informal and initially secretive development of the *classes* caused a defensive reaction from the established church, and this early attempt at Presbyterian government failed with the rejection of their proposed *Book of Discipline* in 1586. Richard Bancroft did not beat about the bush:

> [It] is found out by examination, that this *classicall* and reforming

consort, with their followers, have divided themselves from all the rest of the ministrie, and *Christians* in *England*: and linked themselves into a newe brotherhood, with this lincke, vz. . . . the *desire of the pure Discipline*: thereby sheweing themselves to be the most notorious Schismatickes . . . so have they already seduced her Majesties subjects, by gathering them together into a new societie, whereunto they doe appropriat the name of the Church: as though all other Churches in the realme, were but as *Jewish Sinagogues* or heathenish assemblies. . . .

. . . the parish where they preach, being assembled, is not the Church properly in their sence: but as many thereof onely, as are joyned unto them with that inviolable bond mentioned, vz. *the desire of the godly discipline.*[89]

This expresses as succinctly as any writing of the period the basic issue between Puritanism and the established church—and is remarkably similar to Anglican criticisms of early Methodist polity. The Puritans saw the problem as one of ecclesial discipline; the ecclesial hierarchy saw it as one of schism. It is therefore not surprising, though ironical, to find the argument that scripture does not prescribe any particular form of church government being used *against* the Presbyterians as early as 1584.[90]

Presbyterianism reached its zenith in the Civil War of the 1640s between the English Parliament and King Charles I, culminating in the execution of the king and the formation of a republican government, the Commonwealth of England, over which Oliver Cromwell was later appointed Lord Protector. An important development in the war was the approval by parliament of a *Solemn League and Covenant* with Scotland. This specified that the two nations would work together for the reform of the church "according to the word of God and example of the best reformed Churches," endeavoring to bring the church "to the nearest conjunction and uniformity in religion, confession of faith, form of Church government [and] directory for worship and catechizing."[91] The doctrinal statements which ensued in 1647—*The Westminster Confession of Faith,* the *Larger Catechism*, and the *Shorter Catechism*—are among the most lucid formulations anywhere of Reformed ecclesiology. For the first time, the visible and invisible church is clearly expounded.[92] The true church is invisible, consisting of the whole number of the elect, and the visible church has been given the ministry and ordinance of God "for the gathering and perfecting of the saints, in this life, to the end of the world."[93]

The "Coetus Electorum" and Congregationalism

The Presbyterian system of church government did not, however, give fullest expression to the *coetus electorum*. The Puritan spirit had early raised the question of religious liberty as well as ecclesial discipline, and the failure of the Presbyterians to impose their system nationwide, even at the height of their political influence, was due not least to the resistance of the Independents, who regarded it as a restriction on their freedom of conscience. Their principles of Congregationalism were no less an embodiment of Puritanism.

The origins of "the Congregational way" can be traced back to the reign of Mary Tudor (1553-59), when there were groups who "separated from the reste of the Lande, as from the world, and joyned in covenant, by voluntarie profession, to obey the truth of Christ . . . as they also did even unto death."[94] Gatherings such as the "privye churche" of Richard Fitz in London, the private meetings at the Plumbers' Hall, or the congregations led by Robert Browne and Robert Harrison in Norwich and by Henry Barrow and John Greenwood in London, were all marked by this mutual binding in covenant. Significantly, Browne's description of the congregation at Norwich could easily be that of a Methodist society:

> First therefore they gave their consent, to joine themselves to the Lord, in one covenant and felloweshipp together, & to keep & seek agrement under his lawes & such like disorders & wickdnes, as was mencioned before. Further they agreed off those wich should teach them, and watch for the salvation of their soules. . . . Likewise an order was agreed on ffor their meetinges together, ffor their exercises therin, as praier . . . for noting out anie speciall matter of edifiing at the meeting . . . that all should further the kingdom of God in them selves.[95]

The stated principle of separation, as might be expected, quickly drew ecclesiastical opposition. The leaders of both London groups were arrested in 1567, and the account of the inquisition of the Plumbers' Hall leaders by Bishop Grindal indicates that unlawful gathering, rather than false doctrine, was the concern. As Grindal wrote to Johann Heinrich Bullinger the following year:

> Some London citizens of the lowest order, together with four or five

ministers, remarkable neither for their judgments nor learning, have openly separated from us; and sometimes in private houses, sometimes in the field, and occasionally even in ships, they have held their meetings and administered the sacraments. Besides this, they have ordained ministers, elders, and deacons, after their own way, and have even ex-communicated some who had seceded from their church.[96]

As a result of this and other pressures from the ecclesial authorities, a sizeable number of exiles gathered in the Low Countries, where they developed the first real principles of Congregationalism. They tended at first to retain a concept of ecclesiastical structure, ranging from the "semi-separatism" of John Smyth and John Robinson[97] to the "mutual confederacy" of Henry Jacob and William Ames:

> Yet particular Churches, as their communion requires, and the light of nature and the rules of orderliness and examples from Scripture teach, may and often should enter into covenant relationship and mutual association in classes and synods in order to enjoy common agreement and mutual help as much as fitly may be, especially in matters of greater moment. But this combination does not constitute a new form of church.[98]

Nonetheless, in due course a fully independent ecclesiology emerged, and found expression in *An Apologeticall Narration*, presented to parliament in 1643 by some of the ministers who had returned from exile.[99] And at the Savoy Conference, called in 1658 following the death of Oliver Cromwell, this reached its definitive statement.

The preface to the *Declaration of Faith and Order*, drawn up and agreed at the Conference, used the metaphor, typically vivid, of ships which had been sailing apart and alone on the seas, "exposed to every wind of Doctrine, under no other conduct than the Word and Spirit," yet under the care and power of God they were "found to have steered their course by the same Chart, and to have been bound for one and the same Port."[100] And this sets the tone for a document which, while affirming the general Calvinist principles of the Westminster Confession, goes on to stipulate the further principle of separate gathered churches. As Christ is the only head of the church, he is entrusted with the power of calling out of the world those who are given to him by the Father to "walk together in particular Societies of Churches, for their mutual edification and due performance of that public Worship which he requireth of them in this world."

The underlying principle of this ecclesiology was the doctrine of scripture as the sole rule of faith and practice, the tradition of the church being specifically rejected. John Owen had stated the issue a year earlier in his treatise *Of Schisme*:

> The Church of England as it is called . . . separated herselfe from the Church of Rome [and] in her designe to reduce Religion to its primitive purity, shee always professed, that shee did not take direction from the Scripture only, but also from the Councells and examples of the four or five first Centuries. . . . What I beseech you shall bind my Conscience to acquiesce in what is pleaded from the 4 or 5 first Centuries consisting of men, that could, and did erre; more than did hers, what was pleaded from the 9. or 10. Centuries? Have I not liberty to call for Reformation according to the Scriptures only?[101]

The Conference affirmed this position, stating that the authority of each congregation was scriptural, because Christ, "according unto his mind declared in his Word," had given all that "Power and Authority which is any needful for their carrying on that Order in Worship and Discipline which he hath instituted for them to observe." Apart from these particular churches, there is no other church instituted by Christ for the administration of his ordinances or for the execution of "any authority in his Name." Each church has officers—pastors, preachers, elders, and deacons—chosen by "the common suffrage of the Church itself," with or without the laying-on of hands.[102] And, as John Owen observed, since Christ had granted authority to these churches for their "continuance, increase and preservation in purity, order and holiness," the careful exercise of discipline was of paramount importance.[103]

Dissent and Nonconformity

The Savoy Conference was regarded by many as an attempt to reach agreement between the Presbyterians and the Congregationalists, but events were to overtake such efforts. The short interregnum of Oliver Cromwell's son Richard was rapidly superseded by the restoration of Charles II, and it would have required nothing short of a miracle to have avoided repercussions. While the Presbyterians hoped for some measure of compromise with the re-established Church of England, the Congregationalists intended from the outset to stand firm. A conference was convened early in the new reign, again at the Savoy, to try to incorporate the two groups into the church, but the opportunity passed, and in 1662 the Act of Uniformity was less conciliatory. It restored a Prayer Book which made few concessions to Puritan scruples, and insisted on episcopal ordination for officiating clergy. More than two thousand clergy were unable to subscribe to the Act, and were ejected from their livings as Dissenters, marking the effective beginning of modern Nonconformity.

The next two decades saw these Dissenters persecuted, at times with great severity; and even when the accession of William III brought a measure of relief in the 1689 Act of Toleration, great hardships continued. A Common Fund was established to aid ministers in straightened circumstances, Presbyterian and Congregationalist alike, and it has left us with a very moving record, as needy cases were listed for the distribution of funds.[104] We have already noted that Wesley's forebears knew of these persecutions first hand, and Wesley's Anglicanism did not prevent his vehement censure of the Act of Uniformity:

> So, by this glorious Act, thousands of men, guilty of no crime, nothing contrary either to justice, mercy or truth, were stripped of all they had, of their houses, lands, revenues, and driven to seek where they could, or beg, their bread. For what? Because they did not dare to worship God according to other men's consciences! So they and their families were, at one stroke, turned out of house and home . . . because they could not assent and consent to that manner of worship which their worthy governors prescribed.[105]

Wesley and Richard Baxter

Yet Wesley was far from sympathetic toward what he regarded as the divisive tendencies of an ecclesiology based on the concept of a gathered church. He felt that a discipline could be maintained within the larger ecclesial structure without the necessity of separation, and in this regard the Puritan who came closest to his concept of the church was Richard Baxter.[106] Ordained in 1648 by the Bishop of Worcester, Baxter had early in his ministry been critical of the lax episcopal system in England, and had also begun to question the nature of episcopal authority. While not opposing the episcopacy in principle, his objection was that bishops could not possibly care for the number of souls in a diocese, since there were 9,725 parish churches in his day, but only 25 diocesan bishops and two archbishops.[107] Citing the early church fathers as his authority, he affirmed that presbyters were equal with bishops, and noted that in St. Patrick's settlement of the Irish church, as in the primitive church, there were as many bishops as there were churches, and additionally some ten presbyters to every church. Every pastor thus had the "power of the keys" and the right to govern the spiritual welfare of the people.[108]

This conviction was amply evidenced in Baxter's own ministry, and especially in his guidelines for pastoral visitation. Wesley regarded these as "well worth a careful perusal," and included an abridgement of them in the 1766 Minutes.[109] But while Baxter was concerned for the individual catechizing and religious growth of his people, he was equally concerned for the larger ecclesiastical discipline. He was cautious about any devolution of authority, and even though he approved of small groups meeting periodically for prayer, he opposed the principle of the gathered church.[110] The parish structure was far preferable, since Congregationalism was a building without cement.[111]

Thus, when the episcopacy was abolished during the interregnum of the Commonwealth, and the attempt by parliament to impose Presbyterianism was proving less than effective, Baxter was instrumental in forming the Worcestershire Association in his part of the country. This was officially for the purpose of consultation and debate between pastors, but the intent was to secure disciplinary control over church membership and worship. His vision was a reformation of the church through a comprehensive confederation of parishes, and this to be accomplished in a spirit not only of discipline, but also of ecumenicity:

> I have truly told the World nearly Forty Years ago, that I am past doubt that neither the Episcopal, Presbyterian nor Independant way alone, will well settle the Church: But that each of the three Parties (and those called *Erastians*) have somewhat of the Truth in peculiar, and somewhat of Faultiness, and if ever the Church be well settled, it must be by taking the best, and leaving out the worst of every party, and till that can be done, we must bear with what we cannot amend.[112]

This comes close to Wesley's "catholic spirit," yet the question was by no means as pressing for Wesley as it was for Baxter. Nor yet was the Puritan question of ecclesial authority an issue for Methodist polity. For in spite of the horrendous struggles of the seventeenth century over churchly and political structures, Wesley, as we have noted, was firmly committed to the Church of England as the best national church there could be. With this sure sense of the Anglican *ecclesia*, he was thus able to appropriate the fullest dynamic of the Puritan *coetus electorum*—the immediacy of spiritual experience which the Nonconformists found in fellowship during their period of persecution. It was not the ecclesiology of Puritanism which influenced him, but the Puritan spirit. And even though its most direct influence on Wesley came through Moravian Pietism, it was a heritage as English as the established church. Indeed, it is perhaps the most direct link of all between the early Methodists and their Nonconformist forebears. For, as we shall presently observe, both of Wesley's parents, in spite of their high Anglicanism, were instinctively drawn to the immediacy of fellowship experienced in the *coetus electorum*. The class meeting had a clear precedent in the *ecclesiolae* of English Congregationalism.

The Gathered Church in House Groups

In common with many Christians during times of religious persecution, the Congregationalists developed their concept of the gathered church through the experience of sharing in small house groups. As Geoffrey Nuttall has noted, this perforce was enriching:

> In small groups which have been formed in conscious separation from and in opposition to a larger group, the sense of fellowship is likely to be keen, especially if the small groups are persecuted by the larger; and where in addition the small groups are united in a common devotion to Jesus Christ and have the churches of the New Testament for their model, such fellowship is almost bound to be a prominent feature.[113]

The gatherings evolved distinctive procedures: the sharing of religious experience through testimony; the sense of mutual responsibility between individuals and between the congregation and the minister; the acceptance of personal holiness as the aim of group participation; the insistence on freedom of opinion, with the resultant development of an independent outlook; and what was possibly the most distinctive aspect, the covenant.

The Gathered Church in Covenant

The binding of each to the other and to the Lord in covenant was the major source of comfort and strength for the Congregationalists during their persecution. At Bideford, for example, on April 8, 1658, the following agreement was made:

> This day (we) renewe our former Covenant and Ingagements both with the Lord and one another, purposing (through the Grace and strength of Christ assisting us) to walk up more closely and faithfully in the discharge of all our dutys to the Lord and one another, submitting our selves to all the Lawes and ordinances of his house and yielding obedience to our Pastor and Governors over us in the Lord and watching over and serving one another in Love and making it our main and chief business to promote the Glory of Christ and good of one anothers soules while we shall live together.[114]

Similar wording can be found in a covenant made at Axminster in 1660:

> The Lord having called us into fellowship with his Sonne, And convinced us of the necessity of Church-fellowship: We do solemnly profess, in the strength of Christ, The accepting of the Lord for our God, And the giving up ourselves to him.[115]

Personal Covenants

Just as significant as these corporate agreements were the personal covenants which the Puritans made with God. They understood from scripture that they were bound to God individually as well as collectively, and even though they had the fellowship and support of the gathered congregation, it was not easy to maintain an active Christian witness in a society which, by and large, was hostile to expressions of personal piety. Besides which, the individual Puritan was as vulnerable as any other human being to the sinful tendencies of the will. They found it helpful, therefore, to make explicit in writing the covenant which was "written on their hearts" (Jer. 31:31-4), and at times of stress and falling away, to renew it.

There are many records of such renewals in the Puritan devotional diaries which have come down to us. The Rev. Oliver Heywood, for example, renewed his covenant one year with the following resolutions:

1. By the Lord's help and purpose to be more substantial in secret worship.
2. More sparing of precious time.
3. More constant in reading the Scriptures alone and meditating in them.
4. More careful to improve all opportunities of doing good to souls.
5. Less fearful about events, when in a way of duty, in all which I have lately missed it, but the Lord has pardoned me in Christ Jesus.[116]

The Puritan authors whose directions for personal covenanting were perhaps most widely distributed were Joseph Alleine (1634-68) and his father-in-law Richard Alleine (1611-81). Joseph Alleine's best-known work, *An Alarm to Unconverted Sinners*, published posthumously in 1672, sold 70,000 copies in three years,[117] and a form of prayer which he wrote for the making of a covenant with God, along with rules for daily self-examination, was published as a broadside in 1674.[118] Richard Alleine's major work, *A Vindication of Godliness*, provided very detailed directions for personal covenanting, and incorporated Joseph's Covenant Prayer and Directions.[119]

Wesley's Covenant Service

Wesley's interest in these covenanting disciplines was nowhere more evident than in the fifty volumes he published as *A Christian Library*, culled from what he regarded as the most valuable practical divinity in the English language. The representation of Puritan devotion is extensive, including Joseph Alleine's *Alarm* in Volume 24 and Richard Alleine's *Vindication* in Volume 30, both published in 1753.[120] Two years later, Wesley gave these writings a definitive place in Methodist polity when he instituted the Covenant Service, drawing on materials from the *Vindication*, and incorporating the words of Joseph Alleine's Covenant Prayer.[121] The service soon emerged as an established feature of Methodist worship, and during Wesley's lifetime it became the practice to hold it on the first Sunday afternoon in January along with the celebration of the eucharist. Thereafter it was appropriated by the various Methodist traditions, going through many revisions, but remaining a distinctive liturgical service.[122]

Early Methodist Covenants

Following the introduction of the Covenant Service, there are increasing references in early Methodist literature to the drawing up of personal written covenants. These were usually signed and sealed by the person making the covenant, and took the form of a direct transaction with God in which an existing commitment to discipleship was confirmed and strengthened. They would be renewed from time to time, frequently at a critical point of falling away from the faith, or when a person had experienced a heightened sense of God's presence.[123]

The language of these covenants is strongly evocative of early Nonconformity, and many of the covenants were more detailed than was possible at the corporate Service. Take, for example, the following extract from the diary of John Braithwaite (1770-1822), one of Wesley's preachers, dated October 1-3, 1791:

> As the 29th *ult.* was my birthday, I may here set down the thoughts which then occurred to my mind, but which I have undesignedly omitted on the opposite page: — This is my natural birth-day. I have lived twenty-one long years; but (Oh that I could weep as I write it!) to how little purpose! I am suffering a little from bodily affliction, with a measure of resignation. I want to be thankful in affliction also. Oh, thou dread Majesty of Heaven, who first badest me be, who hast hitherto upheld my uncertain life, and art privy to all my ways, admit me, a worm, this day (in which I commemorate my entrance into existence) into a covenant with thee, ever to be kept in mind. May I take thee and thy cross, in preference to the world, and all its ten thousand allurements. I desire to give myself *wholly* and *always* unto thee. In witness whereof, I have here dared to write (in the presence of I know not how many, and how great, invisible witnesses)
>
> "JOHN BRAITHWAITE"[124]

Even more detailed and searching is an undated fragment of a personal covenant found among Braithwaite's private papers by his biographer, and reproduced as Appendix K.

Yet one of the most eloquent of these covenants is quite brief, drawn up in 1790 by William Baynes, the publisher of Adam Clarke's *Bibliographical Dictionary:*

> I solemnly declare my desire and resolve to be wholly Thine, that my life may be devoted to Thee, that whatever I eat or drink, buy or sell, or whatever I do, I may do all to Thy glory.[125]

The essence of early Methodist discipleship could not have been stated more succinctly. The covenants were a mark of maturity, an expression on the part of seasoned disciples that something was needed to sustain them in their journey; and it is noteworthy that they became more widespread when the movement had been established for some years. The more they practiced their discipleship in the world, the more it became clear that their only mainstay was an active, personal relationship with God. To keep it renewed was therefore of the utmost importance.

The Bedrock of Wesley's Churchmanship

In the final analysis, this was the fundamental principle of Wesley's understanding of the Christian tradition: that when all accountability has been exercised—to scripture, reason, tradition, and the church—the bedrock of the Christian faith is the right relationship of the believer to the living God. He forged his theology from the tensions of the English Protestant tradition: the Puritan spirit and the spirit of Anglicanism. The pattern of the English Reformation had been to sustain both of these emphases—the apprehension of the individual by God in spiritual encounter, and the apprehension of God by human beings within a worldly order. And in his appropriation of this tradition, Wesley applied its dialectic to the full.

Chapter Two

WESLEY'S THEOLOGY OF DISCIPLESHIP

DISTINCTIVE JUSTIFICATION

The Anglican Via Media

Wesley's polity for the United Societies and their various subgroupings reflected not only an ecclesiological dialectic, but also a practical discipleship. They expressed, and in turn affirmed and enriched, his theological emphases on prevenient grace and Christian perfection; and most especially they were an embodiment of his doctrine of justification by faith. For this, Wesley was primarily indebted to the English Protestant tradition, which had resisted the radical Augustinianism of the continental reformers on the question of freedom of the will and irresistible grace. Whether in the enlightened humanism of Colet, Erasmus and More, the covenant theology of Tyndale, or even the Cartwright-Whitgift debates of the later decades, a tradition persisted in England throughout the sixteenth century which would not abandon the necessary function of good works in the order of salvation.[1]

There is no better representative of this *via media* than the monarch who occasioned the English breach with Rome, Henry VIII. At first, he had seemed to be a champion for the Catholic faith. His *Assertio Septem Sacramentorum* (1521), a spirited defense of Roman sacramental doctrine against that of Luther, earned him the title *Defender of the Faith* from a grateful Pope Leo X; and his ensuing dispute with Luther was undoubtedly a major factor in the emergence of the Anglican theological method of scripture, tradition, and reason as opposed to that of *sola scriptura*. Indeed, it can be argued that, quite apart from the political steps which were taken to separate the English church from Rome during the 1530s, the theological debates between English and Lutheran scholars rendered this decade foundational for the English Protestant tradition.[2]

There was genuine hope at Wittenberg during these years that England might be won over to Lutheranism, not least because

Melanchthon seemed to provide a mediating theology which might have resolved the antagonism between Luther and Henry VIII; and a study of the documents emerging from the various negotiations shows the extent to which this appeared to be a real possibility.[3] But the documents also show the extent to which Lutheran doctrine was resisted, most significantly in the *Bishop's Book* of 1537 and the *King's Book* of 1543, both of which were issued as authoritative statements of ecclesial doctrine and practice. The question was whether justification by faith rendered good works unconditional. The Lutheran position did not deny that good works followed from faith, but insisted that they were not a condition of faith. The English position did not deny that justification was by faith, but insisted that good works were a condition of *continuing* in that faith.

In the *Bishop's Book*, for example, we find a clear emphasis on good works as the necessary corollary of justification:

> For although acceptation to everlasting life be conjoined with justification, yet our good works be necessarily required to the attaining of everlasting life.[4]

And in the *King's Book* we find a statement on freewill which stresses human accountability for participation in the *ordo salutis*:

> The commandments and threatenings of Almighty God in scripture, whereby man is called upon and put in remembrance what God would have him to do, most evidently do express and declare that man hath freewill also now after the fall of our first father Adam as plainly appeareth in Romans xii, I Tim. iv, John ii, Matthew xix. Which undoubtedly should be said in vain, unless there were some faculty or power left in man whereby he may, by the help and grace of God (if he will receive it when it is offered unto him) understand his commandments and freely consent and obey unto them. . . . Freewill is a power of reason and will, by which good is chosen by the assistance of grace, or evil is chosen without the assistance of the same.[5]

The continental theologians ultimately made a considerable impact on the English Reformation, but in the Protestantism which was adopted in the Elizabethan settlements of 1559 and 1571, there was a continuing stress on human accountability and good works. Pivotal to these developments was Thomas Cranmer, appointed Archbishop of

Canterbury in 1533. His stamp can be seen on most of the major documents adopted as doctrinal standards by the new Church of England, and in particular in *The Book of Common Prayer* and the *Homilies*. Like Wesley, he was a theologian who wrote for the people, and his writings do not present a clear systematic. But in the homilies entitled *Of Salvation, Of Faith,* and *Of Good Works,* the doctrinal emphasis is clear: a juxtaposition of grace freely given, and good works as a subsequent obligation. The overwhelming impression the reader receives is an attempt to assimilate the full depth and richness of justification by faith as it became the wellspring of Reformation theology, tempered with an instinctive caution as to its implications.[6]

Justification by Faith: That "Much-Controverted" Doctrine

It is no coincidence that these particular homilies were among the earliest of Wesley's edited publications. During the year following his experience at Aldersgate Street, the question of justification by faith became central to his thinking. As he noted in his journal, he began to inquire "more narrowly" into what the doctrine of the Church of England was concerning this "much-controverted point,"[7] and in 1739 he published not only a composite extract from the *Homilies on Salvation, Faith and Good Works,*[8] but also an extract from a work first published in 1531 by the English Lutheran scholar, Robert Barnes: *A Treatise on Jusification by Faith Onely.*[9] The doctrine was prominent on the agenda at the first Methodist Conference in 1744, and it was the very first question to be asked at the second Conference the following year, at which time it was agreed to read through Richard Baxter's *Aphorisms of Justification* as preparation for an even more detailed discussion.[10]

Wesley published an extract from Baxter's *Aphorisms* in 1745, and in many ways it provides a more substantial referent for his thought than the Arminianism with which he is more often identified. Baxter was concerned to counteract the antinomianism which he perceived to emanate from the doctrine of imputed righteousness. His position in the *Aphorisms,* published in 1649, was a double justification—present and final—which stressed the perseverance of believers and the place of moral law in the scheme of salvation. "Justification," he wrote, "is either 1. in Title of Sense of the Law, 2. or in Sentence of Judgment. The first may be called Constitutive, the second Declarative; the first Virtual, the second Actual."[11] Justification was, therefore, dependent on the fulfillment of the new covenant, a breaking of which could result in persons being "unpardoned and unjustified again."[12] It was a "continued Act; which though it be in its kind complete from the first, yet it is still doing, till the finall justification at the Judgment day."[13]

Wesley's position came close to that of Baxter, not least because it reflected the same tensions of faith and works. Yet there was a significant difference between the two, and over precisely the issue which occasioned the storm of protest at the publication of the *Aphorisms* in Baxter's day—imputed rightousness as the formal or meritorious cause of justification. Indeed, this was *the* major issue of the seventeenth-century Anglican theology which was so influential in Wesley's development.[14] But whereas Baxter had been concerned to refute a doctrine of justification which seemed to grant unwarranted license in an age of political and social revolution,[15] Wesley was searching for a doctrine of justification which grounded the accountability of Christian living firmly in God's grace.[16] The distinction is important, not least because the doctrine of justification which Wesley ultimately espoused was forged, not in the seclusion of academic reflection, nor yet in the heat of civil and religious dispute, but rather in the realities of daily Christian living embodied in the class meeting.

Wesley's Early Perfectionism: Inward Holiness of Intent

To understand the importance of this doctrine, we must trace something of Wesley's theological and spiritual pilgrimage through the High Anglicanism of his early years, and through the Moravian Pietism which affected him so profoundly during and following his ministry in Georgia. His Anglicanism, as we have noted, had its origins in his upbringing; but a critical point was reached in 1725 when he was introduced to the writings of Thomas à Kempis and Jeremy Taylor. This was the year when he decided to enter Holy Orders, and the change which took place during these months is regarded by some to have been at least as important as his experience at Aldersgate Street.[17] Wesley was later to observe that his reading of à Kempis led him to see the nature and extent of inward religion as never before. "I saw that giving even all my life to God (supposing it possible to do this, and go no further) would profit me nothing, unless I gave my heart, yea, all my heart, to Him."[18] His reading of Taylor's *Holy Living* and *Holy Dying* had the further influence of prompting him to begin a personal diary for the purpose of better regulating his time, and for spiritual self-examination. Taylor had described the purpose of life as a constant walk with God, so that personal holiness was the necessary concern of the Christian. The goal in life being perfection, even as in Christ, sin had to be strictly analyzed and overcome.[19] Any growth in holiness could only be ascribed to faith in the forgiveness of sins,[20] but faith, "if it be true, living and justifying, cannot be separated from a good life. It works miracles . . . and makes us diligently to do, and cheerfully to suffer, whatsoever God hath placed in our way to heaven."[21]

It was this present purpose of Christian living which prompted the social works of the Oxford Holy Club, the group which Wesley later described as the "first rise" of Methodism.[22] It had its origins in the desire of Charles Wesley and two other students at Oxford, Robert Kirkham and William Morgan, to apply themselves to their spiritual lives more diligently, and their zeal was a direct factor in Wesley's return to Oxford from Epworth in 1729, when he assumed the role of their spiritual mentor. Their visiting of the prisons, helping the tenants of the workhouses, providing education and, in many instances, the basic necessities for destitute families, were a genuine outreach to the victims of an age of social displacement and savage penal retribution, toward whom the established church was largely indifferent.[23]

Yet this outreach was not to the exclusion of a pursuit for inward holiness. Richard P. Heitzenrater, whose work with Wesley's Oxford diaries has illuminated much of his thought at this time, makes the significant observation that these social works were in most cases not initiated by Wesley himself, but by others in the Holy Club. He was actively involved with them in their outreach, but was also concerned to see how the various activities were consistent with the prior objectives of inward and scriptural holiness.[24]

These objectives were further strengthened by Wesley's reading of William Law, a non-juring high churchman.[25] Like Taylor, Law regarded the end of salvation in Christ as the regeneration of the *imago Dei*, perfection in the likeness of God. It was, however, a perfection of purpose rather than achievement, with a focus on the will:

> The doctrine does not suppose, that we have no need of divine grace, or that it is in our own power to make ourselves perfect. It only supposes, that through the want of a *sincere* intention of pleasing God in *all our action*, we fall into such irregularities of life, as by the *ordinary* means of grace, we should have power to avoid. And that we have not that perfection, which our present state of grace makes us capable of, because we do not so much as *intend* to have it.[26]

A right intention, marking a transformation of the will, would change Christians; and through them, the world.[27]

The same emphasis can be found in Wesley's theology during this period. In an essay written at Oxford, dated February 1732, he addressed the issue in the context of the old and new covenants. The covenant of works made with Adam was impossible for a human race to keep in perfect obedience, but the new covenant of salvation in Christ required only sincerity and earnest endeavor:

> Whereas the first agreement was "Do this and live," the second was "Try to do this and live." To man in his strength God said, "Do everything which I command"; to man in his weakness God said, "Use thy best endeavors to do everything which I command." Perfect obedience was made the condition of the first covenant; earnest, hearty obedience of the second.[28]

The Moravian Witness: Gracious Submission

What was absent from this perfectionism of right intention and earnest endeavor, however, was the Augustinian dimension of grace. Law's guidelines consisted of the "stern, objective, moralistic piety of High Churchmanship,"[29] and while this served to strengthen a concept of spiritual self-discipline as the means of finding God through personal holiness, it did little to foster an expectancy of divine initiative toward the believer. It was this which Wesley found so immediately compelling about the Moravians with whom he shared his voyage to Georgia in 1735. At an early stage in the journey, he was sufficiently impressed to learn German so that he might converse with them. He described the group as "men who have left all for their Master, and who have indeed learned of Him, being meek and lowly, dead to the world, full of faith and of the Holy Ghost."[30] Their behavior throughout the voyage seemed to him to be exemplary, as they gave continual proof of their humility "by performing those servile offices for the other passengers which none of the English would undertake. . . . If they were pushed, struck, or thrown down, they rose again and went away; but no complaint was found in their mouth." And when a severe storm arose, Wesley noted that there was now an opportunity to see whether "they were delivered from the spirit of fear, as well as from that of pride, anger, and revenge."[31] As is well known, their Christian spirit more than passed the test.

Shortly after his arrival in Georgia, Wesley turned to the Moravians for spiritual guidance, and the essence of his conversation with one of their leaders, Spangenberg, was to be the focus of Wesley's spiritual pilgrimage leading to Aldersgate Street in 1738:

> [Mr. Spangenberg] told me he could say nothing till he had asked me two or three questions. "Do you know yourself? Have you the witness within yourself? Does the Spirit of God bear witness with your spirit that you are a child of God?" I was surprised, and knew not what to answer. He observed it, and asked, "Do you know Jesus Christ?" I paused, and said, "I know He is the Saviour of the world." "True," replied he; "but do you know He has saved you?" "I hope He has died to save me." He only added, "Do you know yourself?" I said, "I do." But I fear they were vain words.[32]

Spangenberg's questioning was astute. The issue was not only the objective doctrine of justification by faith; it was also the inward regeneration which had been described more than a hundred years earlier by the Puritan divine John Preston as "the testimony of the Spirit . . . such an expression of love and peace and joy, such a thing that no man knows but himself."[33]

In fact, Wesley's spiritual progress was of real concern to the Moravian group in Georgia.[34] In May 1736, he approached them with a request to be admitted fully into their fellowship, but they were not willing to receive a new member with undue haste. Wesley pressed them for their conditions of acceptance, and one of the members, John Töltschig, replied by describing to him the spiritual progression practiced by their community at Herrnhut. The first step was to try to lead people out of themselves, so that the "word of power" might break in on them and "pierce them through." When they were thus "apprehended by grace," their souls were tended so that they might grow in grace from one step to the next. But they were not admitted into full fellowship until they had "genuine forgiveness of sins" and "peace with God," from which would proceed a glad and willing submission to the Moravian discipline.[35]

Even though this effectively denied Wesley's request for membership, he continued to confide in them in spiritual matters. He began a correspondence with Count Zinzendorf, which from the beginning entered into a theological dialogue leading to their future meetings, and, in July 1737, Spangenberg suggested that Wesley should draw up a series of doctrinal questions for further discussion. The spiritual guidance was again astute, in that Wesley himself was encouraged to set the

agenda, and the questions clearly indicated his concern to search out
the significance of the "inner witness" in relation to his ongoing quest for
personal holiness. "What do you mean by conversion?" Wesley asked.
"The passing from darkness to light," replied Spangenberg, "and from
the power of Satan unto God." "Is it commonly wrought at once, or by
degrees?" "The design of passing thus from darkness unto light is
sometimes wrought in a moment, . . . but the passage itself is gradual."
"Ought we so to expect the Holy Ghost to convert either our own or our
neighbor's soul so as to neglect any outward means?" "Many things are
mentioned in Scripture as helps to an entire conversion. So reading
the Scripture . . . hearing it . . . fasting . . . self-examination . . . the
instructions of experienced persons . . . fervent prayer. None therefore
ought to neglect any of these, when it is in their power to use them."[36]

The Crisis of Surrender: Inward Assurance

On his return to England at the end of that year, Wesley's spiritual
quest had reached a point of crisis. His Journal at the close of January
1738 was nothing less than a *cri de coeur:*

> If it be said that I have faith (for many such things have I heard from
> many miserable comforters), I answer, So have the devils—a sort
> of faith; but still they are strangers to the covenant of prom-
> ise. . . . The faith I want is "a sure trust and confidence in God
> that, through the merits of Christ, my sins are forgiven, and I
> reconciled to the favour of God." I want the faith
> which . . . whosoever hath it . . . is freed from doubt, "having the
> love of God shed abroad in his heart, through the Holy Ghost
> which is given unto him"; which "Spirit itself beareth witness with
> his spirit, that he is a child of God."[37]

It was another Moravian, Peter Böhler, who was to provide a decisive
role in resolving the crisis. In a number of conversations with Wesley, he
testified to the living faith which comes through justification. He pointed
to an expectancy of God's grace as the initiative of the new covenant, to
which human obedience was a response rather than a duty.[38] Wesley's
own account of his progression to the evening of May 24, 1738 at
Aldersgate Street is well known, as is his description of the change which
took place.[39] In appropriating what R. Newton Flew has described as
the tradition of the "evangelical succession of believers,"[40] Wesley

came to know for himself what his father had impressed upon him as the essence of the faith: the *inward witness.*[41]

Yet this "revelation of Christ in our hearts," this "divine evidence or conviction of his love," had been an integral part of Wesley's earlier Oxford theology. His 1733 sermon, "The Circumcision of the Heart," made clear that his quest for personal holiness at that time was a searching for the same "distinguishing mark of a true follower of Christ, of one who is in a state of acceptance with God . . . a right state of soul, a mind and spirit renewed after the image of Him that created it."[42] Nor yet had Spangenberg denied the validity of outward means of grace such as prayer, Bible reading, and worship in aiding toward a full conversion, as can be noted in the conversation Wesley had with him in 1737. The question which must be asked, therefore, is in what ways the Moravian emphasis on justification by faith was sufficiently distinctive to impel Wesley, even before his Aldersgate Street experience, to preach with a new vigor, to "declare the love of God to all," and to be banned from several pulpits for so doing.[43]

Illumination of Faith: The Divine Initiative

It is helpful, in addressing this question, to note a distinction made by Umphrey Lee between mysticism and enthusiasm. Mysticism, suggests Lee, is a striving for the union of the soul with the Absolute; enthusiasm is "a vaguer idea of guidance, of impulses, information, commands coming directly from deity to individual."[44] Both concepts can be described as an immediate experience of God, and it was in the nature of his spiritual searching at Oxford that Wesley should have been drawn to writers with a mystical emphasis such as Henry Scougal.[45] William Law had strongly encouraged this pursuit, guiding Wesley toward the German mystics and urging him in particular to read the *Theologia Germanica.*[46] But Wesley returned from Georgia in 1738 with a different outlook, regarding the writings of the mystics as "nothing like that religion which Christ and His apostles lived and taught"; and later he could even refer to the "affected obscurity" of the "unscriptural writer" of the *Theologia.*[47] After a sharp exchange of letters, his relationship with William Law was effectively ended.[48]

It was not that Wesley had come to reject the immediacy of divine illumination.[49] The difference was that he now accepted it as wholly of divine initiative—in short, a significantly new understanding of grace. In *The Circumcision of the Heart*, he had stated this in principle, but had

worked it out in a discipline of self-application rather than in an acceptance of discipleship. Those who are born of God by faith, he had
argued, have the testimony of their own spirit with the Spirit which
witnesses in their hearts. Without the Spirit of God, we can do nothing
but add sin to sin, since it is God who alone works in us either to will or
to do that which is good—or even to think a good thought. But the
Christian "neither apprehends the difficulties of the race set before him
to be greater than he has strength to conquer, nor expects them to be so
little as to yield in the conquest till he has put forth all his strength." It is
by discipline that every good soldier of Christ is to "inure himself to
endure hardship." It is through "daily care," albeit by the grace of God
in Christ, that the Christian purges "the inmost recesses of the soul from
the lusts that before possessed and defiled it." The Christian who does
not run the race in this way, who does not practice such self-denial,
fights the fight of faith to little purpose and merely "beateth the air."[50]

In *An Earnest Appeal to Men of Reason and Religion*, however,
published some ten years later, we find that the emphasis is wholly on
faith as a gift of God. It is

> the eye of the new-born soul. Hereby every true believer in God
> "seeth him who is invisible." Hereby . . . he seeth "the light of the
> glory of God in the face of Jesus Christ. . . ."
>
> It is the ear of the soul, whereby a sinner "hears the voice of the
> Son of God and lives. . . . "
>
> It is the feeling of the soul, whereby a believer perceives, through
> the "power of the Highest overshadowing him," both the existence
> and the presence of him in whom he "lives, moves, and has his
> being" . . . (and) feels "the love of God shed abroad in his heart."

But above all it is the free gift of God. No one is able

> to work it in himself. It is a work of omnipotence. It requires no less
> power thus to quicken a dead soul than to raise a body that lies in
> the grave. It is a new creation; and none can create a soul anew but
> he who at first created the heavens and the earth.[51]

Anglican Criticism: Undue "Enthusiasm"

Wesley's proclamation of justifying faith as an instant gift of God
quickly occasioned Anglican criticism, in spite of the doctrine's Reforma-

tion and Augustinian pedigree. The usual charge was that such claims led to undue "enthusiasm" and thence to antinomianism. Wesley vigorously rejected this. True Christian experience, he rejoined, was grounded in scripture and reason.[52] This was not the same as enthusiasm, which he defined succinctly in a journal entry for January 1739:

> I was with two persons, who I doubt are properly enthusiasts. For first, they think to attain the end without the means; which is enthusiasm, properly so called. Again, they think themselves inspired by God, and are not. But false, imaginary inspiration is enthusiasm. That theirs is only imaginary inspiration appears hence: it contradicts the Law and the Testimony.[53]

The assurance of faith which Wesley preached and taught was a religious intuition, a direct witness of the Spirit of God which enabled the believer to cry "Abba, Father," the moment it was given. It was something immediate, and not the result of reflection or argumentation, for it preceded any human reasoning. Yet it was not an "enthusiastic" experience. It did not obviate the need for an accountability to the law of God, and to the means of grace. The one followed from the other.[54]

Anglican Ambivalence: The Need for Clarification

From the outset of these polemics, the issue was the formal cause of justification. In September 1739, for example, Wesley recorded a discussion in which he had been asked to enumerate his differences on the subject with the Church of England. Making it clear that he did not regard himself at variance with Anglican doctrine, but only with some Anglican clergy, he made the following points:

> First. They speak of justification, either as the same thing with sanctification, or as something consequent upon it. I believe justification to be wholly distinct from sanctification, and necessarily antecedent to it.
> Secondly, they speak of our own holiness, or good works, as the cause of our justification; or that for the sake of which, on account of which, we are justified before God. I believe neither our own holiness nor good works are any part of the cause of our justification; but that the death and righteousness of Christ are the whole and sole cause of it.

Thirdly. They speak of good works as a condition of justification, necessarily previous to it. I believe no good work can be previous to justification, nor, consequently, a condition of it; but that we are justified . . . by faith alone, faith without works.

Fourthly. They speak of sanctification (or holiness) as if it were an outward thing—as if it consisted chiefly, if not wholly, in those two points: (1) the doing no harm; (2) the doing good (as it is called); . . . I believe it to be an inward thing, namely, the life of God in the soul of man; . . . the renewal of our heart after the image of Him that created us.

Lastly. They speak of the new birth as an outward thing—as if it were no more than baptism; . . . I believe it to be an inward thing; a change from inward wickedness to inward goodness; an entire change of our inmost nature.[55]

These tensions are not unlike those to be found in the polemical treatises of the English Reformation, and the issues are precisely what they had been during those pivotal years in the sixteenth century: faith and works, grace and nature, divine sovereignty and freedom of will. Wesley had early to come to realize that faith was primarily a question of the will, but had done so initially in the context of a positive assessment of human reason.[56] Now that he was plumbing the depths of justification by faith, he was encountering the great richness of a doctrine which declared absolutely that God's grace was all things and the human will was nothing. The 1746 Conference recorded that, in ascribing all good to the free grace of God, in denying all natural free will, all power antecedent to grace, and in excluding all merit from man, Methodists came "to the very brink of Calvinism."[57] And in "Justification by Faith," published in the first volume of Sermons on Several Occasions in 1746, there was the clear affirmation that it is God who calls and shows mercy, rather than the sinner who chooses to repent.[58]

Anglican Moralism: Synergistic Faith and Works

The doctrine of justification in Anglican theology, on the other hand, had come to a point in Wesley's day where God's grace and human responsibility were jointly held to be of account in a synergism with strong Pelagian tendencies. The authority most often cited for this position was a treatise published in 1670 by Bishop George Bull: the *Harmonia Apostolica*. Bull argued that people must actively seek to change their lives in order to benefit from Christ's atonement. "Good works are the condition, according to the divine appointment established in the gospel covenant, requisite and necessary to man's justification."[59] It was not that Bull advocated an atonement which could be merited—the merits were solely those of Christ—but he held that repentance was as necessary to faith as justification, and that faith and repentance both included works. Indeed, faith as mere assent or knowledge had little to do with justification.[60]

The position has a particular theological pedigree in the Anglican tradition. It was the outcome of what C.F. Allison has described as a watershed in the middle of the seventeenth century, "an ineluctable movement away from the Christian faith of the earlier divines towards a moralism masquerading as faith."[61] Not that the theologians of the earlier classical Anglicanism had espoused a uniform doctrine of justification. Richard Hooker had viewed it in terms of the regeneration of the will.[62] Lancelot Andrewes had stressed human initiative in appropriating the faith.[63] William Laud had defined faith itself as essentially a human act, as assent of the will and understanding, which did not contradict reason.[64] But in these, as in the other writings of classical Anglicanism, there was a common emphasis on the graciousness of God's atoning work in Christ, and a perception of sin as a profound human condition—a separation from God. Whereas in the later Anglican writers such as Henry Hammond, Jeremy Taylor, Richard Baxter, and George Bull, sin was viewed as a transgression, an action rather than a condition, for which the remedy was the leading of a holy life.[65] Christ's atonement was thus exemplary rather than efficacious. And while Jeremy Taylor, for example, could stress the necessity of grace, especially in his devotional works, the tenor of his highly influential writings and theology was essentially moralistic.[66]

Antinomianism, and the fear of it, were undoubtedly factors in this theological progression, as they had been from the beginning of the English Reformation.[67] Indeed, it can be argued that a concern to guard against the perceived social and political dangers of justification by faith was precisely what rendered Anglican soteriology deficient in its ontological presuppositions.[68] Whether for this reason, or because of the Pelagian tendencies which, as Gerald Cragg has observed, were "always so congenial to the Anglo-Saxon mind, and so prevalent in the eighteenth century,"[69] Anglican theology never did resolve the question of the formal cause of justification. It was an open question in the *Homilies* and the *Articles*.[70] It remained open during the reign of Elizabeth, whose *via media* was even more circumspect than that of her father, Henry VIII.[71] In the seventeenth century, it was at once cause and effect in the development of Anglican thought as a theological method rather than theology *per se*.[72] And in Wesley's day, the enervating diffidence of Latitudinarianism notwithstanding, the issue retained a latent volatility.[73]

Wesley's Critical Insight: Distinctive Justification

In a seminal article for contemporary Wesley studies, Albert Outler has shown why this particular point of doctrine was so important for Wesley, and why his handling of it is the measure of his place as a theologian in the Christian tradition.[74] The formal cause of justification concerns the change which takes place when a person is forgiven and reconciled to God in Christ—in a word, what happens when one becomes a Christian. Given the evangelistic nature of Wesley's ministry, it is hardly surprising that this was the focus of his theological pilgrimage. It is a mark of his sure theological instinct, however, that he began his enquiry into the doctrine by going back to its formulation in the early English Reformation.

Arguing from the *Articles* and *Homilies*, he affirmed that justification was by faith alone, through the merits of Christ, and that good works could only follow this faith, not precede it.[75] At the same time, he affirmed that the necessary consequence of justification was the doing of good works. Instead of linking these necessary good works with the doctrine of justification *per se*, however, he assigned them to the inseparable but quite distinct process of sanctification, an outward holiness which sprang from an inward holiness of heart.[76] This was the touchstone of his theology, and more than anything else provided the shape of early Methodist discipleship:

> But what is it to be justified? . . . It is evident . . . that it is not the being made actually just and righteous. This is *sanctification*; which is, indeed in some degree, the immediate fruit of justification, but, nevertheless, is a distinct gift of God, and of a totally different nature. The one implies what God does for us through his Son; the other, what he works in us by his Spirit. So that, although some rare instances may be found, wherein the term *justified* or *justification* is used in so wide a sense as to include *sanctification* also; yet, in general use, they are sufficiently distinguished from each other, both by St. Paul, and the other inspired writers.[77]

It was a distinction which Baxter's double justification did not adequately emphasize, and the implications were profound. It was not that Wesley saw justification as an isolated doctrine, nor yet as all-encompassing; but he saw the importance of making it a *distinctive* doctrine in the context of Christian discipleship. Distinctively defined, justification was a sense of pardon and acceptance by God, for which the only requisite condition was faith in the merits of Christ's atoning work. This faith was a gift, wholly of God's grace; and with it came the simultaneous gift of the new birth. Yet the two were not the same. "The one is the taking away the guilt, the other the taking away the power, of sin: so that, although they are joined together in point of time, yet are they of wholly distinct natures."[78]

Justification for Discipleship

Without this distinction, the privilege of being children of God is misunderstood, for there is a "wide difference" between being justified and being born again, "the former relating to the great work which God does *for* us, in forgiving our sins; the latter, to the great work which God does *in* us, in renewing our fallen nature." There was no sequence to these two gifts, explained Wesley, but "in order of *thinking*, as it is termed, justification precedes the new birth. We first conceive His wrath to be turned away, and then His Spirit to work in our hearts."[79] The distinction is of the utmost importance. When it is viewed as a sense of pardon and acceptance by God, bestowed as a gift solely by the merits of Christ's atoning work, but not the same as the regeneration of the human will, which is bestowed as the further gift of God so that the believer has the righteousness of the mind that was in Christ, then justification is far from being a formality. Rather it is bestowed with a purpose: *to work out our salvation in the power of the Holy Spirit.*

This distinctive view of justification was affirmed at the Conference of 1745 as the theological basis for a polity of accountable discipleship. On the one hand, it drew on Wesley's Anglicanism, grounded in the realities of the visible church—its ordinances, its sacraments, and its emphasis on the accountability of the human will. He had given himself to this tradition with complete devotion in searching for the inward holiness which was the purpose and fulfillment of these outward means of grace, but had ultimately found it wanting. On the other hand, his distinctive view of justification incorporated the evangelical faith of the Moravians, declaring salvation to be effected wholly by grace, in which the will of the believer was subsumed by the divine imperative. This, too, Wesley had found wanting, in that he could not accept the absolute inability of people to work toward their salvation. Together, however, the two traditions afforded an understanding of God's salvation which affirmed divine initiative and human response in the immediacy of a new relationship—a relationship for which there were no preconditions other than a willingness to be open to God's grace.

Prevenient Grace

The significance of this was twofold. First of all, it extended the efficacy of God's grace to the *whole* of human experience. In this, Wesley appropriated an important dimension of the seventeenth-century Anglican tradition—the doctrine of prevenient grace. It had emerged primarily as a rejection of predestination, and had been formulated especially by Laudians such as Henry Hammond, who propounded a universal redemption in which a real capability of salvation had been restored to all men and women.[80] Widely known as Arminianism, in fact it had its origins in English theology long before the controversy in the Low Countries which led to the Synod of Dort.[81] It was the generally accepted doctrine of the Church of England in Wesley's day, and he never saw the need to depart from it, even though it caused a breach with George Whitefield in 1740 which was never really healed.[82] But whereas in Anglicanism it had developed into the Pelagian tendencies of George Bull's conditional justification, Wesley anchored it firmly to the doctrine of original sin by defining the "natural" human state as one in which God was already active through prevenient grace. There is no one, he argued, in a state of "mere nature" who is "wholly void of the grace of God," unless he has persistently "quenched the Spirit." This was not to deny the depravity of human nature after the fall, but to hold to the Anglican view that the *present* state of the human race was not one of total depravity. Since the fall, a natural conscience had been restored to man, "more properly termed, *preventing grace*," and of this, "no man living is entirely destitute."[83] The Tenth Article of the Church of England said as much:

> The condition of man after the fall of Adam is such, that he cannot turn and prepare himself by his own natural strength and good works, to faith and calling upon God: Wherefore we have no power to do good works pleasant and acceptable to God, without

the grace of God by Christ preventing us, that we may have a good will, and working with us, when we have that good will.[84]

Wesley regarded this prevenient grace as an integral part of the "Scripture Way of Salvation," being "that light wherewith the Son of God enlighteneth every one that cometh into the world," and showing every one "to do justly, to love mercy, and to walk humbly with his God." It was "all the convictions which his Spirit, from time to time, works in every child of man; although, it is true, the generality of men stifle them as soon as possible, and after a while forget, or at least deny, that ever they had them at all." [85]

The first dimension of Wesley's distinction was, therefore, to draw nature and grace into a dialectic rather than a dichotomy, since even the "natural" person had a knowledge of God, imparted by prevenient grace. The tension was between the "drawings" of God and the "stifling" or "quenching" of the Spirit by sinful human beings—in short, the resistance to grace. Wesley's position, contrary to that of George Whitefield and the Calvinists of his day, was that the grace of God in general did not act irresistibly. "We may comply therewith, or may not."[86] There was a process which led to justification: a spiritual searching, a despair, an "emptying" of all self-righteousness, until the human will submitted to God's active grace, and the sinner was justified. Moreover, by making a distinction between justification and prevenient grace, Wesley made this submission of the will an intentional step in which there was an active human participation. By grace, the sinner had been given the capacity to resist God's grace. To cease to resist was thus an act of human responsibility. By the same token, prevenient grace rendered men and women accountable for doing the best they could, whether or not they had the assurance of justifying faith.[87]

Regeneration of the Will

The second dimension of the distinction concerned the relationship between justification and sanctification. Just as the work of God's prevenient grace was to restore the human will to a capacity for repentance, the corollary of which was the capacity to resist, so the work of sanctifying grace was to empower the will for an accountable discipleship, the corollary of which was likewise the capacity to resist. The changes which followed from justification were real as well as relative, and the quest for personal holiness, beginning with the regeneration of the will, was not to be relegated to the mysteries of eternity. It was to be worked out in daily living:

> We allow, it is the work of God alone to justify, to sanctify, and to glorify; which three comprehend the whole of salvation. Yet we cannot allow, that man can only resist, and not in any wise "work together with God"; or that God is so the whole worker of our salvation, as to exclude man's working at all . . . for the Scripture is express, that (having received power from God) we are to "work out our own salvation"; and that (after the work of God is begun in our souls) we are "workers together with Him."[88]

Efficacious Means of Grace

It was in this context that Wesley could not regard as invalid the regulated Christian living developed by the "methodical" years at Oxford. In the initial liberation of his evangelical experience, there was some reaction against these personal disciplines as restrictive works of the law, but it was quickly tempered by an awareness of their importance as efficacious means of prevenient grace and accountable discipleship—something he particularly affirmed about the ordinances of the church.[89] The minutes of the 1744 Conference urged the Methodist preachers to use all the means of grace, "instituted" and "prudential," and to "enforce the use of them on all persons." The instituted means of grace were listed as prayer, searching the scripture, the sacrament of the Lord's Supper, fasting, and Christian conversation. The prudential means were the various personal disciplines for growing in grace—watching, self-denial, exercise of the presence of God—and regular attendance at class or band meeting.[90]

The minutes also included a significant discussion of faith and works:

> Q.11. Are works necessary to the continuance of faith?
> A. Without doubt; for a man may forfeit the free gift of God, either by sins of omission or commision.
> Q.12. Can faith be lost, but for want of works?
> A. It cannot but through disobedience.[91]

The position was reaffirmed in 1746:

> Q.25. Does faith supersede (set aside the necessity of) holiness or good works?
> A. In no wise. So far from it, that it implies both, as a cause does its effects.[92]

This was exactly what was stated in the *Twelfth Article* of the Church of England.[93] As we have noted, however, this position was not developed with sufficient clarity in Anglican theology, not least because it proved to be a major point of dispute with the Calvinism which impacted the English Reformation well before the end of the sixteenth century and throughout the seventeenth. To the extent that the issue was still unresolved in the eighteenth century, Wesley found himself in a constant tension with the Calvinist wing of the Revival, and especially with the Calvinists who had remained in the Church of England. This varied in intensity as the years went by, but came to a head in the early 1770s, and led to the polemics of the closing years of his life.

Calvinist Objections: Imputed Righteousness

Predestination was not the focal point of the dispute.[94] Rather it centered theologically, as had the Anglican criticism of his position on faith, on the formal cause of justification and the nature of imputed righteousness. It is not easy to follow the arguments in Wesley's writings, many of which were couched in the immediacy of his work as an evangelist.[95] Indeed, there were times when he clearly regarded the whole question as a distraction from the central message of the gospel.[96] Yet he kept returning to it throughout his ministry precisely because it *was* central to the proclamation of the gospel. And it was also why, as late as 1778, he founded the *Arminian Magazine* in which some of his later (and much neglected) sermons first appeared.

The Calvinist position that Christ's righteousness is the formal cause of justification had been adopted in the sixteenth century as a safeguard against any insinuation of works righteousness in the doctrine of salvation.[97] Contrasted with the Anglican position that Christ's righteousness is the meritorious cause of justification, it is easy to see how the issue had continued to focus on antinomianism in English ecclesial and social life. If Christ's righteousness is the formal cause of justification, as the Calvinists argued, then the change which occurs in the believer is the imputation of this righteousness as the condition of salvation. Since clearly the forgiven sinner remains a sinner, or at best something less than Christ-like, the force of the doctrine was to affirm that faith in Christ is the assurance of this imputed righteousness, and thereby of remission of sins and eternal life.[98] Since the work of salvation is Christ's and Christ's alone, it does not matter whether or not his righteousness is *imparted* to the believer. To dwell on this question would be to flirt with the idea of inherent righteousness, which the Calvinists would not brook at all. Since only the righteouness of Christ counts before God, the only hope of the sinner, therefore, is to be cloaked in that righteousness. And that indeed was how the Calvinists viewed imputed righteousness—the cloaking of the sinner in the righteousness of Christ as the changed condition, or formal cause, of justification.

The Merits of Christ's Righteousness

Viewed as the meritorious cause of justification, however, the righteousness of Christ takes on at once a more poignant and catholic quality. Such at least is the language of the *Eleventh Article* of the Church of England, in which the merits of Christ's righteousness—what Christ has accomplished for us in his atoning work—count us righteous before God.[99] The changed condition in the believer, or the formal cause of justification, is faith in the merits of that accomplishment; and the imputation of Christ's righteousness is not, therefore, the condition of justification, but rather of regeneration—that which God initially does *in* us. Imputed righteousness does indeed mark a new condition or form. The believer experiences a regenerated will, a new desire and tendency to seek and serve God. And inasmuch as regeneration accompanies justification, this new will is a mark of true faith in the merits of Christ. But it is not the condition of pardon and acceptance by God. Faith, and faith alone, is the formal cause of the justification earned for us by the righteousness of Jesus Christ.

The definitive statement of Wesley's position on the issue is his sermon, "The Lord Our Righteousness," first preached in 1765. In this, he first of all makes clear what he means by the righteousness of Christ. It is twofold, divine and human; and it is the human righteousness of Christ which pertains to the doctrine of imputation. This human righteousness of Christ means his inward purity, his "*every holy and heavenly temper*," and also his outward righteousness, in doing the will of

God on earth "as the angels do it in heaven." Moreover, Christ's obedience implied not only his *doing*, but also his *suffering* the whole will of God, "from the time He came into the world, till 'He bore our sins in His own body upon the tree'; yea, till having made a full atonement for them, 'He bowed His head, and gave up the ghost.' "[100] This is the righteousness which is imputed "to everyone that believes, as soon as he believes: faith and righteousness of Christ are inseparable. . . . There is no true faith, that is, justifying faith, which hath not the righteousness of Christ for its object."[101] Not that faith *per se* is the cause of our justification, but faith in the righteousness of Christ, through which "every believer is forgiven and accepted, merely for the sake of what Christ has done and suffered."[102]

The nub of the argument, however, comes at the conclusion of the sermon, where Wesley makes clear his rejection of Christ's righteousness as the formal cause of justification. What he resists is that "any should use the phrase, 'The righteousness of Christ,' or 'The righteousness of Christ is imputed to me,' as a cover for his unrighteousness."[103] Justification for Wesley is a change in the relationship of the believer to God, for which the only condition is faith in the righteousness of Christ. It is forgiveness and acceptance, not an act of divine self-deception whereby God counts sinners to be what in fact they are not. It is the act of God which, for the sake of what Christ has done, "showeth forth His righteousness (or mercy) by the remission of the sins that are past."[104]

The Dangers of Practical Antinomianism

It is here that we find Wesley the evangelist/theologian at his best. The issue may have been a fine point of theological dispute, but in the field, preaching the gospel to the rank and file of the people of his day, he saw that this Calvinist doctrine often engendered a practical antinomianism.[105] The reason for this was the TULIP formulation which followed inexorably from affirming the righteousness of Christ as the formal cause of justification. Since this righteousness was clearly not imputed to all—for there were many who did not evince justifying faith—then logically there were those whom God did not intend to save. And by the same logic, those who were destined for salvation found the grace of their justification irresistible, since the efficient or moving cause of predestination to eternal life was "not the prevision of faith, or of perseverance, or of good works, or of anything which may be in the persons predestinated, but only the will of the good pleasure of God."[106]

To affirm, as did the Calvinists, that the righteousness of Christ was imputed to the sinner irresistibly by grace, was to imply that no human endeavor at all could be counted as worthy of merit in the *ordo salutis*. Christ's righteousness alone was acceptable to God. And while this provided a powerful assurance for those who took their discipleship seriously, it could, and often did, lead to serious misunderstandings among ordinary people over the nature of grace and salvation. In the form of Quietism, for example, it was the occasion of Wesley's rift with the Moravians at Fetter Lane,[107] and he increasingly saw the mischievous results in his societies when half-understood Calvinist teachings on imputed righteousness led to the doctrinal and ethical confusions which frequently bred a practical antinomianism.[108] Harald Lindström has suggested that it was Wesley's struggle against precisely such dangers which impelled him to reject the notion of imputed righteousness as a fulfillment of the law by proxy. The idea that Christ had met the claims of the law on behalf of the human race seemed to remove any obligation to fulfill the moral law, which is why he dissociated the fulfillment of the law from atonement and justification, and attached it instead to sanctification.[109]

Calvinist Polemics

Wesley made repeated efforts at conciliatory dialogue with the Calvinists, including a series of publications during the 1760s which in many ways constitute his most mature writings.[110] The polemics continued to gather momentum, however, and things were finally brought to a head by the Minutes of the 1770 Conference:

> 3. We have received it as a maxim, that "a man can do nothing in order to justification." Nothing can be more false. Whoever desires to find favour with God should "cease from evil, and learn to do well." Whoever repents, should do "works meet for repentance." And if this is not *in order* to find favour, what does he do them for? . . .
> 4. Is not this "salvation by works?" Not by the *merit* of works, but by works as a *condition*. . . .
> 6. As to *merit* itself, of which we have been so dreadfully afraid: we are rewarded "according to our works," yea, "because of our

works." How does this differ from for the sake of your works? . . . Can you split this hair. I doubt I cannot. . . .

8. Does not talking of a justified or a sanctified *state*, tend to mislead men? Almost naturally leading them to trust, in what was done in one moment? Whereas we are every hour and every moment, pleasing or displeasing to God, "according to our works." According to the whole of our inward tempers, and our behavior.[111]

Wesley felt that these "terrible propositions," as he ironically described them during the uproar which followed, contained "truth of the deepest importance, and such as ought to be continually inculcated by those who would be pure from the blood of all men."[112] But there were so many Calvinist accusations of "salvation by works" that a public clarification had to be made. The 1771 Conference officially conceded that the 1770 Minutes were "not sufficiently guarded in the way they [were] expressed," and affirmed an abhorrence of justification by works as an "abominable doctrine."[113] Yet the statements made in the 1770 Minutes were not rescinded. As Wesley pointed out to the Countess of Huntingdon, the issue was not whether works were the condition of *obtaining* justification, but of *continuing* in the favor of God.[114] Where he parted from the Calvinists was in restricting justification to the distinctive concept of God's *pardon*. It was a change in relationship between God and man, effected wholly by grace through the merits of Christ, a grace which was even irresistible at the critical point of surrender.[115] It was preceded by the drawings of prevenient grace; it was accompanied by the regeneration of the will, the imputed righteousness of the new birth; and it was immediately followed by the real changes worked through sanctifying grace. But justification was specifically and distinctly a sense of acceptance by God in the new covenant, a relationship offered by grace and appropriated by faith at every moment.[116] The new covenant of faith in Christ did not require

any impossibility to be done. . . . This were only to mock human weakness. Indeed, strictly speaking, the covenant of *grace* doth not require us to *do* anything at all, as absolutely and indispensibly necessary in order to our justification; but only, to *believe* in Him who, for the sake of his Son, and the propitiation which he hath made, "justifieth the ungodly that worketh not," and imputes his faith to him for righteousness.[117]

Distinctive Sanctification

The effect of this distinction was to give heightened emphasis to the responsibility of discipleship by imparting a corresponding distinction to sacntification. The new relationship with God, initiated and maintained by justifying grace, brought with it a sanctifying grace which renewed the will inwardly and which led to a transformed life outwardly. The real and relative changes in the believer were interdependent as well as distinct. The changed relationship of justification *necessarily* led to good works, because of the accompanying transformation of sanctifying grace. It was a dynamic necessity, in that a relationship with a living God could not, by definition, be static.

Works of Obedience

Good works which followed justification were therefore those of obedience rather than obligation, of consequence rather than significance. By the same token, disobedience not only impeded the process of sanctification; it affected the immediacy of justification by constituting a breach, however temporary, in the faith relationship with God. It was nothing less than a repudiation of the new covenant. The ongoing, moment-by-moment relationship of justification was exactly that: *moment-by-moment.* It was available at all times by grace through faith, but it was subject to the indiscipline of disobedience until sanctifying grace worked the real change of a sinner's will away from self and toward God:

> Q.26. When does inward sanctification begin?
> A. In the moment we are justified. The seed of every virtue is then sown in the soul. From that time the believer gradually dies to sin, and grows in grace. Yet sin remains in him; yea, the seed of all sin, till he is sanctified throughout, in spirit, soul and body.[118]

The Doctrine of Christian Perfection

The mark of a mature Christian, therefore, was a consistent obedience to God, in which the relationship of justifying faith was no longer interrupted by a wayward will, but firmly grounded in a service of love. It was this which Wesley articulated as the doctrine of Christian perfection: that the inward renewal of the believer could proceed, in this life, to a point of entire sanctification.[119] This was, of course, in conflict with the Calvinist position on justification, which stated quite clearly that it would be presumptuous for the justified sinner to press for any other perfection than that of Christ's righteousness imputed by faith.[120] It was likewise a major point of difference between Wesley and Zinzendorf, who held that Christ's perfection was imputed to the sinner simultaneously with justification.[121] For Wesley, however, Christian perfection was real, not imputed, and it was quite distinct from justification. It was imparted by grace, as was justification, and received through faith:

> [It] appears, beyond all possibility of exception that to this day both my brother and I maintained, (1) That Christian perfection is that love of God and our neighbour, which implies deliverance from all sin. (2) That this is received merely by faith. (3) That it is given instantaneously, in one moment; that now is the accepted time, now is the day of this salvation.[122]

The doctrine has been criticized as Wesley's "pet theory," yet it was no more than the corollary of his distinction between the process of sanctification and the immediacy of justifying faith. It should be noted, first, that he defined Chrsitian perfection as "loving God, with all our heart, mind, soul, and strength," a state in which "all thoughts, words, and actions are governed by pure love."[123] But then it must be observed that this perfection did not exclude "infirmities, ignorance, and mistake." The important qualification was his definition of sin:

> (1) Not only sin, properly so called (that is, a voluntary transgression of a known law) but sin, improperly so called (that is, an involuntary transgression of a divine law, known or unknown) needs the atoning blood. (2) I believe there is no such perfection in this life as excludes these involuntary trangressions which I apprehend to be naturally consequent on the ignorance and mistakes inseparable from mortality. (3) Therefore *sinless perfection* is a phrase I never use, lest I should seem to contradict myself. (4) I believe, a person filled with the love of God is still liable to these involuntary transgressions. (5) Such transgressions you may call sins, if you please: I do not, for the reasons above mentioned.[124]

The perfection which Wesley regarded as attainable in this life was thus one of mature discipleship, a relationship to God in which obedience had become so habitual that the will had lost its tendency to resist the sovereignty of grace.

In this sense, it can be argued that the term *entire sanctification* is not an appropriate description for the doctrine. Indeed, a careful reading of various sermons and treatises on the subject indicate that Wesley had a further distinction in mind. *Sanctification* was a process which preceded *Christian perfection*, and went beyond it, grace upon grace, to all eternity.[125] *Entire sanctification*, on the other hand, was a particular stage in that process, a point at which faithful discipleship culminated in perfect love, a maturity which was as much a gift of God's grace as everything else in the life of the believer. Even though Wesley did not clarify this distinction, the inference is inescapable; *sanctification* and *entire sanctification* are not the same thing. *Christian perfection*, there-fore, is the term to be preferred, understood as maturity of Christian discipleship, but in no way precluding the continued work of sanctifying grace.

Christian Maturity: Consistent Obedience

In point of fact, this is a further significant implication of Wesley's distinctive doctrine of justification, and it sheds important light on the principles he evolved for Methodist discipleship. By restricting justifica-tion to a moment-by-moment sense of pardon, experienced by faith, Wesley infused a divine immediacy into the *whole* of Christian life. As he took the gospel the length and breadth of the land, he saw a wide outpouring of grace. He found, in the richness of Methodist religious experience, a spiritual growth that was analogous to birth, childhood, and coming of age. He saw people brought to the critical point of surrender, their lives changed by justifying grace received through faith. When this was maintained in loving obedience, he saw the develop-ment of religious maturity—a Christian perfection which he came to regard as a "second blessing."[126] When this second blessing was taken for granted, however, there was a falling away—even by the most mature.[127] Obedience could not for one moment be neglected.

The critical question for Christian discipleship, therefore, was how to permit God's grace to foster a maturity of constant obedience, so that sanctifying grace might work with an unimpeded love. It was Wesley's theological understanding of this question which led him to adopt what at first seemed an unbelievably simple solution: a weekly meeting of like-minded persons who would exercise a mutual accountability for their discipleship. This "prudential means of grace" was as profound as it was simple. In adopting the class meeting as the basis for early Methodist polity, Wesley was not only being practical. He was drawing on years of wrestling with that "much disputed doctrine" of the Church of England and its distinctive formulation in his own thought. Its embodiment in the class meeting tempered its formulation, but did not change its substance. The dynamic of early Methodist discipleship was established at the very beginning of the movement on the solid theological principle of distinctive justification—how not to resist the immediacy of God's gracious initiatives. It remains the most important contribution made by Wesley, and by Methodism, to the Christian tradition; and it is time to trace its origin and development in early Methodist polity.

Chapter Three

THE SHAPING OF EARLY METHODIST POLITY

FORMATIVE INFLUENCES AND THE "RISES OF METHODISM"

Wesley was convinced that only through an accountable fellowship could Christian discipleship be nurtured and made effective, and it is in such a context that the development of Methodist polity must be understood. His theological foundations for this were important, as we have observed, but he was also influenced during his formative years by two specific patterns of disciplined Christian living, each an expression of the concept of *ecclesiola in ecclesia*.[1] Before arriving at the Methodist order of *societies, classes,* and *bands,* he had direct experience of the religious societies of the Church of England and the communal piety of the Moravians, applying many of their ideas and practices in what he later described as the three "rises" of Methodism:

> On Monday, May 1 (1738) our little society began in London. But it may be observed, the first rise of Methodism, so called, was in November, 1729, when four of us met together at Oxford; the second was at Savannah, in April 1736, when twenty or thirty persons met at my house; the last was at London, on this day, when forty or fifty of us agreed to meet together every Wednesday evening, in order to a free conversation, begin and ended with singing and prayer.[2]

To comprehend the distinctive characteristics of the class meeting in Methodist polity, we will need to trace the formative influences of these "rises" in some detail. Each in turn provided a component for the dynamic of accountability which has such important implications for twentieth-century Christian discipleship.

1. DISCIPLINED CHURCHMANSHIP
The Religious Societies

The first "rise" of Methodism, the Oxford Holy Club, followed a precedent established some fifty years earlier by the religious societies of the Church of England. These had first appeared in the latter part of the seventeenth century, when the "spirit of celebration" following the restoration of the monarchy in 1660 had seemed to persist for much of the reign of Charles II, resulting not only in the eclipse of Puritan religion, but also in the decline of Puritan morality. The societies were organized through the influence of Dr. Anthony Horneck, a Lutheran minister who had settled in England,[3] and consisted mostly of young men from the High Church of England who were seeking to develop a more disciplined spiritual life. Around the year 1678, they began to hold evening services at St. Clement Dane's Chruch, and to converse together on matters of practical religion.[4]

Horneck drew up a set of rules for the societies, reproduced as Appendix A, which stipulated that all members should be aged at least sixteen and be confirmed Anglicans. A minister of the Church of England had to be chosen as a "director," to be responsible for spiritual guidance and to approve the admission of new members. The societies were to "keep close" to the Church of England in all things, and were to avoid "controversial points of divinity" or discussion of church or state government in their meetings. Practical piety was to be encouraged by the collection of regular contributions for distribution of money to the poor, and the selection of two stewards to deal with this marked the beginning of a strong lay leadership which was to develop as the movement spread.

The standard history of the societies was published in 1698 by Josiah Woodward, who served as minister for the Poplar Society in London, and it is clear from his account that the movement became more strictly regulated as it developed.[5] In the Poplar rules (reproduced as Appendix B), the purpose of the society was specifically declared to be a quest for perfection and holiness through self-examination; and an important function of meeting together was to provide the mutual support and encouragement necessary for such a purpose. The pattern of the meetings was quite structured, with a liturgical as well as a spiritual emphasis. If the director was absent, the stewards were to begin the meeting, or "conference," with an invocation, the opening words of which were: "My Brethren, we are commanded of God, *That our Communication be such as tends to the edifying of one another; and such as ministers*

Grace to the Hearers, Eph. 4.29"[6] Then, all kneeling, three collects were to be repeated, followed by a scripture reading and exposition, allowing comment from any member. This was to be followed by a "discourse," the purpose of which was to further the practice of Christian duty and to promote holiness of life. And the stewards, again in the absence of the director, could propose a subject at each meeting for discussion the following week. The list of suggested topics indicates the marked emphasis on personal religion—the duty of self-examination, the duty of self-abasement, evangelical repentance, trust in God, mortification, humility, prayer and praise, contempt of the world, etc.[7]

The stewards were also instructed to guide the discussion, so that "no Person speak above three or four Sentences, without a convenient Pause, to give room to others to speak their Mind." And to prevent undue digression, specific questions were to be put to the members, so that "every one's Discourse may be the more directly practical." Each member was to be asked about the nature of a particular Christian duty each week—how they were to practice it, the discouragements they experienced in it, and their motives for undertaking it—in a clearly catechetical format.[8] Following the "conference" there was a devotional service, for which an Anglican liturgy was again supplied, and in which singing played an important part. The members were exhorted to "strain up (their) affections to the highest Pitch, and so sing the Praises of God in Heart and Spirit, that Angels and Saints may join with (them)."[9]

Woodward was in no doubt about the advantages of the weekly meetings. They placed young communicants, most of whom were under the age of thirty, in a position where, under the direction of a minister, they could

> admonish and watch over each other, and . . . fortifie each other against those Temptations which assault them from the World and their own Corruptions. . . . And these Persons knowing each other's manner of Life, and their particular Frailties and Temptations, partly by their familiar Conversation, and partly from their own Experience, can much better inspect, admonish, and guard each other, than the most careful Minister usually can.[10]

Woodward further observed that in the society meetings there was a freedom and openness which enabled the members to

> speak more suitably to each other's Capacity, and consequently more effectually to one another, than more learned Persons

ordinarily do. And besides, they can more freely ask and debate
their Queries one among another, more frequently have Recourse,
and more familiarly open their Minds to one another, than with
such as are not of such familiar Acquaintance, or of a Rank superior
to them.[11]

This *Account* was written at what was probably the height of the
societies' effectiveness. The role of lay leadership had become more
prominent than in Horneck's original format, and it was no longer
stipulated that there should be a religious director. In the absence of a
minister, the stewards were named as leaders of worship, and Woodward states that it would only be "very expedient" to have a minister
present "to preserve Order, excite Zeal, and resolve Doubts."[12] This
probably indicated that the rapid proliferation of the societies had made
it difficult to find clergymen willing to accept this responsibility, which,
along with the developed role of lay leadership, opened the groups to
suspicion of schismatic tendencies. Woodward felt the need to include
in the *Account* a detailed response to such allegations, using language
which came close to that of Wesley when answering similar charges a
generation later:

> Whereas it has been objected, That there is danger of *Schism
> and Dissention* by their Weekly Meeting, and conferring together
> about Religious Matters.
> They answer, 1. That they cannot conceive where this Danger
> lies; since no Persons do more professedly own the holy Doctrine
> and Constitution of the Church of England than themselves . . .
> that none do more sincerely reverence and esteem the *publick
> Ministry*, nor more constantly and reverently attend upon the *pub-
> lick Ordinances* . . . and have procured (thro' the Assistance of
> several pious Divines) the benefit of *weekly Communions* in many
> Churches which they frequent in great Numbers.[13]

Far from encouraging their members toward Dissent, Woodward
pointed out that the societies had been the means of bringing several
Dissenters into the Church of England, and had furthermore "preserved
from *Popery* several unsteady and wavering people." Since the sole
purpose of meeting together was to promote practical holiness, and
since points of doctrinal controversy were specifically forbidden by their
rules, the work of the societies could not in any way be said to encroach

upon the offices of the ordained ministry. For twenty years or more it had been "very rarely found that any Member of these Societies had left the Communion of the Church of England for any other," and that "ill designing men" such as "popish emissaries" had been unable to infiltrate the membership.[14]

In spite of such criticisms, by the turn of the century the societies had gained the approval of the highest authorities, as had a parallel movement known as *The Societies for the Reformation of Manners*. These functioned in the main from 1690 to 1710 and had close connections with the religious societies; indeed, they had a sizeable membership in common. But their objectives were markedly different, in that the reforming, or "regulated," societies devoted their energies to the enforcement of law and order in the land. They actively encouraged civic officials in their duty to this end, supplying prosecutors, constables, and even informers to ensure that this was done. There were eight such societies in London alone, and they have rightly been described as "vigilance committees."[15] It is not surprising, therefore, that Woodward should have been at pains to draw a sharp distinction between their aims and those of the religious societies:

> [The] *Societies for Reformation* bent their utmost Endeavours from the first to suppress *publick Vice*; whilst the *Religious Societies* endeavour'd chiefly to promote a due Sense of *Religion* in their own Breasts, tho' they have since been eminently instrumental in the publick Reformation. The *former* endeavour'd to take away the Reproach of our Religion by curbing the Exorbitancies of its Professors; the *latter* attempted to retrieve that holy Vigor in the Practice of Religion, which becomes *Christians*.[16]

The inference drawn by Woodward proved correct, for the regulated societies were relatively short-lived. Rather than the legal constraint which they attempted to exercise, it was the piety of the religious societies which prevailed, and which increasingly led to the practical social works of caring for the poor, relieving debt, visiting the sick, providing for orphans, and setting up about a hundred schools in London and the suburbs. Their work further led to the founding of the *Society for Promoting Christian Knowledge* (SPCK) in 1699, and the *Society for the Propagation of the Gospel in Foreign Parts* in 1701. If the regulated societies had any part to play in these developments, it was by showing the limitations of social coercion, and thereby encouraging the pursuit of "a more excellent way, that of education."[17] As

Woodward observed, while the regulated societies could pluck up the weeds and prepare the ground, it was the promotion of Christian knowledge which planted the seed.[18] It is noteworthy that a subsequent attempt to revive a regulated society in 1756 was also short-lived, even though Wesley gave it his support.[19]

Wesley became a corresponding member of the SPCK in August 1732, and must have been familiar with the work of the religious societies through his father.[20] Samuel Wesley's interest was initially in the regulated societies, for whom he preached a sermon in 1698, relentlessly censuring contemporary morals.[21] His zeal was quickly tempered, however, and channeled into the more positive approach of the religious societies. In 1699 he published *A Letter Concerning the Religious Societies*, in which he urged the need for pastoral care and spiritual growth, and noted their value in this regard.[22] He observed that there were precedents for such societies, including those of the Marquis de Renty, and stressed that their purpose was neither to gather new churches out of existing churches, nor to foment schisms or divisions, nor yet to imply that other Christian brethren were heathen, but rather to promote the glory of God in the practice of humility and charity. After reading Woodward's *Account*, he resolved to form a society at Epworth to improve the state of his people's religion.[23]

The first meeting was held in the rectory on February 7, 1701, with eight persons present in addition to Samuel Wesley himself. Meetings were held on Saturday evenings in order to prepare for the Lord's Day, and Wesley began the practice of using for his Sunday sermon the subject for discussion the following Saturday. Membership was granted only by consent of all, "lest a little Leven should spoil the whole Lump," and was restricted to no more than twelve. When more sought admission—as many as thirty or forty in due course—two members were separated to start a new society, with authority vested in the original body.[24] The results were quite marked. Wesley observed that his people were becoming "much more careful of their lives and conversations," and were taking Communion each month, showing "great devotion" and proving "more zealous for the glory of God, and the welfare of their own souls."[25] (An extract from his account of the society is reproduced in Appendix C).

It is not clear whether these societies survived Samuel Wesley's imprisonment for debt in the summer and fall of 1705, but in 1712, while he was attending the Convocation of the Church of England in London, his wife Susanna began holding what she described as "enlarged family prayers" in the rectory kitchen at Epworth.[26] During the winter of 1711-12, she had undergone a deep religious experience after reading an account of the work of two Danish Moravian missionaries, and she resolved, even though she was "not a man, nor a minister," to "do somewhat more [by speaking] to those with whom I converse with more warmth of affection." She set a time each evening to talk with her children in turn, Thursday being the night for Jacky, the young John Wesley. She also discussed with those neighbors who came to the rectory the "best and most awakening sermons."[27] The numbers in attendance gradually increased, eventually exceeding two hundred, and while the format was that of religious society meetings, the atmosphere was less formal. One reason for this more relaxed atmosphere might well have been the admission of women which, though not specified in Mrs. Wesley's account, can be inferred from her observation that she dared "deny none that ask admittance." In other ways, however, the format of the religious societies was maintained. "Temporal concerns" were disallowed. "We keep close to the business of the day, and, when it is over, all go home."[28] Her use of the word *society* to describe these gatherings cannot have been without significance in view of her husband's previous work.

Nor can the gatherings have failed to make a lasting impression on John.[29] There were many aspects of the religious societies which proved to be direct precedents for Methodist polity: admission procedures, for example, the mutual oversight of personal and public conduct, the weekly meetings, the restriction in some societies to a limited number of members and the use of terminology such as *society* and *steward*. Perhaps most important of all, there was the growing role of lay leadership, something which the correspondence files of the SPCK make very clear. Frequent requests for literature and information indicate that the societies not only continued to function well into the eighteenth century, but that the stewards had emerged even more strongly as pastoral leaders.[30]

The religious societies not only provided a number of precedents for Methodism; initially they were its immediate context. Although in decline when the Revival began, and not commanding the level of support they had enjoyed at the turn of the century, they had by no means disappeared, and there are continued references to their activities alongside those of the Methodist Societies.[31] Wesley was indebted to them in many instances for the incipient structure of his own organization, for they often were receptive to his evangelical message when parish clergy were not, and they provided the first Methodist societies with an important nucleus of membership.[32]

And yet there was an important difference, which can best be described as the "spirit" of the Revival. Where Methodism infiltrated a religious society, there was a transforming process, as new life was infused into the old, and the need for new societies was quickly created.[33] The difference between the religious societies and Methodism was the liberating dynamic of discipleship. It was what James Hutton described as the "joy and wonder" of justification by faith:

> This was to us all something so new, unsuspected, joyful, penetrating; for the most of us had sorely striven and fought against Sin without profit or result, and the teaching in the Churches from the pulpits was so formulated, as if Christ and his Merit, his coming on Earth and Incarnation and his Eternal Redemption, which he obtained for us through his bitter suffering and dying, were not the main thing. It was much forgotten and Pelagianism was the breath of the Pulpits, and dry miserable morality reigned everywhere, and we who were awakened were just as far from Christ as the general run of preachers, for we sought to help ourselves, and dreamt not nor heard nor knew that our salvation lay alone in Christ. So began the evangelical period in England.[34]

That this marked a new departure for the old societies is evidenced by the fact that correspondence between the SPCK and the religious societies ceased quite abruptly as the Revival began. Apparently the SPCK regarded Methodism as dangerously "enthusiastic."[35]

Wesley was indebted to the religious societies for the discipline of Methodism, not least because they maintained the structural link with the Church of England which he regarded as crucial for the United Societies. But it was to the Moravians that he owed the concept of spiritual nurture—the guiding to maturity of a faith which was received as a gift, by grace. It was no coincidence that his mother's "enlarged family prayers" were begun after she learned of the work of Moravian missionaries, for they practiced a spirituality which placed the weight of Christian discipleship firmly with God's initiative. As Julia Wedgwood has put it, with mixed but vivid metaphors: "The religious societies supplied only the body to Methodism, the Moravians gave it a soul; under their influence the empty vessels were again filled, but the wine was different."[36]

2. SPIRITUAL NURTURE
The Moravian Bands

The history of the Moravian church has its roots in the radical movements of late medieval Christianity, and in particular the followers of John Hus.[37] The Romanization of the Bohemian Church had never been thorough, and during the Papal Schism of the fourteenth century, there was a strong undercurrent of patriotic fervor which expressed itself in a desire to purify the church by returning to primitive Christianity.[38] The execution of Hus in 1415 removed the uniting influence of this very diverse movement, leading inevitably to religious wars; and one of the dissident groups to break away from the papacy named themselves the *Unitas Fratrum*, holding their first synod in 1467.[39] In spite of constant persecution during the next century and a half, they continued to grow in strength, and in 1609 achieved a temporary degree of religious toleration, brought to an end, however, by the Thirty Years' War. The defeat of the Protestants at the Battle of the White Hill in 1620 removed all hope of freedom of worship, and the Brethren were expelled from Bohemia.

Lacking official identity, the scattered church nonetheless kept alive the "hidden seed" of their fellowship—a concept which they derived from the biblical notion of "remnant." This was of great significance when their tradition was revived by the renewed *Unitas Fratrum* at Herrnhut in the eighteenth century, a tradition which included an episcopacy in succession from the Waldenses, and a markedly ecumenical perspective.[40] A further component of their tradition was the influence of seventeenth-century German Pietism, the movement largely associated with Philipp Jakob Spener. Spener was a Lutheran pastor who served at Strassburg and Frankfurt, and in the general moral laxity of German Lutheranism following the Thirty Years' War, found a ready response to small groups which he organized for disciplined fellowship, naming them *collegiae pietatis*.[41] His work was continued by August Hermann Francke, who later became professor of theology at the University of Halle, and under whose leadership Pietism took a more practical turn, with the provision of an orphan home, a charity school, a dispensary, and a publishing house.[42] It is not insignificant that Francke took a lively interest in the work of the Anglican religious societies, letting Josiah Woodward know that the Chaplain to the King of Prussia had translated his *Account* into German. Francke himself was elected a corresponding member of the SPCK in June 1700.[43]

The *Unitas Fratrum* found a new home at Herrnhut through the hospitality of the man who was to become their foremost leader in the eighteenth century, Count Nikolaus Ludwig von Zinzendorf. His father had been a personal friend of Spener, and he himself had studied at Halle under Francke. The death of his father when he was only six weeks old had led to his upbringing in the home of his grandmother, the Baroness Katherin von Gersdorf, a woman well educated in theology and biblical languages, who maintained a wide contact with religious leaders and held numerous meetings on her estates for the Pietist movement. From his earliest years, Zinzendorf assimilated two of the movement's important concepts: that of *ecclesiola in ecclesia*, regarded by Spener and Francke alike as a means of reviving the church without occasioning separation; and that of a personal relationship with Christ as the bedrock of the Christian faith. As Zinzendorf recorded many years later, he learned to love his Savior as a child, and had "carried on a friendship with Him, quite in a childlike way, sometimes talking with Him for whole hours, as we talk with a friend, going in and out of the room quite lost in my meditations. I have enjoyed this close personal relationship with Jesus for fifty years, and I feel the happiness of it more and more every day I live."[44]

Zinzendorf spent six formative years in Francke's *paedagogium* at Halle, during which time he developed the firm conviction that, without the unity of fellowship, Christianity was ineffectual. It also led him to develop a broad ecumenical perspective, and when he bought the estate of Berthelsdorf from his grandmother in 1722, it was with the specific intent of creating what he hoped would be a place of refuge for oppressed and persecuted Christians of every kind. He installed a Pietist, Johann Andreas Rother, to be minister of the Lutheran church on the estate, and through him met Christian David, a Moravian preacher in fellowship with a "hidden seed" group of the *Unitas Fratrum*.[45] Zinzendorf's immediate response to David's account of the group's persecution was an offer of land at Berthelsdorf, and by the end of 1722 a community was established, named Herrnhut—"Watch of the Lord."

The growth of the renewed *Unitas Fratrum* at Herrnhut was not, however, without its tensions. Zinzendorf, who adhered to Lutheran doctrine, expected the refugees to merge with the existing congregation at Berthelsdorf, whereas the Moravians were primarily concerned to establish a place in which they could practice their religion in freedom. Initially they nurtured the hope of an eventual return to their homes, but by 1725 it was clear that their stay was likely to be prolonged, and their religious identity thus became an issue. They began to adopt some of the distinctive features of the old *Unitas Fratrum*—the appointment of *helpers*, for example, to exhort their members in their work, their service and almsgiving, the visiting of the sick, and especially for the guidance of souls. The *helpers* were appointed according to spiritual stature rather than their rank, learning, or seniority. They were to manifest the discipline which, as Christian David put it, equipped them to "wrestle, walk and fight gallantly, and thus seize for [them]selves the kingdom of God."[46]

As more refugees continued to arrive on the estate, the question of identity led to further dissension and, in 1727, to the threat of withdrawal from Herrnhut. It was only through the concern and diligence of Zinzendorf in the summer of that year that a compromise agreement was reached, permitting the apostolic disciplines and fellowship of the *Unitas Fratrum* to be recognized as an *ecclesiola* within the *ecclesia* of the religious life of Berthelsdorf.[47] Two major documents were drawn up, the one granting the residents of Herrnhut free citizenship under the protection of the Count, like all the other residents at Berthelsdorf; and the other, signed only by those wishing to enter into an inner religious fellowship—the *Gemeine*.[48] In practice, the whole congregation came under a religious discipline to the extent that the officers of the community concerned themselves with spiritual as well as physical welfare, elders being appointed to keep watch over the maintenance of good order and discipline under the authority of two wardens, one of whom was the Count himself.

One author has gone so far as to describe this system of supervision by elders as monastic.[49] The members were divided into groups, or *classes*, according to age, sex, and marital status, each with a director chosen by the members themselves. Within these *classes* there was a mutual oversight for the furtherance of spiritual growth, each member being visited daily by one of the class to provide exhortation and to take note of the state of his or her soul, in addition to frequent meetings of the classes and of the leaders, all for the purpose of spiritual direction. Spiritual growth was to be assessed, and members identified as "dead," "awaked," "ignorant," "willing disciples," or "disciples that have made a progress." Similar terminology appears on early Methodist class papers—a language of spiritual awakening and discipleship, of dynamic growth rather than inward endeavor.[50]

The initial "classification" of the Herrnhut membership soon developed a twofold division. Groups which were divided according to sex, age, and marital status became known as *choirs*, adopting a residential pattern as the community expanded. At the same time, within the *choirs*, those who wished to further their spiritual growth formed smaller groups, known as *bands*.[51] These had been a feature of the old *Unitas Fratrum*, and the criterion for membership was spiritual affinity. They consisted originally of only two or three persons, each under the direction of a *band-keeper* accountable personally to Zinzendorf, and they grew rapidly in number. In 1732 there were 77 *bands*, and by 1734 they had increased to 100.[52]

The informality of the bands provided a degree of flexibility which the *choirs* did not possess. For example, if a member or leader did not derive benefit from one band, he or she could move to another. Zinzendorf himself was in no doubt as to the significance of their fellowship experience, which he regarded as highly important for the spiritual life of the community. It was, he said, "productive of such blessed effects that I believe without such an institution, the church would never have become what it is now."[53] He expended a large amount of care in their nurture, regarding them as informal associations of those who felt drawn together for prayer and intimate discussion of religious experiences—"a few individuals met together in the name of Jesus, amongst whom Jesus is; who converse together in a particularly cordial and childlike manner, on the whole state of their hearts, and conceal nothing from each other, but who have wholly committed themselves to each other's care in the Lord."[54] The hermeneutic principle is arresting: that two or three gathered in the name of Christ find him present in their midst in the power of the Holy Spirit. Zinzendorf even went so far as to describe the visit of Mary to Elizabeth (Lk. 1:39-56) as the first biblical expression of such Christian fellowship. To meet together in a band was not merely to exercise self-examination, nor yet to engender a mutual growth in spiritual self-awareness; it was to occasion the presence of Christ and thus to provide a sure and efficacious means of grace.[55]

Yet behind all of this quest for spiritual growth, the tensions remained. It had been the practice of the old *Unitas Fratrum*, for example, to classify members according to spiritual maturity; and the early emergence of the bands, with their voluntary association and emphasis on spiritual enrichment, was in this tradition. While the Count shared this concern for spiritual advancement, however, he wished to incorporate the community into a Lutheran parish structure, and to this end his concept of supervision was more rigid. Even more significant, the Pietism of the old *Unitas Fratrum* had an ethical quality which stressed conduct as well as experience. Zinzendorf, on the other hand, brought to the renewed *Brethren* an emphasis on inner religious experience through intensive spiritual enquiry.[56]

By the 1730s, therefore, not only did the domestic arrangements of Herrnhut reflect the views of the Count, but the bands too had begun to acquire a degree of compulsion, with an emphasis less on mutual sharing and support and more on the segregated pattern of the choirs.[57] Moreover, members of the aristocracy had come to hold positions of secular power in the community out of all proportion to their numbers.[58] The tradition of the old *Unitas Fratrum* embodied a concept of spiritual growth which Martin Schmidt has described as "a Pietist correction of Lutheran prosiness."[59] It was effected through the spontaneous fellowship of the bands, which were not a part of the community at Berthelsdorf before they arrived. Zinzendorf's pietism, by contrast, was that of a community organized by house neighborhoods in the Lutheran tradition, and ultimately realized in the rigidly stratified systems of the choirs.

The tensions were further reflected in the question of ecclesiastical order. As we have noted, Zinzendorf viewed the Moravians as an *ecclesiola in ecclesia* at Berthelsdorf, and it remained his conviction that they should not become an autonomous church, not least because of their legal position with regard to the state church of Saxony. In 1729 a further document was drawn up, defining the relationship of the new settlement to the civil and ecclesiastical authorities, on the basis of which it could be shown that there was no intention of founding a new sect, but only the renewal of an ancient *Gemeine*.[60] The Moravians, however, stood firm. They had no intention of being absorbed by the Berthelsdorf church, and in March 1735 they sent one of their members, David Nitschmann, to be ordained bishop in Berlin by Daniel Jablonski, grandson of Comenius. In 1737 Zinzendorf accepted the fact of their separation in his own ordination as their second bishop.[61]

As events proved, the Count's concern for ecclesiastical legality was not unwarranted. Some Schwenkfelders to whom he had given asylum at Herrnhut were banished by the Elector of Saxony, and Zinzendorf was genuinely concerned that the Moravians might also be expelled.[62] After negotiating the admission of the Schwenkfelders to the English colony of Georgia, he arranged for a group of the Renewed Brethren to settle there under the leadership of August Gottlieb Spangenberg, a professor from Halle who had joined with the community after being dismissed from his post at the university. They were received with sufficient hospitality to encourage a second group, who set out with

Bishop Nitschmann in the fall of 1735, and it was with these that John and Charles Wesley sailed to Georgia.

We have already noted the importance of the theological dialogue which ensued, but of equal importance was Wesley's introduction to Moravian church order. The second "rise" of Methodism at Savannah indicated his adoption of the practice of meeting in bands for mutual edification, and his acknowledgment that, in addition to their value as a means of ecclesial discipline, such intimate groups could also be a means of grace:

> Not finding, as yet, any door open for the pursuing our main design, we considered in what manner we might be most useful to the little flock at Savannah. And we agreed, (1) to advise the more serious among them to form themselves into a sort of little society, and to meet once or twice a week, in order to reprove, instruct, and exhort one another. (2) To select out of these a smaller number for a more intimate union with each other, which might be forwarded, partly by our conversing singly with each, and partly by inviting them all together to our house; and this, accordingly, we deter-mined to do every Sunday in the afternoon.[63]

Wesley did not use the word *band* to describe the smaller grouping, and in his description there is not yet an appreciation of the immediacy which was the dynamic of Moravian fellowship. But clearly there had been an impact. In the third "rise" of Methodism, the formation of the Fetter Lane Society, we find that bands were one of the distinctive features.

3. THE METHODIST ORDER
Ecclesiola in Ecclesia

The society formed at Fetter Lane in London on May 1, 1738, met initially at the home of the Rev. John Hutton, a Non-Juror whom the Wesleys had come to know in the early 1730s when their older brother, Samuel, had been a tutor at the Westminster School and had lived next door. In those days Hutton actively sponsored an Anglican religious society, and his son James was so influenced by the Wesleys that he formed his own society when they departed for Georgia. This new society, however, was a direct outcome of the fellowship which Wesley shared with a Moravian named Peter Böhler during the spring of

1738.[64] Böhler had arrived in London in February with a group of Moravians on their way to Georgia, and had quickly become convinced that much could be accomplished in England. "O how good it would be," he noted in his diary, "if there were a brother or sister in Herrnhut who understood English and who could be sent to guide these poor folk. The poor people are awakened but do not know what they want. They toil at reading books and their prayer book, but they know nothing of the Savior."[65] Accordingly, he set about the organization of small group fellowships patterned after the Herrnhut bands, meeting with some success, though not realizing his hope of reproducing the Herrnhut congregational model.[66]

The Fetter Lane Society evidenced this Moravian influence by adopting bands as an integral part of its organization, even though it was structured as an Anglican religious society.[67] In fact, James Hutton subsequently became the first member of the Moravian church in England, and one of its important leaders.[68] Describing the Fetter Lane Society in his journal, Wesley listed eleven "fundamental rules," though initially there were only two: that the members would meet weekly to share in mutual prayer and confession, and that others of like purpose should be allowed to join them. Subsequent rules, numbering 33 in all (reproduced as Appendix D), were for the most part concerned with the subdivision of the society into bands, and with other Moravian practices, such as unbroken intercession and lovefeasts. The bands were to number no fewer than five persons and no more than ten, with all members of the society to be so divided. Everyone was to speak "as freely, plainly and concisely as he [could] the real state of his heart, with his several temptations and deliverances, since the last time of meeting." Prospective members were to be formed into trial bands, to be "assisted" for a period of two months before admission, at which point they were admonished to be "entirely open," using "no kind of reserve."[69]

Wesley supported Böhler's insistence on the necessity of bands, but already we can discern something of the rigidity in the Moravian discipline by which the freedom and immediacy of the original band fellowship had been restricted, and when Wesley visited Herrnhut later that year, his Aldersgate Street experience behind him, it was precisely in this area that he expressed reservations.[70] His account of the visit is an interesting historical document, not least because he was assisted in his observations by an early meeting with an old Georgia acquaintance, Baron von Hermsdorf, who made it his business that Wesley should see as much as possible of the community.[71] He was present at a lovefeast, took part in a Bible conference, and met with several of the bands. The intimate conversations he had with a number of the leading members were especially significant, and his meticulous record makes clear the extent to which the segregation of the community had already become more regimented than originally envisaged in 1727.[72]

Although he could write enthusiastically to James Hutton that "we are here compassed about with a cloud of witnesses that the Ancient of Days waxeth not cold," and that "the same gifts are still given unto men, the same holiness and happiness, and same freedom from sin, the same peace and joy in the Holy Ghost,"[73] he was sufficiently concerned with some of the restrictions to pen a letter to Herrnhut shortly after his return. The points are worth noting in detail as an indication of the impending direction of Methodist polity. After expressing approval of the pastoral oversight and instruction of the Moravian community, and especially their bands and conferences, Wesley continued:

> But of some other things I stand in doubt, which will mention in love and meekness. And I wish that, in order to remove these doubts, you would on each of these heads, (1) plainly answer whether the fact be as I suppose; and if so, (2) consider whether it be right.
>
> Do you not wholly neglect joint fasting?
>
> Is not the Count all in all? Are not the rest mere shadows, calling him Rabbi, almost implicitly both believing him and obeying him?
>
> Is there not something of levity in your behaviour? Are you in general serious enough?
>
> Are you zealous and watchful to redeem time? Do you not sometimes fall into trifling conversations?
>
> Do you magnify your own Church too much?
>
> Do you believe any who are not of it to be in gospel liberty?
>
> Are you not straitened in your love? Do you love your enemies and wicked men as yourselves?
>
> Do you not mix human wisdom with divine, joining worldly prudence to heavenly?
>
> Do you not use cunning, guile, or dissimulation in many cases?
>
> Are you not of a close, dark, reserved temper, and behaviour?
>
> Is not the spirit of secrecy the spirit of your community?
>
> Have you that childlike openness, frankness, and plainness of speech so manifest to all the Apostles and first Christians?[74]

It can readily be noted that Wesley's objections were centered on those aspects of Herrnhut life which were the results of Zinzendorf's overlordship rather than the older traditions of the *Unitas Fratrum.* The rigid system of spiritual supervision was leading, as Wesley astutely observed, to an immaturity of secrecy rather than an openness of mutual responsibility which, in his view, should be the true purpose of group fellowship. He was willing to accept the division of bands according to sex and marital status—but as a means of furthering such openness, and not as an end in itself.[75]

Later that year, in the same vein, he strongly disapproved of the appointment of monitors at Fetter Lane. Writing to James Hutton, he listed the reasons:

> First, it seems needless. Every man in my band is my monitor, and I his; else I know of no use of our being in band. And if anything particular occur, why should not the leaders (as was agreed before) delegate a monitor *pro tempore?* Secondly, I doubt it would be hurtful; and, indeed, many ways: by lessening the care of every member for every other, when so great a part of his care was transferred to another: by lessening mutual freedom. . . . Thirdly, I have seen it has produced these effects. Sin (as they esteemed it) was suffered in me at Savannah, first seven months, afterwards five months, without one breath of reproof; notwithstanding the command of God, notwithstanding earnest, continual entreaty on one side, and solemn, repeated promises on the other. And how should this be? Why, there were stated monitors to reprove. Others, therefore, judged reproof to be a thing quite out of their way. But I fell not under the care of the monitors.[76]

In the *Rules of the Band-Societies* which Wesley drew up for the Methodists in December of the same year, he stressed precisely the quality he felt was lacking in the Moravian system of monitors: mutual confession and accountability. The leader of the band, "some person among us," was to "speak his own state first, and then ask the rest, in order, as many and as searching questions as may be." A series of such "searching questions" was suggested:

> Have you the forgiveness of your sins?
> Have you the witness of God's Spirit with your spirit?
> Has no sin, inward or outward, dominion over you?
> Do you desire to be told of all your faults?
> Do you desire that, in doing this, we should come as close as

possible, that we should cut to the quick, and search your heart to the bottom?

But at every meeting, there were five questions to be asked of everyone:

What known Sin have you committed since our last Meeting?
What Temptations have you met with?
How was you delivered?
What have you thought, said or done, of which you doubt whether it be a Sin or not?
Have you nothing you desire to keep secret?

These rules (reproduced in full as Appendix E) have been described by one biographer as an indication of the "still unhealthy tone of Wesley's piety . . . no doubt put with the best intentions, but . . . like a prurient spying into secrets which properly belong to man and his Maker." [77] Yet this is to misunderstand the purpose of the bands, and to overlook the interdependence of Wesley's theology and practice. We have noted the significance of the distinction which he drew between the immediacy of justifying faith and the process of inward sanctification, but in 1738 this was by no means fully developed in his thought. In the months following his experience at Aldersgate Street, his overwhelming concern was with the assurance of the "inner witness" and the impact it had on the religious societies he visited. [78] Yet he was clearly concerned, during those same months, to work through the implications of this religious assurance for the doctrine of justification by faith, as indicated by the summary of his differences with some of the Anglican clergy in September 1739, and his publication of edited versions of the relevant Anglican *Homilies* and Robert Barnes' *Treatise.* [79] The point at issue— and, as we have noted, it proved to be of profound significance for the development of Methodist doctrine and polity—was whether justifying faith occasioned merely a formal change in the believer or was the beginning of a substantive change occasioned by the reality of a new relationship with God.

It is by no means coincidental that 1739, the year in which Wesley worked through this seemingly fine theological question, was also the year in which he ventured into "field preaching." He had agreed to preach in the open air near Bristol only as a favor to George Whitefield, and the account he gives in his journal indicates that he did so with considerable reluctance and even trepidation. [80] The response, however, was such as to convince him of its efficacy, and the ministry he had in the area proved to be extremely fruitful. He worked to build up a society at Bristol with the help of existing religious societies, and, as at Fetter Lane, divided the members into bands in order to ensure their spiritual growth.

The events of the following year, however, both in Bristol and in London, led him to a serious questioning of the bands as a normative pattern for the emerging Methodist societies. First of all, he was confronted in London with "Quietism," an extreme form of inward spiritual exercise introduced to the Fetter Lane Society by Philipp Heinrich Molther, a Moravian who had arrived from Germany while Wesley was in Bristol. Wesley notes that, on his return to London in November 1739, a woman whom he had left "strong in faith and zealous of good works" was now fully convinced that she "never had any faith at all." She had been advised "till she received faith, to be 'still,' ceasing from outward works."[81] A Mr. Bray "likewise spoke largely of the great danger that attended the doing of outward works, and of the folly of people that keep running about to church and sacrament, 'as I,' said he, 'did till very lately.' "[82]

This Quietism seems not to have been disputed by Spangenberg, who happened to be in England on his way back from Georgia, and with whom Wesley discussed the problem.[83] While agreeing with him that "whoever is born of God doth not commit sin," Wesley could not agree that "none has any faith so long as he is liable to any doubt or fear; or, that till we have it, we ought to abstain from the Lord's Supper or the other ordinances of God."[84] The issue for Wesley was whether the inward assurance of justifying faith was coterminous with salvation, or whether there were other ways in which the sinner could be drawn to the forgiveness and reconciliation of a justified relationship with God in Christ:

> (1) There are means of grace—that is, outward ordinances— whereby the inward grace of God is ordinarily conveyed to man, whereby the faith that brings salvation is conveyed to them who before had it not; (2) that one of these means is the Lord's Supper; and (3) that he who has not this faith ought to wait for it in the use both of this and of the other means which God hath ordained.[85]

The implications of this were pastoral as well as doctrinal, indicating a basic incompatibility between the Moravian spiritual disciplines as they had developed at Herrnhut, and Wesley's evangelical ministry. It led eventually to his separation from the Fetter Lane Society; but perhaps more important, it raised questions about the efficacy of the bands as a basic structure for the embryonic Methodist movement. In the refined seclusion of Herrnhut, a "stillness" in waiting for the assurance of faith was a practicable if questionable exercise, with all the advantages of accumulative community support. But in the realities of eighteenth-century England, this was not the privilege of the great majority of people who were hearing Methodist field preaching and beginning to respond. As the Revival touched those sections of the population which even the religious societies had largely failed to reach, the unreality of maintaining a "once-for-all" doctrine of imputed righteousness became clear. As Martin Schmidt has perceptively observed, Wesley left his followers in their original situations, in contrast with German pietism, which set out to make the rebirth of the justified sinner visible in a holistic new creation which included the material sphere. Wesley gave full emphasis to the order of creation as it already was.[86]

In so doing, he affirmed a fundamental theological truth: that the imputed righteousness of Christ was the occasion, but only the occasion, of an imparted righteousness which demanded of the justified sinner an accountable obedience to God's gracious initiatives. And it was at this point that the bands proved inadequate. Wesley himself acknowledged that, "as much as we endeavoured to watch over each other, we soon found some who did not live the gospel," and that "several grew cold, and gave way to the sins which had long easily beset them," placing "a stumblingblock in the way of others."[87] In his rejection of Molther's "stillness," Wesley had affirmed that there were degrees of faith antecedent to the full assurance of justification,[88] and the corollary was already clear in the practical experience of the bands—that degrees of faith proceeded from this assurance, for which a life of accountable discipleship was the necessary condition.

The problem was that the bands, patterned after the Moravian disciplines, presupposed an environment of outward as well as inward change which the new converts to Methodism, unlike the inhabitants of Herrnhut, did not have the opportunity to effect in their social context. The same can be said of the religious societies, whose methods of personal discipline could never have provided spiritual guidance for the Methodist membership in general, many of whose daily labors and economic hardships were already a discipline of the harshest kind. The point is made tellingly, if unwittingly, by William Law in his *Serious Call*:

> Great parts of the world are free from the necessities of labour and employments, and have their *time* and *fortunes* in their own

disposal. . . . But as no one is to live in his employment according to his own humour . . . the *freedom* of their state lays them under a greater *necessity* of always chusing and doing the best things.

They are those, of whom *much will be requir'd, because much is given unto them.*

A *slave* can only live unto God in one *particular* way; that is, in religious patience and submission in his state of slavery.

But all ways of holy living, all instances, and all kinds of virtue, lie open to those, who are masters of themselves, their time and their fortune. It is as much the duty, therefore, of such persons, to make a wise use of their liberty, to devote themselves to all kinds of virtue, to aspire after every thing that is holy and pious . . . as it is the duty of a *slave* to be *resign'd* unto God in his state of slavery.[89]

The genius of Wesley's organization of the Methodist societies lay in his recognition that Christian discipleship was first and foremost a response to God's grace, and not a striving for virtue, nor yet an expectation of instant salvation. Confronted by the alternatives of a secluded pursuit of doctrinal and behavioral absolutes, or a pragmatic acceptance of human regeneration in its social reality, he unhesitatingly opted for the latter and formulated this theology accordingly. He could not regard those who "did the best they could" as being beyond the plan of salvation any more than he could regard those "groaning for full redemption" as falling short of it.[90]

The differences with the Moravians came to a head at Fetter Lane in July 1740. Some months earlier, Wesley had leased the ruined Foundery in Moorfields in order to form a new society, which had rapidly grown in size; and, having failed to reach some basis of doctrinal agreement with Molther at Fetter Lane, Wesley read a short paper to the members and withdrew with eighteen or nineteen others to the Foundery.[91] The anguish which this caused him, and the efforts he took to reach a compromise with Molther, are only too evident in the letter of explanation he sent to Herrnhut and his subsequent conversations with Zinzendorf.[92] But the break was inevitable, and salutary; for it gave Wesley the freedom to work with the emerging Methodist societies more directly, and in due course to adopt what became the basic structural unit of the movement—the class meeting.

Given Wesley's pragmatic approach to new situations, it is not surprising to find that the class meeting had its genesis at a gathering of the Bristol society with the most mundane of agendas—the clearing of a building debt. The mortgage had been obtained for the building of new premises, "large enough to contain both the societies of Nicholas and Baldwin Streets, and such of their acquaintance as might desire to be present with them."[93] The first stone had been laid at the site in the Horsefair on Saturday, May 12, 1739, and by the following October, Wesley was already referring to them as the *United Society*, a term he subsequently applied to the Methodist societies as a whole.[94]

In acquiring the separate premises of this "New Room" in Bristol, and, later that year, of the Foundery in London, Wesley was assuming a leadership which he could not have provided for the emerging Methodist movement had he attempted to contain the societies in Moravian or Anglican High Church piety. As he later recalled the sequence of events, he felt compelled to "convince those who would hear what true Christianity was, and to persuade them, to embrace it," and equally compelled to respond to ensuing requests for spiritual guidance and oversight:

> Many of those who heard [my brother and I preach] began to cry out that we brought "strange things to their ears"; that this was doctrine which they never heard before, or at least never regarded. They "searched the Scriptures, whether these things were so," and acknowledged "the truth as it is in Jesus." Their hearts also were influenced as well as their understandings, and they determined to follow "Jesus Christ, and him crucified."
>
> Immediately they were surrounded with difficulties; — all the world rose up against them; neighbours, strangers, acquaintances, relations, friends, began to cry out amain, "Be not righteous overmuch; why shouldest thou destroy thyself?" Let not "much religion make thee mad."
>
> One, and another, and another came to us, asking, what they should do, being distressed on every side; as every one strove to weaken, and none to strengthen, their hands in God. We advised them, "Strengthen you one another. Talk together as often as you can. . . ."
>
> They said, "But we want you likewise to talk with us often, to direct and quicken us in our way. . . ." I asked, Which of you desire this? Let me know your names and places of abode. They did so. But I soon found they were too many for me to talk with severally, so often as they wanted it. So I told them, "If you will all of you come together every Thursday, in the evening, I will gladly spend some time with you in prayer, and give you the best advice I can."

Thus arose, without any previous design on either side, what was afterwards called *a Society*.[95]

In the *Rules of the United Societies* (reproduced in full as Appendix F), Wesley dates this request for spiritual guidance at "the latter End of the Year 1739,"[96] which places the emergence of his leadership in the context of the tensions at Fetter Lane, and links it to the critical formulation of his theology during the same period. The prolific output of his publications in the early 1740s indicates that his Moravian apprenticeship had been quickly served, and that the tradition of English Protestantism was once again shaping the dimensions of his thought and practice. He was ready to provide leadership for the Methodist movement, not only because he saw the dangers of permitting the seeds of evangelical preaching to be scattered rather than sown, but also because he saw the frustrations of trying to implement what he perceived to be inadequate concepts of nature and grace.[97] The discipline of the religious societies was not only formal and credal; it was socially selective. The piety of the Moravians demanded a withdrawal from the world which led to the extremes of "stillness," while Calvinism, which increasingly characterized the other wings of the Revival, was doctrinally selective, and frequently proved to be a source of fraction in the societies.

It is worth recounting an early anecdote which reveals the distinctive understanding of the faith which Wesley was to preach for the next fifty years, and shows why he felt the need to exercise a different approach from that of the Moravians, the Anglican societies, and the Calvinists. In June 1740, a Mr. Acourt, whom Charles Wesley had refused to admit to the Foundery society, hoped to get a more positive response from John. Accordingly he took up the matter on an occasion when Charles had left town. It soon became clear that the reason for his exclusion by Charles was his avowed intent to set the members of the society straight on the question of election and predestination. Wesley suggested that an argument about it would cause unnecessary trouble, but Acourt was adamant; and so the decision not to admit him was confirmed. Following his account of the episode, Wesley added this significant observation:

I mentioned this to our society, and, without entering into the controversy, besought all of them who were weak in the faith not to

"receive one another to doubtful disputations," but simply to follow after holiness, and the things that make for peace.[98]

For Wesley to refer to the avoidance of disputation and the pursuit of
holiness was not, of course, an innovation, having been a cardinal rule
of the religious societies from their inception, and likewise of the Moravian bands. What was significant was Wesley's understanding of being
"weak in the faith"—something which ultimately governed the whole
of Methodist polity. The Moravians dealt with it in the intensive nurture
of communal piety; the religious societies tended to subordinate it to
moral endeavor; and Calvinism regarded it as something of a doctrinal
contradiction. But Wesley perceived it as a spiritual condition closely
linked to social realities. He sensed that educational and behavioral
barriers could be just as debilitating to a person's faith as doctrinal or
credal requirements; and that they could even be one and the same
thing. Indeed, in Wesley's day, the Nonconformist churches had
adopted an attitude toward the common people as disdainful as that of
the established church, and when the noted congregationalist Philip
Doddridge showed interest in the work of Wesley, he met with dis-
couragement and disfavor from his friends and colleagues.[99]
Wesley did not have the benefits of social theory to analyze these
factors, but he sensed instinctively that the niceties of doctrinal dispute
were not the stuff of discipleship, and that they could even be a weighty
impediment. Common people who came to a knowledge of the gospel
needed their own peculiar pattern of spiritual nurture, a building up in
the faith which had no prerequisites other than commitment to obedience in the service of Jesus Christ. The answer clearly lay in some
form of mutual encouragement and guidance; for time and again, as he
noted, "the far greater part of those who had begun to 'fear God and
work righteousness,' but were not united together, grew faint in their
mind, and fell back into what they were before. Meanwhile the far
greater part of those who were thus united together [into a society]
continued 'striving to enter in at the strait gate,' and to 'lay hold on
eternal life.' "[100]
As Methodist preaching reached those who were "utterly inaccessible
every other way . . . the multitudes . . . both in Kingswood and the
fells about Newcastle,"[101] so the societies received them with no other
condition than that they should "desire to flee from the wrath to come,
to be saved from their sins."[102] A United Society was defined as "no
other than a *Company of Men* having the Form, and seeking the Power
of *Godliness.*" The rules went on to affirm, however, that "wherever this

[desire] is really fix'd in the soul, it will be shewn by its Fruits," and in order that it "may the more easily be discern'd, whether [the members] are indeed working out their own Salvation, each Society is divided into smaller Companies, called Classes, according to their respective Places of abode."[103]

The distinctive pattern of Methodist polity had emerged. The class meeting was at once the expression of an inclusive concept of salvation in which men and women participated with freedom and responsibility, and a supportive structure for discipleship grounded in the realities and the common sense of worldly living.

Chapter Four

THE DEVELOPMENT OF THE CLASS MEETING

THE SINEWS OF METHODISM

1. THE WEEKLY MEETING

A Prudential Means of Grace

Once he perceived its usefulness and its validity, the class meeting was adopted for Methodism as readily as other means of grace which Wesley found to be "prudential." As we have noted, the debt on the New Room was being discussed at Bristol on February 15, 1742, a debt which, not untypically, Wesley had assumed personally; otherwise, as he put it, "the whole undertaking must have stood still."[1] A retired seaman, known to us only as Captain Foy, proposed that each member of the society should give a penny a week toward clearing it. The identity of Foy has not been established, though his place in the Methodist tradition is assured for no other reason than this far-reaching suggestion.[2] When it was pointed out that a penny a week was beyond the means of many members, he replied that he would personally accept responsibility for collecting the weekly amount from ten or twelve members, and would himself make up any deficiencies. Others offered to do the same, and so it was agreed to divide the whole society into "little companies, or classes—about twelve in each class," with one person, styled as the leader, to collect the weekly contributions.[3] What began as a financial expedient soon presented an opportunity for pastoral oversight. One of the leaders reported to Wesley that he had found instances of misbehavior on his rounds—a man quarrelling with his wife, another drunk—and "it immediately struck into Mr. Wesley's mind, 'This is the very thing we wanted. The Leaders are the persons who may not only receive the contributions, but also watch over the souls of their brethren.' "[4]

He shared this idea with several trusted members of the Foundery society in London the following April, and they readily agreed with him that the classes would be an excellent means of coming to "a sure, thorough knowledge of each person."[5] Every society from that time, noted Wesley, willingly followed the same example, and before long there was a further development. The weekly visitations of the leaders proved to be not only time-consuming, but frequently inconvenient. Many persons, for example, lived as servants in houses where the master or mistress would not permit visitors; and even when visits were permitted, class leaders were unable to talk with the members alone. There was the further difficulty of misunderstandings between members, which could not be resolved without face-to-face meetings.[6]

It was therefore agreed that the members of each class should meet together once a week, not only to collect the weekly contributions, but also to give advice, reproof, or encouragement as needed. A dynamic of Christian fellowship quickly developed, as members began to "bear one another's burdens," and to "care for each other." The openness which was engendered by the meetings led to "a more endeared affection" between the members, and they felt free to be honest with each other. "Speaking the truth in love, they grew up into Him in all things, who is the Head, even Christ."[7]

Classes and Bands

These descriptive phrases of Wesley come close to what was already expected of the bands. Indeed, as the class meetings developed, the distinction between the two forms of group fellowship became imprecise, especially where the class leader had become skilled and spiritually perceptive. Even Wesley, in one of his later accounts of Methodist polity, confuses the chronology of their respective developments.[8] Yet there were important differences, and even as the classes became the basic unit of Methodist organization, the bands were by no means neglected. Continuing to follow the Moravian pattern, these were structured according to age, sex, and marital status. The classes, on the other hand, were divided more pragmatically, according to the topography of the society membership and the exigencies of available leadership. In new societies, for example, there might initially be only one class, consisting of all the members, men and women; in the larger societies, there would often be separate classes of men or women as well as those of mixed membership. The only rule in this regard was that female classes at no time had a male leader. Otherwise, the society lists indicate that the division into classes was made solely on the basis of where the members lived, in order to facilitate the weekly meetings. A good example of this is the class list of the Bingley society in 1763, when the membership numbered about thirty (reproduced as Appendix G).[9]

There were further differences between the two groupings. The bands, though an integral part of the Fetter Lane society and strongly encouraged by Wesley in the early Methodist societies, had not been imposed as a condition of membership. Classes, on the other hand, were made a prerequisite for society membership, and consisted of a division of all the members on the society lists. Perhaps most significantly, the bands had been structured for mutual fellowship and spiritual oversight, with the leader chosen from the members; whereas the classes were formed around appointed leaders. Even though the meetings subsequently became what have been described as "family circles,"[10] their purpose, as Wesley saw it, was to implement an accountable discipleship among the society members.

A Description of a Class Meeting

There are many personal experiences of class attendance to be found in early Methodist biographies,[11] but one of the most succinct descriptions of the format of a class meeting occurs in Joseph Nightingale's *Portraiture of Methodism*, published in 1807. The author, a Methodist who turned Unitarian, states at the outset that he is drawing on his own "personal knowledge of the Methodists [from which] I have been able to produce much original and interesting information: original, at least, to the public at large; and even, I may add, to numbers of the Methodists themselves."[12] The fact that he is clearly no longer in sympathy with the movement renders his account all the more interesting, as innuendo mingles with objective detail:

> A class-meeting, at present, consists of an indefinite number of persons, generally from twelve to twenty; though sometimes fewer even than twelve. This meeting is designed for the spiritual advantage of members only, or of those that are desirous of becoming such. It is composed either of persons of both sexes, of men only, or of the fair sex. In the two first cases, the leader is always a brother, in the last case, the leader is chosen out of the sisterhood. These meetings are generally holden at private houses, and commence at eight in the evening. The leader having opened the service by singing and prayer, all the members sit down, and he then relates to them his own *experience* during the preceding week. His joys, and

his sorrows; his hopes and his fears; his conflicts with the world, the flesh, and the devil; his fightings without and his fears within; his dread of hell, or his hope of heaven; his pious longings and secret prayers for the prosperity of the church at large, and for those his brothers and sisters in class particular. This *experience* is generally concluded with some such language as the following: — "After all, my dear brethren, I still find a determination in my own soul to press forward for the mark of the prize of my high calling of God in Christ Jesus. He is still precious. His word is an ointment poured forth. After all my short-comings — my doubts and anxieties — my wanderings, weakness, and weariness, his spirit still whispers to my heart — 'Thou art black but comely. Open thy mouth wide and I will fill it. Make haste, my beloved, and be thou like to a roe, or to a young hart, upon the mountains of spices!' so I still may say to my sweet Jesus —

> 'I hold thee with trembling hand,
> And will not let thee go.' "

After some such harangue as this, the leader proceeds to inquire into the state of every soul present; saying, "Well sister, or well brother, how do you find the state of *your* soul this evening?" The member then proceeds, without rising, to unbosom his or her mind to the leader; not, as has often been said, by particular confession, but by a general recapitulation of what has passed in the mind during the week. Such advice, correction, reproof, and consolation, is then given, as the state of the case may require; so the leader passes on to the next, and the next, until every one has received a portion of meat in due season.

After this, the leader, or some other on whom he may be pleased to call, gives out a stanza or two of a hymn, which being sung, standing, they proceed with prayer; when such thanksgivings, deprecations, or petitions, are poured forth as the different *experiences* may have suggested.

Any one is at liberty to exercise the gift of prayer, and no strangers being present, a freer vent is given to the effusions of the mind and the soft meltings of the soul, than is usual at a public prayer-meeting. Those who are still unconverted, or who labour in the pangs of the new birth, lay their unhappy case before God; and in the most pressing manner, beseech the merciful Jehovah *then* to pity them — at least to lend a willing ear to their complaints — to bow the heavens of his love and come down — to open the bowels of divine compassion towards them — to look upon the bleeding wounds of his suffering Son; and to pardon all their sins upon the consideration of his merits.

Those who are groaning for *full redemption*—who seek to have their robes washed and made white in the blood of the Lamb—who will not be comforted until the last remains of sin are removed from their hearts, and God declares that they "are all fair, that their [sic] is no spot in them," are more than commonly solicitous that the Holy Ghost would come and dwell in their souls without a rival; and that the enemies they had seen that day they should see no more for ever.

For the careless, the formal, and the lukewarm, the most earnest prayers are put up, lest the Almighty, in disgust, should "spue them out of his mouth."

. . . . .

As singing forms a considerable portion of the service at a class meeting, I must give you one or two specimens of their hymns. . . . They are poured forth in the most soft, soothing, languishing, and melting strains that music is capable of; and music, you know, has charms to soothe a savage breast.[13]

The leader having closed the meeting, in the usual manner, by benediction, proceeds to call over the names of every member present; and to collect what they are disposed to give towards the support of the *work of God*. The usual sum is one penny each; but some, who can afford it, pay two-pence, three-pence, or even six-pence, as they may be able, or willing. These several sums are entered on the class-paper: a sheet being provided for that purpose, rules and divided into columns and squares for every separate account; the leader himself always contributing his proper share.[14]

Accountability and Pastoral Oversight

Two important characteristics of the class meeting emerge from this account. The first is that the dynamic of the class, as opposed to that of the band, was clearly one of *giving an account*. Nightingale stresses that it was not the purpose of the dialogue between the leader and each member to press for an intensive confessional, but rather a straightforward accounting of what had taken place during the preceding week. This rendered the meetings a process of mutual response and support rather than inward enquiry, and we shall note the importance of this for the distinctive contribution of the classes to early Methodist discipleship. The second characteristic is the centrality of the class leader. From the very beginning of the class system, this position was a crucial element in a line of authority and communication extending from Wesley to the Methodist membership as a whole—the connectional system of Methodism which, as E. P. Thompson has rightly observed, broke so sharply with the traditions of Dissent in England.[15] It was through this connection that Wesley maintained the direct pastoral oversight of his *episkopé*, and which, in the final analysis, made Methodism an *ecclesiola in ecclesia*.

2. THE CLASS LEADER

Nowhere was this more evident than in the appointment and instruction of class leaders. To begin with, their duties were specified in the *General Rules*. It was the business of the class leader:

> (1) To see each person in his class once a week at least, in order to inquire how their souls prosper; to advise, reprove, comfort, or exhort, as occasion may require; to receive what they are willing to give toward the relief of the poor. (2) To meet the Minister and the Stewards of the society once a week; in order to inform the Minister of any that are sick, or of any that walk disorderly, and will not be reproved; to pay to the Stewards what they have received of their several classes in the week preceding; and to show their account of what each person has contributed.[16]

Then it was made clear that the appointment or removal of such persons was the prerogative of Wesley himself or his assistants.[17] "As long as I live," he wrote to John Mason in 1790, "the people shall have no share in choosing either stewards or leaders among the Methodists. We have not and never had any such custom. We are no republicans, and never intend to be."[18]

In practice, of course, the training of so many lay people to such a high level of pastoral skill was bound to create tensions in the societies. Wesley himself constantly upheld the necessity for the grounding of Methodism in the visible church, with pastoral authority resting in himself. Yet so much of this pastoral authority was delegated to laypersons, who rubbed shoulders with Dissenting congregations where local autonomy was normative. Perhaps the most direct confrontation he had with class leaders in this regard was at Dublin in 1771, where there had been "a continual jar for at least two years." Wesley used the occasion to define the order of authority in the Methodist organization. It passed down from himself to his assistants, thence to the preachers, and thence to the stewards, the leaders, and the people. The authority of the class leader was reaffirmed according to their duties in the *General Rules*; but thereafter, their role was advisory. The spiritual affairs of the society were to be regulated by the assistant, the temporal affairs by the stewards, and any unresolved issues were to be referred to Wesley himself.[19]

Not that Wesley was unresponsive to the dynamics of leadership. There is no way that he could have fostered the connectional system of the movement had he not been sensitive to local particularities and exigencies. This emerges clearly from his handling of the objections raised when classes were first introduced. Among the reasons given against their introduction, he regarded as most plausible the fear that the leaders who were appointed would not be able to handle their assignments, and would not have the necessary gifts for spiritual oversight. His reply was that God had clearly blessed the work of those who had been appointed, and that if any leader was "remarkably wanting in gifts or grace," then that person was quickly removed. "If you know any such," he enjoined, "tell it to me, not to others, and I will endeavor to exchange him for a better."[20]

Role of Class Leaders

Wesley was aware that the authority of class leaders would depend to a large degree on the respect accorded by the class, not least because they were in touch with the members at precisely the point of accountability for discipleship. Leaders met weekly, therefore, with the preacher appointed by Wesley as minister of their society, both to report on their members, and to receive advice and instruction. Moreover, Wesley's correspondence indicates time and again how sensitively and lovingly he guided these men and women in their pastoral role. This was especially evident in his closing years, as in the perceptive rebuke to a class leader in Yorkshire who had asked his advice on dealing with refractive members: "John White, whoever is wrong, you are not right."[21] Or in the gentle reminder at the end of a letter to John King: "If any of the class-leaders teaches strange doctrine, he can have no more place among us. Only lovingly admonish him first."[22] Perhaps most pointedly, in his advice to John Cricket: "I positively forbid you or any preacher to be a leader; rather put the most insignificant person in each class to be the leader of it."[23]

Selection and Appointment of Class Leaders

The selection of leaders tended to evolve naturally as an acknowledgment by societies of their potential, and in particular to mark their spiritual development. Thus the progression from class leader to preacher was not uncommon.[24] A good example is the Irishman, Thomas Walsh, who left the Roman Catholic Church, not only to become an Anglican, but a Methodist to boot—something which convinced his relations that he had "turned heretic altogether."[25] He joined the society at Limerick in 1749, and the following is extracted from the earlier part of his biography in Jackson's *Lives*:

> The treasure of light and love which God had put into the soul of His servant began now to shine clearly to others. They could easily discern an amazing change in his very aspect, as well as tempers and conduct in general. The calm, and at the same time divine, cheerfulness and serenity of his soul rendered him a desirable, as well as useful, member of their religious meetings. And the loving zeal which he felt for promoting the glory of his dying God prompted him to exert himself with much fervour in the service of his neighbour.
>
> Thus, with a heart set on fire to pay, at least, some small returns for all that ocean of mercy and love which he had experienced in himself, he sought opportunities, and embraced every occasion, of imparting all the good which he possibly could to others; till it seemed good to those who directed their religious exercises to appoint him leader of a class (so called): that is, a little company of Christian friends, mutually agreed to meet together weekly in order to their furtherance in the way of godliness; one person of which was styled "leader."[26]

Shortly after this, Walsh began to wrestle with the call to preach; and on asking Wesley's advice, received the reply in June 1750:

My Dear Brother,
 It is hard to judge what God has called you to, till trial is made. Therefore, when you have an opportunity, you may go to Shronil, and spend two or three days with the people there. Speak to them in Irish.[27]

By the same token, Wesley and his assistants were quick to discern leadership qualities, and this resulted not infrequently in what seemed to be an arbitrary choice. The appointment of William Smith at the Orphan House in Newcastle upon Tyne is a case in point. Smith was in the congregation on an occasion when Wesley was preaching, and at the close of the sermon was surprised to hear the announcement that he was being appointed a leader. Moreover, he was expected to form a class "on such a day and at such an hour." We are given to understand that Smith was dressed at the time as a typically fashionable young man of the day, having on "a waistcoat richly embroidered, and frills adorning his wrists." Nor, the account continues, was he lacking the "customary silver buckles." His reaction to this appointment by Wesley was at once to regard his dress as inconsistent with his new office, and forthwith to assume a "plainness and almost elegant simplicity." He subsequently became one of the prominent leaders of the Orphan-House society—an indication that Wesley had assessed his vocation and his capabilities correctly.[28]

Spiritual Leadership

The position of the class leaders has been variously described as "sub-pastor,"[29] "non-commissioned officer,"[30] and even as "spiritual police,"[31] but there is little question that they became as skilled a group of spiritual mentors as the church has ever produced. What Wesley looked for in a leader was a combination of disciplinary and spiritual discernment, so that fellowship in the classes would be a means of growing discipleship. Appointment to the position was an important advancement in a society, and those who occupied it were aptly described in Joseph Nightingale's contemporary account as the "body politic" of Methodism.[32] Their spiritual acumen was matched by a capacity for pastoral and administrative leadership, and strong loyalties developed between leaders and their class members. Wesley's account of the death of Elizabeth Vandome in 1769, for example, tells of her request to have the members of her class summoned to her bedside, in order that she might speak her last words with them.[33]

This strong attachment to the class leader, already evident in Wesley's day, became even stronger in the post-Wesleyan phase of the move-ment. Social historians have been quick to point out that the dynamics of this were not always healthy; and indeed, it was a notable feature of the various schisms of the nineteenth century that members tended to follow their leader's stand unquestioningly.[34] Yet it should not be forgot-ten that the class leader functioned in the community at large, as well as in the Methodist society, and that the relationships engendered by the class meetings were tempered by the grist and grind of daily living. There may have been sublimation of feelings, as amply illustrated by the poems reproduced in Appendices L and M; but the classes remained very much in the world, even when, in their decline, they succumbed to an inbred religiosity.

The Class Leader as Institution

In the nineteenth century, Methodism became more institutionalized; and, not surprisingly, directions for class leaders became very elaborate, as illustrated by the following item from *The Wesley Banner and Revival Record* in 1849:

The Duties of Class Leaders

Class Leaders occupy a vital position in our Connexion. Pious, intelligent, active leaders always have healthy and prosperous classes. Know the leader, and you may to a great extent judge what his members are.

His duties are weighty. He ought himself to be a man of clear and sound religious experience, having the abiding witness of the Holy Spirit to his adoption, constant power over sin, and steady growth in grace. It is indispensably necessary that while caring for the vineyard of others, his own is kept in a state of high and improving culture.

He should aim to make himself a master of theology, well acquainted with the sacred Scriptures, having lucid views of doc-trinal truth, of Christian experience, and of moral and religious duties. In order to teach, he must learn; to attain this, he should study well; the Bible, and such works of human authority as throw light upon the work of grace in man's heart.

He should seek to discriminate between his members, and by careful observation to discern and ascertain their particular character, the peculiarities of their experience, and the spiritual dangers to which they are severally and specially liable. General observations from week to week, having no particular adaptation in them to the variety of character and condition presented by a class, will be tedious, monotonous, and unedifying.

He should be solicitous that every one of his members lives in the light of God's countenance, as athirst for Christian holiness, conscientiously discharges all the obligations of Christian morality, and patiently endures his various crosses; — aiming himself to be a pattern to his class, he should do his best that his members may be patterns to the world.

While dealing tenderly and kindly with the timid, the tempted and tried, he should be faithful, and healing a wound slightly, not allowing his members to express themselves in terms so general that no indication is given of their personal possession of saving grace, and not withholding necessary reproof from fear of offending a member and driving him from the class.

He should urge his members to a weekly attendance upon their class, insisting, in spite of the excuses which some make for their iregular attendance, that, generally, where there is a will, there is a way; to a weekly contribution in support of the cause of God, as most persons will find it much easier to contribute a small sum every week than a fourth of the amount at the end of the quarter; to personal attendance at every quarterly visitation of the classes, that each member may receive from his chief pastors a renewed token of his connexion with the body.

IF POSSIBLE, the Leader should see every one of his members once every week, and if in consequence of affliction or neglect, any member is absent from his class, that member should be without delay visited. As it will often be extremely difficult, and sometimes quite impracticable, for the leader to do this, it is desirable, in such cases, that there should be an assistant leader, who in addition to visiting absentees, shall by occasionally leading the class be in training for the office itself.

The leader should every week fill up his class book in the way directed. Careful attention to this is creditable to the leader, and enables a preacher at sight, to form a tolerable judgment of the state of the class. The leader should urge his members to unite with him in zealous efforts to increase the class. He should make it a point of conscience as regularly to attend the leaders' meeting, as he urges upon his members regular attendance at their class. If he neglect this, he neglects a duty, he pains the minds of his co-leaders, he loses oneness of feeling with his brethren, and generally becomes an inefficient leader whose class dwindles away under his hands.

Class leaders, continue faithful, earnest, living to God, and urging your member to advance in the divine life; and may he multiply you a thousand fold! Selah.[35]

3. CONNECTIONAL DISCIPLINE

The injunction on class leaders to report to the minister if there were "disorderly members" who would not accept reproof was, as we have noted, a stipulation of the very first *General Rules* in 1743; and there was a good reason for it. In an intimate fellowship, any lack of commitment or discipline on the part of an individual member was bound to be disruptive. If Methodists were to "seek the power of Godliness" by uniting to "pray together, to receive the Word of Exhortation, and to watch over one another in Love," so that they might "help each other to work out their Salvation,"[36] then any member failing to provide this mutual support was certain to be a hindrance. The wide range of religious experience which the societies perforce had to accommodate as a consequence of their rapid growth necessitated a constant supervision of membership, first by selective admission to the societies, and then by ensuring that those who were admitted did in fact follow the *Rules*.

Class Tickets and Quarterly Examination

Wesley effected this with a relatively simple procedure which at the same time provided society members with an important symbol of identity: the class ticket (see Appendix H). In this, he was adopting a practice of the early church, where the supplying of commendatory letters—a practice widespread in the Graeco-Roman world—was adopted by the primitive Christian community.[37] Wesley introduced them at Bristol and Kingswood, initially as a disciplinary measure to guard against "disorderly walkers," some forty of whom were expelled in February 1741. He quickly perceived the effectiveness of the measure, and similar disciplinary action was taken in London the following April.[38] Thereafter he stipulated them for all the societies, combining the issue of tickets with a quarterly examination of the classes by himself or one of his preachers. Those who were keeping the society rules were thereby provided with a visible means of encouragement, and at the same time those who were "disorderly" could be removed in a "quiet and inoffensive" manner simply by withholding their new ticket.[39]

Supervision of Leaders

This quarterly examination was a further means of supervising the leaders themselves. They were required to meet weekly with the preacher appointed as their minister to hand in class monies and to give a report on the progress of their members. But an examination of members by the preacher each quarter also provided an important check on how a leader was performing his or her task. Wesley makes this clear in his account of a visitation to Gateshead in 1747:

On *Monday*, *Tuesday*, and *Thursday* I examined the classes. I had been often told it was impossible for me to distinguish the precious from the vile, without the miraculous discernment of spirits. But I now saw, more clearly than ever, that this might be done, and without much difficulty, supposing only two things: first, courage and steadiness in the examiner; secondly, common sense and common honesty in the leader of each class. I visit, for instance, the class in the Close, of which Robert Peacock is leader. I ask, "Does this and this person in your class live in drunkenness or any outward sin? Does he go to church, and use the other means of grace? Does he meet you as often as he has opportunity?" Now, if Robert Peacock has common sense, he can answer these questions truly; and if he has common honesty, he will. And if not, some other in the class has both, and can and will answer for him. Where is the difficulty, then, of finding out if there be any disorderly walker in this class, and, consequently, in any other? The question is not concerning the heart, but the life. And the general tenor of this I do not say cannot be known, but cannot be hid without a miracle. . . .
The society, which the first year consisted of above eight hun-

dred members, is now reduced to four hundred; but, according to the old proverb, the half is more than the whole. We shall not be shamed of any of these when we speak without enemies in the gate.[40]

The references in Wesley's journal and diary to such visitations are myriad, and the preachers were constantly directed to be thorough and conscientious in this aspect of their duties, even to the point of visiting door-to-door those who had not been meeting in class—an injunction which they found demanding on their time and energies, however indefatigable Wesley himself might have been.[41]

Trial Membership

Even so, the immediate means of effecting discipline in the societies remained the class meeting itself. The leaders were the initial point of contact for those who wished to join a society, and their judgment of potential members was indispensable in the trial period of three months which followed. During this time, on the recommendation of the leader, a note would be issued for admittance to society meetings, and at the end of the three months the leader would again be consulted about full membership.[42] We have a detailed description of this procedure from a first-hand account written in 1790, when the class meeting was at the height of its effectiveness:

> When a person first visits a Class on trial they are asked "Do you know the design of our meeting together?" The Rules of the Society are given them with some such Remarks as these: "If you continue to meet with us, you will observe these Rules, both [for the] End you ought to have in view & the Conduct you are expected to manifest. Take them Home with You—consider them alone, as in the Sight of God. Consider with much Prayer what you are about to do, & if you do not sincerely intend, with divine help, to forsake your Sins, to take up your cross & follow Jesus Christ, do not increase your Guilt by professing to belong to his followers. But if you do indeed feel the Burden of Sin & want to be saved *from* it, However, weak you feel, be not afraid. Give up yourself in sincerity to God—Whatever your determination be—Be sincere in it. Consider it thoroughly in Solitude with much prayer & if you

conclude that Your union will help you & are sincerely purposing to walk by these Rules we shall rejoice to receive you."

An exhortation to this purpose being given with the Rules, if that person returns, some Questions similar to what follows are proposed them. "Have you seriously considered these Rules? Are you conscious that your Sins have Exposed you to the wrath to come & is it your chief concern to flee from it? Do you conclude that it is your duty to walk by these Rules, & will you esteem it a Privilege to meet here? Do you understand that it is the duty of your Leader to speak with the utmost plainness to you?[43]

Regular Attendance

Just as the class meeting was the occasion of membership, it was also the condition. As the "sinews" of Methodism, the formation of the first class was the immediate priority when a new society was established.[44] Attendance at the weekly meetings was always a condition for the renewal of the quarterly tickets, and preachers were given clear instructions to withhold them from those who were irregular. Writing to Joseph Benson in 1776, he was nothing if not specific:

> We must threaten no longer, but perform. In November last I told the London Society, "Our rule is to meet a class once a week, not once in two or three. I now give you warning: I will give tickets to none in February but those that have done this." I have stood to my word. Go you and do likewise wherever you visit the classes.[45]

The general, though unwritten, rule was that three consecutive absences constituted self-expulsion from a class,[46] and leaders were required to keep a record of attendance on a special class paper, or later, in a class book (see Appendix I). If any member was absent, the leader was to make enquiries, and enter the letter D opposite that person's name if distant—i.e., away from home, an S if sick, a B if on business, and N if it was felt that the reason was mere neglect. If no reason could be found for the absence, then the letter A was to be entered.[47]

The General Rules

This meant that, once a week, a society member had to give an account of his or her discipleship, for which the initial referent was the

General Rules. Wesley never ceased to affirm these "outward rules" as the disciplinary framework within which the spiritual growth of the early Methodists was effected, and without which it was inevitably impeded.[48] Members were not admitted in trial without affirming their willingness to accept the rules, and there were many instances of tickets being refused each quarter to those who failed to abide by them. Some specifics of these rules might be regarded today as expressive of a dated casuistry, but their purpose was clear. Since there was no prerequisite for Methodist membership other than a desire for salvation, the societies were open to all, regardless of their spiritual state. But to remain in membership, there had to be an evidence of the desire for salvation in the doing of outward and visible good works. These were at once a manifestation of faith, and a condition of continuing in it.

The *Rules* accordingly stipulated three criteria. First, members were enjoined to do no harm, and to avoid "evil in every kind." Second, they were to do good "of every possible sort, and as far as possible, to all Men." Third, they were to attend upon "all the Ordinances of God: Such are The publick Worship of God; the Ministry of the Word, either read or expounded; The Supper of the Lord; Private Prayer; Searching the Scriptures; and Fasting, or Abstinence." Wesley regarded this third criterion, the attending on the ordinances of God, as availing oneself of the "instituted means of grace," the disciplines, the practices of the church, without which any attempt to pursue a Christian discipleship was fallacious. It indicates not only that he perceived worldly service in the name of Christ to be ineffectual without the power of the Holy Spirit, but also that the inner discipline of Methodism was inexorably linked to that of the Church of England. He developed the polity of small group fellowship on the assumption that the wider questions of doctrine and order were already established. Members of Nonconformist churches who joined the societies were expected to fulfill their congregational obligation no less than parishioners of the Church of England.[49]

Other leaders in the Revival were less concerned about this aspect of society discipline. One of Wesley's assistants, John Nelson, records such an example. He had preached for a week to some of Benjamin Ingham's societies in the North of England, during which time "nine or ten were brought to experience the love of Jesus. . . . Those that were of the Church of England, I exhorted to keep close to the Church and Sacrament; and the Dissenters to keep to their own meetings, and to let their light shine before those of their own community. But soon after, I learned that Mr. Ingham advised the contrary, and several began to stay at home on the Sabbath; which made me very uneasy."[50]

4. SPIRITUAL MATURITY

Wesley's insistence that the instituted means of grace not be neglected by the members of the Methodist societies is particularly important in the context of the complementary function of the class meeting—the nurture of spiritual growth. For just as the weekly meetings held Methodists accountable for their discipleship in the world, so they fostered the development of a spiritual maturity as the members "watched over one another in love." Class leaders were encouraged from an early date to evaluate the spiritual state of their members, as in a report to Wesley from one of the leaders at the Foundery society, Abraham Jones, dated December 13, 1742:

> My Class (except John Moss, for I know not how he walks) do all walk orderly, & keep close to the Word, and the means of grace. E.J. the Elder, in my Class, complains much, as being under strong temptations, as to doubt the being of a God, or of ability to hold out, that if the Lord did not destroy the man of sin in her that it would destroy her, & yet acknowledges, that at every one of these assaults of the enemy, The Lord appears in the promises to her relief and she is delivered.[51]

The same concern for detailed evaluation can be seen in a 1747 communication from another Foundery leader, John Hague, who reports to Wesley that seven persons "seem to retain their confidence in the Lord;" that six others "seem to be shut up in a fog, and are not able to get out on any side," being "very dead and yet very sore;" nine others "seem to be in earnest, seeking the Lord;" and two "appear to have a desire, and to be widely seeking something."[52]

Spiritual Discernment

As the classes developed, so did the language of spiritual discernment. Class papers required the leader to insert in a separate column the "state" of each member with an appropriate sign: the letter (a) for one who was *awakened*; a question mark (?) for one whose state was *doubtful*; a period (.) for one who professed *justification*; and a colon (:) for one who professed *the perfect love of God*.[53] The extent to which this was accepted as a normative classification can be further discerned in the headings of the hymn book published in 1780, which included sections on: *Formal Religion; Inward Religion; Praying for Repentance; for Mourners Convinced of Sin, Brought to Birth, Convinced of Backsliding,* and *Recovered;* and for *Believers Rejoicing, Fighting, Praying, Watching, Working, Suffering, Groaning for Full Redemption, Brought to the Birth, Saved,* and *Interceding for the World.*[54]

By the same token, the quarterly renewal of class tickets became not only a disciplinary examination, but also an occasion when all of the members, including the leader, were questioned about their spiritual growth. This was not, of course, the sort of intensive questioning which took place in the bands. There were too many variables in a class meeting for the searching confessionals of a band to be either practicable or prudent as a normative procedure. In many instances, the fellowship in a class did develop to a point where there was deep spiritual sensitivity; but in general there had to be a pragmatism in the format which could respond to the basic requirements of discipleship in the world as well as to the mysteries of sanctifying grace. As Wesley himself noted, the class meetings were "merely prudential, not essential, not of divine institution. We prevent, so far as in us lies, their growing formal or dead. We are always open to instruction; willing to be wiser every day than we were before, and to change whatever we can change for the better."[55]

The Danger of Formalism

Wesley's concern to prevent the meetings from becoming a mere formality was by no means an empty warning. By their very nature, the classes had a fixed agenda, which at once provided a structure for the meetings and a danger that the catechetical format of question and answer would become repetitive and routine. An account of a class meeting published by the Methodist Conference Office in 1813 gives a good indication of the ways in which class leaders were expected to respond to the answers they received from their members, precisely to avoid such repetition and formality.[56] The author warns at the outset that in a class of twelve members, each person will be different, ranging from one who has only "some faint desires to be religious," to one who is "rejoicing in that perfect love which casteth out fear." There may even be one who has "fallen into open sin," to say nothing of one who is "dull and suspicious." The task of the leader, therefore, is to vary the advice and instruction given to each, providing mutual encouragement so that each might learn something from the experiences of the others.

An Example of Class Meeting Catechesis

This account is worth excerpting in some detail as an example of how class meetings were conducted. We shall need to make some allowances for the language, and for the fact that it is a hypothetical model. It must also be remembered that, by virtue of joining a class, each member was bound by the *General Rules* with regard to many aspects of personal and social behavior which are not specified in the dialogue. Even so, what follows is an evocative and instructive example of how the early Methodists "watched over one another in love."

Specimen of a Class Meeting

In giving a *specimen* of the ordinary process of a class-meeting, it will be proper to suppose twelve persons met together . . . ; and after singing and prayer, suppose the following statements made by the members, in answer to inquiries made by the leader, as to their state and experience in religion: and the following advices or reproofs given, founded on these statements.

First. "I trust the Lord hath taught me to seek my happiness in him; the world appears to contain nothing in it sufficiently interesting to engage my heart: I am weary with its vanities, and now desire a better country; nothing is so desirable to me as the knowledge of God's ways, and I wish to forsake all, that I may follow on to know the Lord." Hosea vi.3.

Leader. "I rejoice with you in the favourable change which has taken place in your views and feelings, and that you have at length consented to walk in that path where true joys alone are to be found; and that the Father of mercies hath begun to allure your wishes, and engage your affections to himself: be careful, however, that you do not by indifference hinder, or by rebellion defeat, the gentle allurements of grace; be decided; come out from the ungodly, and be ye separate, saith the Lord: think how important it is to make a good beginning in religion; and while we hope that the wishes and desires which you have expressed arise from sincerity and truth, let us have the happiness also to see, that your actions agree with your words." 2 Cor.vi.17.

Second. "My soul is in heaviness. I am oppressed: Lord, undertake for me! I am made to partake of deep sorrow, and the terrors of the Lord make me afraid. I have sinned against Heaven, nor can

I answer for one sin: O, wretched man that I am! My sins are very great, and the remembrance of them is very grievous. O that I knew where to find redemption! God be merciful to me a sinner!" Luke xviii.13.

Leader. " The Lord God is gracious and merciful, slow to anger, and of great pity, forgiving iniquity, transgression, and sin; to that man will he look, who is humble, and of a contrite heart, and that trembleth at his word. Fear not, believe only; thou are not far from the kingdom: behold the Lamb of God, that taketh away the sin of the world. I have nothing to say to thee, my brother, but what is encouraging. And now why tarriest thou? Arise, and wash away thy sins, calling on the name of the Lord." Acts xxii.16.

Third. "Blessed be God, I feel his mercy to my soul. I can say to the glory of his grace, that though he was angry with me, his anger is turned away, and now he comforts me. I know in whom I have believed, and have a blessed testimony; bearing witness that I am passed from death unto life, and that God, for Christ's sake, hath forgiven me my sins." Ephes. iv.22.

Leader. "Rejoice with trembling; be thankful, and continue humble: stand fast in the liberty wherewith Christ hath made you free. Sin no more, lest a worse thing come unto thee."

Fourth. "I want a brighter evidence of my interest in the pardoning love of God. Once I had no doubt on this subject; the candle of the Lord shone on my head, and my title to heaven was clear: but now I am in heaviness through manifold temptations, weeping, and saying, 'Verily thou art a God that hidest thyself.' " Isaiah xlv.15.

Leader. "It is well, when we have lost any of the blessings which we once enjoyed, to be sensible of their absence, and to mourn their loss. It would be an additional evil to lose religious good, and be insensible of the loss. To be sensible of our loss here, is to be in the way of recovery. Continue to seek the return of your evidence, that you may again be filled with all joy and peace in believing." Rom. xv.13.

Fifth. "As the hart panteth for the water-brook, so my soul panteth for the living God. I want to be sanctified throughout body, soul, and spirit, and to be filled with all the fulness of God. I cannot rest in present attainments: this one thing I do, forgetting the things which are behind, I go on to perfection." Heb. vi.1.

Leader. "This is the duty and interest of believers. There is a fountain open for sin and uncleanness: the blood of Christ cleanseth from all sin: without holiness, no man shall see the Lord:

therefore, he saith, 'Be ye holy, for I am holy'; and learn what this meaneth: 'I will sprinkle clean water upon you, and ye shall be my people, and I will be your God.' " Ezek. xxxvi.25.

Sixth. "I feel myself nothing before God, and all the world is as nothing to me. God is the supreme object of my love: he knoweth all things, he knoweth that I love him above all things, and in all things. I have given my total heart to him, and he is the unrivalled ruler of my affections. My fears are lost in perfect love, my heart is fixed. I will sing and give praise." Psalm lvii.7.

Leader. "Happy are the people who are in such a case; yea, blessed is that people whose God is the Lord. What hath the world to equal this? Who would not gladly exchange the toys of life for this *better part*, and count all things but as dross, when compared with these *true riches*? And this I pray, that 'being rooted and grounded in love, you may be able to comprehend with all saints, what is the breadth, and length, and depth, and height, and to know (i.e., approve) the love of Christ which passeth knowledge, that ye may be filled with all the fulness of God.' " Eph. iii.17-19.

Seventh. "I have had painful trials, and severe temptations: fightings without, and fears within. The frowns of providence, and the wiles of the devil, have alternately pierced and alarmed me. O that it were with me now, as in days past!" Job xxix.2,3.

Leader. "Many are the afflictions of the righteous, and many are the conflicts of a christian soldier. To be tried and tempted, are the common lot of all the truly faithful; nor should you think it strange concerning the fiery trials which happen unto you, as though some strange thing had occurred: you have not forgotten the exhortation that speaketh to you as children: 'My son, despise not thou the chastening of the Lord, neither faint when you art rebuked of him: for whom the Lord loveth, he chasteneth, and scourgeth every son whom he receiveth.' Be patient then, knowing the rod, and who hath appointed it." Micah vi.9.

Eighth. "My faith is feeble, and my consolations are small. I cannot as I wish lay hold of the promises; unbelief robs me of my peace, and fills me with doubt; and my constant prayer is, 'Lord, forgive, and help my unbelief.' " Mark ix.24.

Leader. "This is one of the most common snares of the devil, as well as one of the most successful ones. His constant endeavour is to excite suspicion, perplex with doubt, and embarrass with evil reasonings, the faith and hope of God's people. I advise you to refer again to the *truth* and *faithfulness* of God's word. Remember, you have more reasons to believe than to doubt; think on the endless mercy of Almighty God, and be not faithless, but believing." John xx.27.

Ninth. "My heart is dull and comfortless; I can neither hear, nor read, nor pray, as I did once: God has either departed from me, or I have departed from him, or both, and I am tempted to go back again to the world." Heb. x.38.

Leader. "Painful state! dangerous condition! You have then suffered declension in your soul, and are a backslider in heart from the Lord. Can you rest in this state, and feel no apprehension of the danger to which you are exposed? You have been unwatchful; you have not been as fervent in prayer as you should have been; you have nearly lost your religion, and are not far from losing your soul. 'What meanest thou, O sleeper? Call upon God, that thou perish not.'" Jonah i.6.

Tenth. "I am ashamed of myself; I have been overtaken in a fault; nor should I have had courage to come to my class again (much as I love class-meetings) had it not been that I owe it, to God and to you, to confess that I have sinned against heaven, and am no more worthy of a name or a place among the people of God: my heart bleeds; it will break; men and brethren, what shall I do?" Acts xvi.30.

Leader. "To have sinned against God is an evil and a bitter thing, and should penetrate the offender with the deepest remorse; as it not only grieves the saints, but gives the enemies of the Lord great occasion to blaspheme. The Lord, however, hath made you sensible of your sin, and, we hope, hath put away your sin: learn, then, your own feebleness, and be more watchful, and as thou art made whole, sin no more, lest a worse thing come unto thee." John v.14.

Eleventh. "I can truly say that I desire to press forward; I endeavour to do all I can. I hope and trust that I should love religion more and more. I was brought up rather gay in life, and am obliged to go to those places where others go; but I do not feel that I am as right any where as in the way of true religion."

Leader. "Ah! my brother! how little religion has done for you! and how little you have done to gain religion! If you cannot give up the world for the sake of Christ; if you are not affected with your sin and danger; if you have never felt repentance towards God, and faith in our Lord Jesus Christ; you are still in your sins, you have neither part nor lot in this matter; nor have I any advice to give you at present, but that you should turn from your evil ways, and seek the Lord while he may be found, and call upon him while he is near." Isaiah lv.6.

Twelfth. "I had departed from the fountain of living waters; I had wandered back again to the beggarly elements of the world; but God hath restored to me the joys of his salvation, and now I feel him precious to my soul, and present with me again." Isaiah xii.1.

Leader. "I am glad that your soul is restored, and that you have proved the patience and forbearance of God towards you. Ah! do not grieve him again; be on your guard against the enemy by whom you have been ensnared: cleave to the Lord with purpose of heart. What I say to you, I say to *all*, 'Watch.'" Mark xiii.37.

Thus it will appear, that in a class of twelve members, every case may be different; and that therefore the leader of such a class will have to render his advices as various as are the states of his people.

It does not follow, however, that the manner of a class-meeting must always be the same; variations may be safely, and have been successfully adopted. . . .

Hence arises the importance of the station in which a leader is placed. His duties are arduous, and his responsibility great: not only is it necessary that he should have a deep experience of God's mercies to his own soul, but that he should have a fervent love for the souls of others, and an extensive knowledge of the workings of the heart, of the wiles of the wicked one, and of the word of God.[57]

It quickly becomes clear from this account that the exchanges in the class meetings were essentially catechetical between the leader and each member of the group. The process was one of question and answer, with the leader articulating what was felt to be the point which would most profitably be shared by the other members—a method which served to emphasize that the initial purpose of the meeting was for each person to give an account to the others of his or her discipleship. We shall presently note that the tendency of such catechesis during the nineteenth century was away from accountability for good works, and more toward an inbred pietism which marked the decline of the class meeting—a tendency already evident in this early post-Wesleyan account. But as Wesley introduced and developed them, the classes exercised accountability for the *General Rules* as well as for inward spiritual growth; and it is a serious, though common, error to assume that they were intended primarily for fellowship. Nothing could be further from the truth.[58]

Weekly Fellowship amd Accountability

   This is not to say that fellowship was not engendered by the weekly gatherings. On the contrary, this is the title given by Leslie F. Church to the chapter on class meetings in his book, *The Early Methodist People*, which remains one of the finest compilations we have of source materials. The metaphor he adopts is highly evocative: The classes were "the 'fireside' round which members of the 'family' shared a common experience and kept their sacred tryst."[59] This imparts at once the informality of the meetings and the nature of the accountability to which they called the members. To give an account of one's spiritual journey— inward discernment and practical discipleship—while gathered round a fireside is much more the spirit of the early classes than that which Nightingale's account implies, however much they might have become formalized in their post-Wesleyan phase.

   Nonetheless, the point to be made is that the classes enjoyed this fellowship precisely because they did have the prior purpose of accountability. Initially there would be some awkwardness as the catechetical process was implemented, and people would be diffident about answering such direct and evaluative questions. But as the accountability was exercised, they began to realize that they were indeed on a common journey—and that their mutual accountability was not pejorative, but supportive. The fellowship was rich because they understood the real purpose of their gathering; and the meetings were informal because their structure was assured.

5. FELLOWSHIP BEYOND THE CLASS

The Bands: Mutual Confession

   In the bands, on the other hand, there was a less structured but more intensive exchange, due in large part to the greater intimacy afforded by Wesley's restriction of membership to those who wanted and needed "some means of closer union." It was here that the spiritual quest for perfection was fostered and guided. Wesley described band members as those who, being justified by faith, had peace with God through Christ, and

> felt a more tender affection than before, to those who were partakers of like precious faith; and hence arose such a confidence in each other, that they poured out their souls into each other's bosom. Indeed they had great need so to do; for the war was not over, as they had supposed; but they had still to wrestle both with flesh and blood, and with principalities and powers: So that temptations were on every side; and often temptations of such a kind, as they knew not how to speak in a class; in which persons of every sort, young and old, men and women, met together.[60]

With the same pragmatism which led him to adopt the classes as the basic requirement of membership in his societies, Wesley retained the bands for those who wanted and needed this more intimate form of fellowship. Continuing the pattern of segregation by sex and marital status, membership in a band was strongly recommended as a means of being strengthened in love, and more effectually "provoked to abound in every good work."[61]

Band members were subjected to a more rigorous disciplinary oversight than the classes. The early *Rules of the Band Societies* were supplemented in December 1744 with a series of *Directions* (also reproduced in Appendix E), which took the *General Rules* of the societies and gave them a very particular focus. Band members were to abstain from evil *carefully*, to maintain good works *zealously*, and to attend on all the ordinances of the church *constantly*. They received a special notation on the quarterly class tickets, initially the word *band*, and later the letter *b* in the corner. Such a ticket was not granted without a trial period of three months, and it distinguished those members within a society as those who were committed to the quest for Christian maturity.[62]

The "Body Band"

The assistants and helpers were instructed to give the band leaders, or "keepers," special oversight, and to be especially vigilant in enforcing the *Rules* and *Directions*.[63] Furthermore, they were to meet with all of the band members weekly, quite apart from the general society meetings and the quarterly visitations—a practice introduced early in the movement by Wesley himself:

> That their design in meeting might be the more effectually answered, I desired all the men-bands to meet me together every Wednesday evening, and the women on Sunday, that they might receive such particular instructions and exhortations as, from time to time, might appear to be most needful for them; that such prayers might be offered up to God, as their necessities should require; and praise returned to the Giver of every good gift, for whatever mercies they had received.[64]

Known as the "public" meeting of the bands, or the "body band," these gatherings became an established part of the Methodist connectional polity. In due course, the women's and men's meetings were combined, and often reached large numbers as society memberships increased.[65] At such meetings, observed Jonathan Crowther, "people are not spoken to, one by one, as at a class-meeting, but every one speaks, or remains silent, as they are disposed."[66]

Meeting "In Band": Intensive Experience

It was assumed that an experience of justifying faith was shared by all those who met in the bands—those who had "long walked in the way," to use the description of John Valton, one of Wesley's preachers who was first admitted "into band" in 1764.[67] The purpose of meeting together was to provide the mutual confession and encouragement conducive to advanced spiritual growth. As Joseph Nightingale noted, band members were "generally those who have either attained or are earnestly seeking, a state of perfection or complete sanctification;"[68] and, as further observed by Jonathan Crowther, they were those whose "attainments in religion [were] supposed to be nearly equal."[69] There was accordingly a greater degree of openness, and the intimacy which this afforded takes the reader of early Methodist biography on to holy ground.

The correspondence between John Braithwaite and his biographer, Robert Dickinson, is a case in point, demonstrating on almost every page what it meant to be "band-fellows." When Braithwaite came under appointment as an itinerant preacher, for example, he noted that "Brother R. Dickinson and I still continue like David and Jonathan, and . . . when he comes to Whitehaven, we generally hold a little band-meeting, and Brother Sykes makes a third."[70] The correspondence becomes poignant when the two men wanted to seek the hand in marriage of the same young woman in the Whitehaven society. But this was resolved with expedition, and with grace.[71] The letter reproduced in Appendix K evinces a pride so sensitive as to border on true humility, and could only have come from a total trust in the mutual working of the Spirit.[72]

In the many accounts where bands are contrasted with classes, the former are frequently identified as experiential, and the latter catechetical.[73] Indeed, it is this very quality of the bands which has been seen by some critics as an unhealthy procedure, whereby "every incipient feeling, every lighter thought that would have been passed over . . . and been forgotten, is to be remarked and remembered, that it may be renewed and rivetted, and *burnt in* to the heart by the pain and shame of confession."[74] It is not surprising, therefore, that in Wesley's day they were alleged to be "mere popery."[75] On more than one occasion he defended the mutual sharing which took place as being in no way analagous to the confession made by a single person to a priest.[76] Rather than a preoccupation with sin, the emphasis was on a growth in grace. Rather than a probing for hidden faults, the openness of fellowship was a means of mutual guidance toward a perfection of love, in which, as he put it, "the chains were broken, . . . and sin had no more dominion over them."[77] He regarded band leaders, men and women alike, as those with "a deep fear of God, a continual consciousness of His presence, and a stronger thirst after his whole image, and observed, significantly, that many of the poor were of this number, but "extremely few of the rich or honourable Methodists."[78]

Lovefeasts

The earnest pursuit of the bands for Christian perfection led in turn to the adoption of further "prudential means of grace," such as the lovefeast. Wesley had been introduced to this early Christian practice by the Moravians while he was in Georgia,[79] and had commended it from the days of the Fetter Lane society as a regular observance. The format was simple: bread and water served at tables while the participants shared in prayer and testimony. Yet the fellowship engendered by this humble meal was intense, and Wesley's record of the feast held at Fetter Lane on New Year's Day, 1739, indicates that it had an immediacy and an impact which could easily be misunderstood by those not aware of the nature of the gathering.[80]

Wesley regarded love-feasts as an extension of band fellowship, and as a means of stimulating it. They were held each quarter for men and women, separately and jointly, and were the occasion of admitting new members into the bands.[81] When attendance was extended to all society members after 1758, it remained a highly coveted privilege, with admission strictly by class ticket only.[82]

Select Societies

An even more restricted grouping was the *select society*, in which the doctrine of Christian perfection was most demonstrably experienced and practiced. Wesley regarded these members as "outrunning" the greater part of their brothers and sisters, "continually walking in the light of God, and having fellowship with the Father, and with his Son Jesus Christ."[83] His purpose in forming such groups was not only to direct them "how to press after perfection," how to "incite them to love one another more, and to watch more carefully over each other." He also looked upon them as "a select company, to whom I might unbosom myself on all occasions, without reserve; and whom I could propose to all their brethren as a pattern of love, of holiness, and of good works."[84]

There were no rules for these groups, since they had "the best rule of all in their hearts." They had only three basic guidelines:

> First. Let nothing spoken in this society be spoken again. (Hereby we had the more full confidence in each other.) Secondly. Every member agrees to submit to his Minister in all indifferent things. Thirdly. Every member will bring, once a week, all he can toward a common stock.[85]

In all other respects, the select societies had a completely free agenda, each member able to speak openly, and with no leader appointed. The status of the groups within the movement was affirmed by the 1744 Conference, and Wesley urged them to meet regularly, examining them separately and insisting on their strict oversight.[86]

Backsliders and Penitents

Since they were in many ways an expression of the doctrine of Christian perfection,[87] it is important to note that the progression to membership of select societies seems frequently to have been that of "backsliding" and then "recovering." Those who "fell from the faith, either all at once, by falling into known, vileful sin," or "gradually, and almost insensibly, by giving way in what they called little things," as well as those "whose fall was not checked by 'exhortations and prayers used among the believers,'" were classified by Wesley as *penitents*, and given special instruction and advice. Those who "recovered the ground they had lost" proved even stronger in the faith, "being more watchful than ever, and more meek and lowly."[88]

The significance of these penitents is that they had already advanced to be "in band," and were not just rank-and-file class members.[89] In the broader spectrum of the class meeting, where the condition of membership was merely a *desire* to seek the accountability of Christian discipleship, inconsistencies were to be expected. But in the bands, where justifying faith was the common experience, discipleship was no longer merely a commitment of intent. It was a condition of continuing faith. The striving for perfection was the conscious desire on the part of the band member to reach a continuous and unbroken relationship with God in love; and the experience of the penitents was precisely to have discovered how crucial this was for the maturity of their faith. They had come to know that at any time the relationship of the believer with God in Christ can be broken by disobedience to the known will of God, and that such a breach resulted not only in the lack of spiritual progress. It occasioned a falling away—and even *the loss of faith*.[90]

The Path to Perfection

Wesley did not lose sight of the nature of Christian perfection as a gift. It was received by faith, as was the new birth of justification; and the language he used to describe it made clear that both were a work of the Holy Spirit:

> When, after having been fully convinced of inbred sin, by a far deeper and clearer conviction than that . . . experienced before justification, and after having experienced a gradual mortification of

it, [the believer] experiences a total death to sin, and an entire renewal in the love and image of God, so as to rejoice evermore, to pray without ceasing, and in everything to give thanks. Not that "to feel all love and no sin" is a sufficient proof. Several have experienced this for a time, before their souls were fully renewed. None therefore ought to believe that the work is done, till there is added the testimony of the Spirit, witnessing his entire sanctification, as clearly as his justification.[91]

But Wesley placed this perfection in a doctrinal context of *accountability*. Those pressing on to perfection were to wait for the gift of the fullness of love, "not in careless indifference, or indolent inactivity; but in vigorous, universal obedience, in a zealous keeping of all the commandments, in watchfulness and painfulness. . . . It is true we receive it by simple faith: But God does not, will not, give that faith, unless we seek it with all diligence, in the way which he hath ordained."[92] Christian perfection proceeded from Christ, but had to be maintained in obedience to his Spirit, moment by moment. It was not like a tree, which "flourished by the sap derived from its own root, but . . . like that of a branch which, united to the vine, bears fruit; but, severed from it, is dried up and withered."[93] And in the closing months of his life, he reaffirmed the point in a letter to Edward Lewly: "My Dear Brother, — I do not believe any single person in your Select Society scruples saying, Every moment, Lord, I need The merit of thy death."[94]

Basic Spiritual Nurture

All of which served to emphasize the importance of the class meeting, not only as the basic unit of Methodist organizational structure, but also as the most effective means of spiritual nurture for the membership as a whole. All Methodists, whether starting out as "awakened" sinners or having received the gift of perfect love, whether they were meeting in band or even in a select society, had to meet once a week as members of their class to give an account of their discipleship. It was an inclusive requirement, and it was egalitarian—the necessary complement to the bands and select societies which have been described as evidence of Wesley's "virtuoso religiousness."[95] The "path to perfection" began *and continued* with an accountability for the basics of Christian discipleship—the means of grace and the works of obedience—without which no genuine progress could be made in the Christian life.

It was precisely such an accountability which the class meeting sought to foster; and we shall argue in the concluding chapter that it was this *purpose*, rather than any effect it might have had within the Methodist movement or on society at large, which constitutes its real significance.

Chapter Five

THE SIGNIFICANCE OF THE CLASS MEETING

ACCOUNTABLE DISCIPLESHIP

1. THE CLASS MEETING IN WESLEY'S ECCLESIOLOGY

The focus of our study thus far has been the origins of the early Methodist class meeting in the Christian tradition. Accordingly we began with Wesley's understanding of the church as he himself stood in that tradition. We noted that he affirmed the authority of the visible *ecclesia* as normative for Christian faith and practice, and the *Articles* and *Homilies* of the Anglican church as referents for that authority in England. He censured unnecessary schism, arguing strongly against ecclesial divisions which seemed to him a diversion of energies away from the gospel into fruitless pursuits after non-essentials in the faith. The pragmatism which marked his oversight of early Methodist polity was ultimately governed by the principle which guided his ecclesiology—that the Church of England was closest to the early church in faith and practice. It was the church which he knew, and he loved it. Unless there was a very good reason to depart from its doctrines and ordinances, therefore, he saw no point at all in so doing.

At the same time, he affirmed the supremacy of scripture when it contradicted ecclesial teaching and practice. And since scripture did not, in his view, articulate any particular form of church order, he was open to varieties of opinions and practices in such matters. Moreover, while he resisted any contravention of Anglican discipline which seemed unwarranted by this larger purpose, he was willing to concede the point when he saw the grace of God flowing through non-ecclesial channels, even though his peers and superiors in the church regarded them as highly irregular. He firmly subordinated the rubrics of the church to what he regarded as its overriding purpose: the saving of souls.

Wesley's ultimate authority, however, was his obedience to the indwelling Spirit of God, the essence of the Puritan spirit. When all other ecclesial and theological maxims had been given their due, this was the

125

overriding imperative—the criterion of direct religious experience which
he added to the Anglican theological method of scripture, tradition, and
reason. It was this same imperative which led him to develop the polity
of the Methodist societies, classes, and bands under his *episkopé*,
fostering an obedience to the will of God as experienced by the prompting of the Holy Spirit.

Spiritual Obedience and Catholicity of Grace

The wellspring of this obedience was the grace of God; and in the
catholicity of grace as Wesley perceived it, there were no limits to God's
initiatives. Indeed, the first gift of God's grace was the freedom to resist
it, a freedom restored preveniently to a depraved human nature. Likewise by prevenient grace, each person was afforded the opportunity to
act responsibly according to conscience, that gift of God which enabled
people to "do the best they could" while seeking the fullness of a
restored relationship with God in Christ. Justifying grace brought the
consciousness of pardon and acceptance by God through the merits of
Christ—the critical point of surrender, where the human will finally
submitted to God's initiatives, and where the sinner, experiencing the
new birth of the Spirit, was adopted as a child of God. The relative
change was then worked out through sanctifying grace, as the Christian
maintained the new relationship in works of obedience. This too was
God's gracious gift. But in the same way that justification was received
when the sinner, with the freedom of prevenient grace, decided not to
resist the forgiveness of God, so sanctification came through accepting
the will of God in conscious obedience. No less distinctive was Christian
perfection, the maturity of consistent obedience, whereby the new
relationship with God in Christ was bonded in a perfection of love,
received by grace through an accountable discipleship.

The Christian Tradition and the Means of Grace

Wesley felt it was important to ground this catholicity of grace in the
Christian tradition, and specifically in the instituted means of grace
afforded by the disciplines of the church. In this way, the societies,
classes, and bands fulfilled their true purpose. Precisely because the
ecclesia provided the doctrinal structure for the Christian faith, those in
the *ecclesiolae* were free to respond to the inner promptings of the

Spirit. The "little churches" were formed with the avowed purpose of remaining within the larger church in order to call it back to its own essentials; and their members were given guidance in religious experience and spiritual nurture only to the extent that the doctrines and ordinances of the Church of England were pre-supposed.

Ecclesiola in Ecclesia

In short, Wesley practiced the concept of *ecclesiola in ecclesia* with integrity: the freedom of small groups, focused on the immediacy of obedient Christian discipleship; and the necessary structure of the larger church where doctrine and order were established in the realities and uncertainties of the world. The inference is clear: The structure of the larger *ecclesia* must be affirmed as inherently valid and necessary if the freedom of the *ecclesiola* is to be exercised responsibly.

2. CONTEXTUAL TRADITIONING

As we turn to assess the significance of the class meeting, however, we must do more than view it in the context of Wesley's theology and churchmanship. We must take into account the realities of our own context, within which we are perforce obliged to do our traditioning. This means that first of all we must view the ecclesiological dialectic of early Methodist polity through the contemporary perspectives of social psychology and group dynamics. Not to do this would be to deny the post-Marxian and post-Freudian reality of the late twentieth century. And if we take care not to superimpose twentieth-century perceptions onto eighteenth-century religious experience, the exercise will permit us to discern the distinctive pattern of Methodist discipleship in the light of behavioral patterns which, though analyzed comparatively recently, are now widely accepted as endemic to the human race.

Spontaneous Community and Social Structure

To begin with, the tension between spirit and structure is now seen to be a social axiom, as in Victor Turner's analysis of social relationships in contrast with social systems.[1] Relationships between "concrete, historical, idiosyncratic individuals" are *communitas*—spontaneous community, unstructured and free from the restrictions of role and status. This cannot, however, be maintained for very long. "Communitas itself soon develops a structure, in which free relationships between individuals become converted into norm-governed relationships between social personae. Thus it is necessary to distinguish between: (1) existential or spontaneous communitas . . . ; (2) normative communitas, where . . . the existential communitas is organized into a perduring social system; and (3) ideological communitas . . . utopian models of societies based on existential communitas."[2]

Utopian models of spontaneous communitas as they have appeared in history, argues Turner, have ultimately proved unrealistic. They can and should occur from time to time between people who are otherwise socially structured, punctuating the social life of a complex and institutionalized society, and offering an "existence" as opposed to the organization of society. Indeed, structured social patterns quickly become arid and mechanical without such a periodic regenerative immersion. But communitas should not be a substitute for the careful ordering of human relationships within the context of nature. True social wisdom, he concludes,

> is always to find the appropriate relationship between structure and communitas under the given circumstances of time and place, to accept each modality when it is paramount without rejecting the other, and not to cling to one when its present impetus is spent. . . . Spontaneous communitas is a phase, a moment, not a permanent condition . . . [it] is nature in dialogue with structure, married to it as a woman is married to a man. Together they make up one stream of life, the one affluent supplying power, the other alluvial fertility.[3]

Wesley's organization of Methodism incorporated this social wisdom. He perceived that an *ecclesiola* which rejects the structure of the *ecclesia* must perforce provide its own, thereby losing the freedom of its spontaneity. He also perceived the necessity for a disciplined order, without which the immediacy of Christian experience could lead to the excesses of an otherworldly enthusiasm. In the societies, classes, and bands, there was the communitas of the "gathered church," called out of the world. But there was also the firm grounding of the Anglican tradition and structure, with its positive approach to human reason and the visible reality of the church in the world.

The Class Meeting and Interpersonal Dynamics

Understandings of interpersonal dynamics have likewise made clear that many of the characteristics of the class meeting are common to all small groups. For one thing, they provided a sense of security, thereby meeting some basic social and personal needs of their members. Sociological studies have shown that all people have three needs in common: the need for *inclusion*—the degree of commitment, belongingness, and participation an individual requires in human inter-action; the need for *control*—the degree of influence and power an individual requires; and the need for *affection*—the degree of closeness and intimacy an individual requires.[4] And in meeting these needs, the early Methodist classes could not avoid a further dimension of group dynamics—that any genuine human interaction inevitably involves feeling and emotion, the "basic raw data of interpersonal rela-tionships."[5]

The analysis of emotional expression as it occurs in small groups has been an important development in interpersonal dynamics. Not only has this led to more detailed correlation between feelings and human needs; it has also provided a new awareness of personal change as it takes place in groups, where emotional expression is caught up in a highly distinctive dynamic through a process of feedback and interac-tion.[6] Moreover, as the work of Carl Rogers has demonstrated, self-expression can be the means of meeting the need for personal growth and of achieving emotional maturity. The class meeting quickly acquired such a dynamic. As members were asked by the leader each week to articulate their religious experiences and feelings, they grew in self-assurance and self-perception.[7]

Social Needs and Eighteenth-Century English Society

These insights raise the sociological question of the extent to which Methodism was supplying some basic needs for its members in response to a society which was suffering from radical change and depersonalization. Rogers, for example, is convinced that, in a broader social context, personal growth achieved through a process of self-expression is a concept of a new kind of life, particularly suited to a society where people must develop skills to exchange deep feelings through relationships of a comparatively short duration. "At the present time [the encounter group experience] is the best instrument I know for healing the loneliness that prevails in so many human beings. It holds forth a real hope that isolation need not be the keynote of our individual lives."[8] By the same token, Kurt Back has observed that "the search for groups in which intense and emotional experience can be enjoyed is a sign of disturbance in many societies, occurring at times of deep social unrest and especially during the rise of new religions."[9]

It is widely agreed that the eighteenth century in England was just such a time.[10] There was ferment in the intellectual climate which questioned many aspects of the established order, the Age of Reason being remarkable "less for the doctrine which it propounded than for the manner of thought which it encouraged. It was secular in spirit and destructive in effect. It diffused a scepticism which gradually dissolved the intellectual and religious pattern which had governed Europe since Augustine."[11]

This was accompanied by economic unrest. Domestic industries were replacing the old trade guilds, and monopolistic practices were beginning to encroach on those trades which remained established. Rapid colonial expansion added further commercial pressure to a domestic industry not yet equipped to serve and use a growing empire to advantage—added to which there was a great deal of social displacement. As the century progressed, enclosure of common land rendered many of those who had tilled the soil for generations little more than casual laborers, and ripe for transition into the proletariat which fueled the incipient Industrial Revolution.[12] Under Elizabethan Poor Law, enacted as far back as 1601 and administered locally by Justices who could fix wage scales and even restrict the movement of workers from one community to another, resources proved increasingly inadequate for the thousands who gravitated from the country to seek work in the towns, causing a drastic increase in the numbers of the poor.[13]

The results were slum conditions created by cheaply-produced tenements in crowded municipalities, with bad hygiene, poor health, and the absence of any real sense of community for a large section of the population. Indeed, the major contrast between pre- and post-Industrial Revolution England was "less that of capitalism or bourgeois economic control, than the transition from small, family-type social units to the larger society of undifferentiated equals."[14] Not surprisingly, discontent was prevalent, serious disorder was a frequent occurrence, and the method of dealing with these symptoms was a savage penal code which did nothing to resolve the problems.[15]

Methodist Membership and Social Identity

In this context of social deprivation, Methodism brought to many a recognition and identity. "For the crushed and despised classes to be told over and over again that God loved them, that Christ died for them, that there was forgiveness of sins [and reconciliation] through the wondrous cross, sounded strange in their ears and brought a marvel to their hearts."[16] There can be little doubt that those who joined the Methodist societies found, in their weekly class meetings, the human relationships which provided the means of achieving their identity.

Yet a word of caution is in order. Methodist membership seems for the most part to have comprised artisans or tradespeople, persons who were in possession of at least a rudimentary education and who, while living in the midst of social unrest, were usually not among those hardest hit by the changes. Moreover, while Methodism under Wesley's leadership became the most significant component of the eighteenth-century evangelical revival, it was never a mass movement. The following statistics show that, in any given year, Methodists constituted only a fraction of 1 percent of the populace:

Year	Population of England and Wales[17]	Membership of Methodist Societies[18]
1760	6,664,989	19,267 (1766)
1770	7,123,749	25,701
1780	7,580,938	35,680
1790	8,216,096	53,691
1801 (First Census)	9,168,000	85,063

Methodist influence went far beyond its membership, of course, reaching the common people through its preaching and its witness,[19] and the educated classes through its literature and the polemics which surrounded the movement from the very beginning.[20] Likewise it is true that this influence increasingly focused on those areas where there was demographic concentration. The doubling of society membership during the last two decades of the century was in precisely those places where industrial development was most advanced.[21] Yet the statistics make clear that by no stretch of the imagination can Methodism be said to have fulfilled a need for society at large. We shall return to this point later in the chapter, but in view of the prominence which group dynamics continue to receive in the life and work of the contemporary church, it is important to note that the class meeting must be considered primarily in terms of what it did for its members rather than for eighteenth-century English society as a whole.

The Class Meeting and Behavioral Change

By the same token, it should be noted that the format of the class meeting was not intentionally conducive to an intensive group experience. Rather than the fostering of interpersonal relationships, which was quite specifically the dynamic of the bands and select societies, the class meeting was at once more pragmatic and more task-oriented. It was first and foremost what Kurt Lewin has defined as an instrument of planned behavioral change, a context or "field" in which a process of change through interpersonal relationships can be effected and sustained. Lewin, whose work in the mid-twentieth century pioneered the study of group dynamics, describes this process of behavioral changes in three stages: *unfreezing, changing,* and *refreezing.*[22] While the class meeting provided the potential for all three, it seems to have been primarily a means of refreezing—the integration of a new way of life following the change brought about by the commitment of the members to an accountable discipleship.

Not that the unfreezing and changing which took place should be discounted; nor yet the depth of interpersonal relationships which was engendered by the regular mutual catechesis. On the contrary, time and again early Methodist biography reveals that the fellowship of the class meeting was a major influence in bringing people to the point of Christian commitment as well as confirming them in it afterwards. Conversions were usually a climactic point in a process of gradual awakening to the truth of the gospel, in which attendance at class meetings played a pivotal role.[23] But it must be reiterated that the context, or "field," of this unfreezing and changing was the accountability required of all members for works of obedience and for using the means of grace. Wesley constantly affirmed the efficacy of these practices for all members, whatever their level of commitment to the faith. Accountability was preparation for commitment no less than its outworking in discipleship. The means of grace were converting as well as sustaining ordinances.[24]

Group Cohesiveness and Cognitive Dissonance

The theories of group interaction have further made clear that the influence of the class meetings on members was directly related to their cohesiveness as disciplined groups.[25] Members of highly cohesive groups will tend to influence each other more, thereby making a greater effort to reach agreement; and there were many aspects of the class meeting which engendered precisely the conditions which have been found to induce such cohesiveness. There was the class ticket, for example, which restricted membership to those who affirmed the same values and pursued the same goals; there was obligatory weekly attendance; and perhaps most of all, there was regular instruction in the purpose and function of the group provided by the catechetical questioning of the leader. In addition to all of which, it seems clear that the classes functioned according to the theory of *cognitive dissonance:* that "the simultaneous existence of cognitions which in one way or another do not fit together (dissonance) leads to effort on the part of the person to somehow make them fit better (dissonance reduction)."[26] There could have been no more direct instance of this than the searching catechism of the weekly meetings.

Communication in the Class Meeting

A final insight into the function of the class meeting is the place which it occupied in early Methodist polity as a means of communication among Wesley, his preachers, and the members of the societies. Modern studies in communication theory illustrate that the most effective pattern proves to be that which communicates information initially one-to-one through individuals, who then disseminate it to groups of people.[27] As we have noted, there was just such a pattern of authority from Wesley, to his preachers and leaders, and thence to the classes. This at once facilitated the thoroughness of Wesley's *episkopé* and made the class meeting an extremely effective means of instruction as well as nurture.

3. PURPOSE OF THE CLASS MEETING

To be aware of these group dynamics, however, is only to make clearer the distinctively Christian characteristic of early Methodist polity. Social and psychological observations help us to understand how the class meeting functioned, and to some extent why it functioned. What they do not give us is its *purpose* in relation to the ongoing task of Christian discipleship. Whenever Christians meet together in the name of Christ to search out God's will for their lives, they remain, of course, human beings. As such, meeting in a social context, they will occasion group dynamics; but something else will happen. The Spirit of God will be present, working in and through the dynamics, to empower those Christians in service for the coming New Age of Jesus Christ.

In other words, the church as *ecclesia* cannot be viewed merely as social structure; nor yet can the *ecclesiola* be viewed solely as communitas. Only when the church finds its distinctive identity in the world is it the church properly so called. And this means that the significance of the early Methodist class meeting must be determined by its role as well as its origins in the Christian tradition, viewed against the panorama of human history.

Church and Sect

At this point it is still helpful to be reminded of the seminal work of Ernst Troeltsch, whose distinction between *church* and *sect* has been the basis for so much of the sociology of religion in the West. The church type of Christian society he defines as

> a universal institution, endowed with absolute authoritative truth [with] values which have arisen out of the relative Natural Law, and are adapted to the conditions of the fallen state; the whole of the secular life, therefore, is summed up under the conception of a natural stage in human life, which prepared the way for the higher supernatural state, . . . for the spiritual and hierarchical world-organization.

The sect type, on the other hand, has evolved its social ideal

> purely from the Gospel and from the Law of Christ. . . . Therefore, either it does not recognize the institutions, groups, and values

which exist outside of Christianity at all, or in a quietly tolerant spirit of detachment from the world, it avoids them, or under the influence of an "enthusiastic" eschatology it attacks these institutions and replaces them by a purely Christian order of society. . . . [In this way, the] champions of the "Church" theory were able to discard the ideal of a strict Christian perfection, . . . [and] the supporters of the "sect" theory upheld the ideal of Christian perfection as binding on all Christians alike.[28]

Troeltsch's assessment of Methodism is that it was a combination of two forms of the sect-type—the religious order and the voluntary association:

Nothing was altered in Church dogma, its supernatural character was only intensified, and its general meaning was summed up in conversion and its presuppositions, and in sanctification with its heavenly results. The continuance of the Church was taken for granted, but in spite of that its spirit was denied. This necessarily led to external separation, in England itself last of all.[29]

Methodism as an Anglican Order

As a verdict on Methodist history as a whole, this conclusion is arguably warranted. But it does not give sufficient weight to Wesley's churchmanship, which affirmed the Church of England as the taproot of the societies and classes in the Christian tradition, however much this has subsequently been taken for granted. Even if the sociological criteria are the same, this necessitates a very different form of analysis, as Michael Hurley makes admirably clear in his edition of Wesley's *Letter to a Roman Catholic:*

In understanding Wesley's own attitude, however, the very nature of a religious society within the Church would seem to be of decisive importance. Franciscans and Dominicans and other religious orders do not—and precisely because they are religious societies rather than separate churches—have distinctive dogmas and Church doctrines of their own. They do . . . have distinctive spiritualities: distinctive approaches to the service of God and of his world, distinctive emphases in their conception of the Christian life of prayer and work. Against this background Wesley's seeming indifference to sound doctrine becomes more meaningful and understandable. Because his aim was not to found a separate Church he had no need or reason to concern himself much with creeds and confessions. Because on the contrary his aim was to found a religious society whose members would remain loyal to their own church or chapel with its particular tradition of essential Christian belief and worship, he had every reason and right to concern himself chiefly with his particular spirituality and its propagation, the spreading of scriptural holiness over the land.[30]

From Society to Church

The aim, as we know, proved abortive. Whether this was due to Anglican intransigence or Wesley's pragmatism is ultimately of less concern than the fact that it remained but a vision as Methodism progressed from society to church. And it is a continuing problem of Methodist ecclesial self-understanding that this particular change of identity has not been fully assimilated into its various traditions.[31] Not least among the reasons for this was Wesley's resistance to separation from the Church of England to the very end of his life. In nineteenth-century British Methodism, it made the transition from society to church highly problematic and divisive;[32] and in American Methodism, the steps taken in 1784 proved to be quite indecisive in terms of an ecclesial identity.[33] There remains an ill-defined feeling in the various branches of the denomination that those who call themselves Methodists should be as disciplined and as committed as were the members of the early societies. To aspire to this, while at the same time attempting to be an inclusive church in which there are many levels of commitment, is bound to occasion a high degree of vocational discomfort which the mainstream of Methodism has eased by assuming the more relaxed role of social institution—though not without serious challenge from the separatist Methodist churches, whose social stance, especially in the nineteenth century, has often stood in sharp contrast.[34]

Not only was this progression from society to church contrary to Wesley's reforming intentions: it proved to be debilitating for the class meeting. In an important study, Henry Rack has traced its decline in England primarily with respect to the ambivalent question of church membership.[35] The weekly class became increasingly difficult to sustain in the nineteenth century, argues Rack, because of a lack of common religious experience which, coupled with the endemic problem of indifferent or incompetent class leadership, meant that "it was always liable to suffer from other popular and perhaps less 'official' means of grace." As Wesleyan Methodism became more socially acceptable, preference was increasingly expressed for a "less personalized and exacting form of religious exercise."[36] Given the lack of any clear Methodist doctrine of the church, the class meeting became a central means of fellowship rather than the basis of church membership, and the Wesleyan standards of personal holiness became more broadly social. This led to a bitter conflict in the latter half of the century, culminating in the findings of a Conference committee in 1889, which recommended retaining the class as the traditional basis of membership, but not to insist that failure to attend justified loss of membership. The peculiar character of Methodism was thus changed "from the condition of a society with some marks of a holiness sect to the more conventional and less demanding character of a church."[37]

The contrasting view of William W. Dean is that the decline of the class meeting was due to a change in its basic functions.[38] It is important, he argues, to distinguish between what Wesley wrote about the class meeting and what actually happened in them; and in Wesley's day, they were primarily a means of "evangelism and conservation—the *recruitment* and *assimilation* of new members." The first half of the nineteenth century saw the loss of both of these functions, however, in part due to the changes identified by Rack, but also because of the acceptance by British society, albeit superficially, of evangelical values.[39] References to class meetings in early Methodist autobiography decline quite abruptly during the 1830s, and the role they had hitherto served as a door into the societies was taken over by the prayer meeting—especially the after-preaching prayer meeting at the Communion rail or in the vestry. Indeed, spiritual vitality in general became more frequently related to prayer meetings than to classes. They were less structured and more spontaneous gatherings, and were more readily adaptable to the institutional activities of the chapel than the interpersonal spirituality of the class meeting.[40]

Christian Tradition and Human History: The Halévy Thesis

Helpful though both of these assessments are in pointing to the role the class meeting played in Methodism *per se*, we must also consider the broader perspective of the Christian tradition in human history. The starting point for this continues to be another seminal work: Elie

Halévy's *England in 1815.*[41] The thesis is well known: that evangelical religion, and especially that of Methodism, prevented England from the sort of revolutionary upheavals which were prevalent on the continent of Europe in the late eighteenth and nineteenth centuries. It was most clearly argued in two articles published in 1906 under the title "La Naissance du Méthodisme en Angleterre."[42] Halévy found an inescapable link between the commercial crisis of the late 1730s and the religious revival of the same period, and on the premise that it was the bourgeoisie of the country who determined the direction of the agitation emanating from the crisis, he argued that the English middle class, remembering the horrors of the Civil War in the preceding century, gave the discontent a religious and conservative form.[43]

This was quite in keeping with the British national character as Halévy saw it. "The English are a nation of Puritans, and Puritanism is Protestantism in all the strictness of the dogma which constitutes its theological core—adherence to the doctrine of 'justification by faith' propounded by Saint Paul . . . the immediate and mysterious relationship of the individual soul with the Deity."[44] "Even today," he concluded,

> whenever a Methodist preacher brings a popular audience together at a street corner to read the Bible, sing hymns, and pray in common, whenever he induces a "revival" of mysticism and religious exaltation, in a region or throughout the nation, the great movement of 1739 is being repeated in the pattern fixed by tradition, with climactic changes of mood that everybody—passionate participants and disinterested spectators—can foresee in advance. A force capable of expending itself in displays of violence or popular upheavals assumes, under the influence of a century and a half of Methodism, the form least capable of unsettling a social order founded upon inequality of rank and wealth.[45]

Political Self-Awareness

It is this negative connotation of Halévy's thesis which is often used to brand Methodism as an obstacle to the much-needed social reforms of the nineteenth century. But Bernard Semmel, in his substantial historical essay, *The Methodist Revolution*, argues on the contrary that the positive conclusions of Halévy are far more important.[46] Because Methodism saw people as good, its enthusiasm was a transforming influence. It summoned people "to assert rational control over their own lives, while providing in its system of mutual discipline the psychological security necessary for autonomous conscience and liberal ideals to become internalized, an integrated part of the 'new men' awakened and regenerated by Wesleyan preaching."[47]

Not only is this a weighty theological argument; it has a great deal of corroborating historical evidence. It was with this new self-awareness, emanating in large part from the classes and class leadership, that Methodism contributed to the radical political movements of the nineteenth century. Much of their leadership was drawn from Methodist circles, and in many instances they adopted Methodist polity for their emerging structures. The early Union and Reform Societies in England, for example, were organized into classes of twelve members, each with a leader. The society in Stockport established weekly meetings in 1818

> for the purpose of reading any political or other books, papers, &c., &c., or conversation upon the best practical mode, according to the exigency of the time. . . . Each member shall pay weekly to his class leader, at the time of meeting, one penny, for the purpose of carrying into effect the object of the Union, viz., that of obtaining Political Liberty and Universal Freedom.[48]

The National Union of Working Classes was later organized along similar lines, a special committee recommending in 1831:

> 1. That you should appoint class leaders for the different districts of the metropolis and its vicinity.
> 2. That there should be on average twenty-five members to each class, so that there may be forty class leaders to 1,000 members.
> 3. That every member should call, or leave his name at the residence of his class leader, once a week, or the class leader on the members, if more convenient.
> 4. That the list of class leaders be read over in the first general meeting of the Union every month, and, that each class leader be then either continued, or changed, according to the meeting.
> 5. That each class leader shall keep a list of the names, and residences of the different individuals, who leave their names with him, and that he shall receive their monthly subscription and send it to the secretary.
> 6. That the services of the class leaders be perfectly gratuitous.
> 7. That the class leaders constitute a committee, which shall meet once every week. . . .[49]

And in 1839, the Chartists in Sheffield posted placards on walls throughout the city, announcing that, since the magistrates had suppressed their "legal and peacable meetings," they had resolved to hold small class meetings, similar to the Methodist class meetings, to concentrate their strength.[50]

Methodism and Social Division

This contrasted markedly, however, with the official stance of the Wesleyan Methodist Conference, which was to disapprove of involvement in the political reform movements, and to discipline those members who so transgressed.[51] The tensions which this occasioned, most especially with rebellious local preachers, were not only an important factor in the divisions which occurred within the movement, but served also to alienate Wesleyan Methodism from many of its grassroots origins, provoking the incipient working-class movement to identify with the breakaway groups, such as the New Connexion, the Primitive Methodists, the Bible Christians, and the Independent Methodists.[52] The more Wesleyan Methodism seemed to gravitate toward an ecclesial establishment, the more its preachers were perceived to be professional clergy, as opposed to the voluntarism of these offshoots, where the preachers were largely unpaid. Moreover, the Wesleyan Methodist hierarchy was increasingly perceived to be aligned with the existing social order.[53] Semmel's argument notwithstanding, the case made by E.P. Thompson that the piety of Methodism was manipulated by those with social power to divert the energies of its members from self-improvement to otherworldly concerns has been presented with a documentation and a social poignancy yet to be matched from within the tradition.[54]

Wesley and Radical Protestantism

All the more welcome, therefore, is the direction set by Howard Snyder's incisive study, *The Radical Wesley*. Writing out of the Free Methodist tradition, Snyder views Wesley from the perspective of Radical Protestantism, according to which the church must be "a distinct, separate, countercultural covenant community" if it is to speak prophetically to the world and the institutional church.[55] He identifies seven elements in this ecclesiological model: (1) voluntary adult membership, emphasizing obedience to Jesus Christ as necessary evidence of faith in him; (2) a disciplined community in conscious separation from the world as the primary visible expression of the church; (3) a life of good works expected of all believers, thereby emphasizing the ministry of the laity; (4) the Spirit and the Word as the sole basis of authority, thereby de-emphasizing church traditions and creeds; (5) the early church as model and goal, implying some view of the fall of the church and the need for it to be restored to its essential elements; (6) a pragmatic, functional approach to church order and structure; (7) a belief in the universal church as the Body of Christ, of which the particular visible believing community is but a part.[56]

The Witness of the Ecclesiola

Showing how much of Wesley's ministry incorporated these criteria, Snyder argues convincingly that the *ecclesiola*, as embodied in Methodist polity, is the most effective form of churchly witness, since it provides supportive affirmation for the alternative lifestyle offered by the gospel; which, in the final analysis, is the decisive Christian challenge to the world. He is careful to stress that Wesley adopted this form of outreach as an established churchman, who refused to surrender "both-and" for the seeming inevitability of "either-or."[57] But the weight of his argument is to place the class meeting at the interface of Christian witness with the world, and to suggest that those who comprise the *ecclesiolae* witness to their faith with a directness which comes first and foremost from commitment to a lifestyle consistent with the gospel. They may ground this commitment in the scriptures and teachings of the *ecclesia*, but their participation in *ecclesiolae* gives them a role which is ultimately more important for the world than for the church. This is a pivotal issue in any evaluation of the class meeting, and Snyder has performed a signal service for Methodism by making it an unequivocal challenge to a church which remains divided as it embarks on its third century of witness to the world.

The crux of the issue is that the call to accountable discipleship as evinced by contemporary *ecclesiolae* continues to present not only Methodism, but the institutional church as a whole, with a deep and frustrating predicament. The witness of radical Christianity in our time is powerful primarily because it consists of persons who take their obedience to the gospel seriously, and who, in a very real sense, manifest the "virtuoso discipleship" of Wesley. It is no coincidence that some of the most powerful writing in the church today has come from such communities: *Solentiname* in Nicaragua, *Sojourners* in Washington, D.C., *Jubilee* in Philadelphia.[58]

The Witness of the Ecclesia

The institutional church, on the other hand, is religiously inclusive and thus by definition culturally conditioned. Its membership is by and large reflective of its social context, and its witness is inevitably filtered through the exigencies of structural maintenance, human and material. Confronted by the radical discipleship of these contemporary *ecclesiolae*, there are many members of mainline North American churches who are only too aware of being challenged by a call to further commitment, but in all sincerity do not know how to answer it without rejecting most of what they have hitherto known as churchly activity. To become *ecclesiola* seems to present an unavoidable alienation from the *ecclesia*, however much a structural relationship is sought and maintained. It is not too much to say that for some, the tension of this dilemma is sufficiently intense for them to opt out of the struggle, and to settle for the blandness of folk religiosity. But for others, the hunger for spiritual fulfillment remains, and the summons to costly discipleship persists, as they wrestle with a call which they sincerely, even desperately, need to know is coming from the God whom they worship week by week.

Not only are these questions of some consequence for North American Christians. Increasingly the world church is asking them of Western Christianity as a whole. As the gospel is traditioned in a wide range of global contexts, the Western church, and Protestantism in particular, is perceived to be highly enculturated in its theology, its ecclesial practices, and its social function. The confronting issue raised by the *ecclesiolae*, therefore, and most especially for North American churches by the *comunidades de base* of Latin America, is quite fundamental: In which form does the church witness most effectively to the world?[59]

The Witness of the Class Meeting

It is at this point that the significance of the class meeting comes sharply into focus. But in seeking the answer, we must not put the cart before the horse. We must look at the class meeting, not as a paradigm for Christian witness to the world—for that was its *effect*—but rather as a means of seeking obedience to God's will—for that was its *purpose*.

Put differently, if we ask what it was that the early Methodists *sought* in their class meetings, we might better understand what it was they *accomplished*.

Take, for example, the Halévy thesis in either of its interpreted modes—that Methodism fostered or hindered the social reforms of the nineteenth century. There is no doubt that the seriousness with which the early Methodists took their discipleship made an impact on society: directly, through their participation in traditional forms of philanthropy such as charity schools, hospitals, and the maintenance of a "lending stock" by the societies; and indirectly through the pervasiveness of their presence in the industrial cities of the late eighteenth and nineteenth centuries. Yet the social and political impact of the class meeting, and the rich opportunities it afforded for personal development and self-awareness, were ancillary to the purpose of Methodist polity as Wesley saw it. His concern was that there should be a means of effecting faithful discipleship, a pattern of living in the world, which was accountable first and foremost to the will of God.

Wesley himself had no blueprint for political involvement. His social ethics were essentially individualistic, the practical and necessary outcome of a relationship with God.[60] And in eighteenth-century England, that was social witness enough. The members of the United Societies lived out their discipleship in the rough and tumble of what was often a vicious social context. To declare themselves as Methodists was thus a mark of high courage. If they took the three-fold emphasis of the *General Rules* seriously, as the great majority did, it singled them out in the towns and villages where they lived and worked as people to be watched, and often persecuted. To desist from certain practices, personal and social, frequently meant ostracization or at least the ridicule of one's neighbors; while to do good to every possible person in every possible way often occasioned the active opposition of those who saw this as a social threat.

Mere resolve to make such a witness, therefore, was not enough in and of itself. Nor yet would it have been sufficient to know—which, of course, they did not and could not—that they were laying any sort of theological groundwork for social reform or for its obstruction. Their immediate priority, rather, was how to sustain their witness against the bruising and the buffeting of a hostile world. To pursue faithful obedience in such a context required constant spiritual nourishment, which is why the weekly class meetings were, above all, a point of accountability. Without the disciplines of Christian living, the early Methodists could not for long have sustained their witness. They needed the means of grace, instituted in the ordinances of the church, and experienced in the society and class meetings. They watched over one another in love, not so much to deepen their spiritual experience—which, of course, they did—but rather to hold fast to the task in hand. For what ultimately gave Methodist discipleship authenticity was Wesley's emphasis on faith and works alike as appropriate responses to God's gracious initiatives. To the great advantage of the Christian tradition, and in spite of the ill-informed invective of enemies and the well-meaning excesses of friends, he never swerved from this twofold principle: True Christian discipleship can spring only from faith received by grace; and true faith in Christ can be sustained only by obedient discipleship in response to grace.

Purpose of the Class Meeting

It is at this historiographical juncture that the Halévy thesis proves inadequate for the purposes of our study. If we regard the class meeting primarily as a socio-historical phenomenon, we perforce limit our investigations to its effects, and thereby invite conflicting interpretations. Detailed studies have now shown that the role of early Methodism in English society must ultimately be determined town by town and village by village; and even then it is unclear to what extent it was the *locus* of any influence.[61] If we seek to *tradition* the class meeting, however, then its significance emerges primarily with regard to its purpose—that the members were enjoined to watch over one another in love, lest they should make shipwreck of their faith. God's grace thereby moved through their lives and made a distinctive impact on their social context; but only because they were first of all obedient in their discipleship, the occasion and the dynamic of which was the relationship with God which they sought to maintain through the mutual accountability of their weekly meetings.

Significance of the Class Meeting

The importance of this in assessing the significance of the class meeting is that Wesley charged the early Methodists with a twofold traditioning of the gospel in the immediacy of their worldly context. They were to hand *on* the gospel within their community of faith and hand it *over* to the world. Obedience to the gracious initiatives of the Holy Spirit, therefore, was constantly determined, not only by the scriptures and teachings of the church and the promptings of the inward witness, but also by the exigencies of living out a faithful discipleship. Precisely because they were faithfully obedient to God, the early Methodists understood their world better than any social historian has subsequently been able to infer from the records of their witness to that world. Works of Christian obedience are determined to a large degree by social context, and the early Methodists found themselves in the front line of service for the coming New Age of Jesus Christ as long as they held one another accountable for their discipleship.

The significance of the class meeting is not to be found in its efficacy for Methodism as movement or church, nor yet in its impact on society as instrument or obstacle of reform. It was a prudential means of grace whereby Christians in witness to the world could sustain one another in their distinctive tasks assigned by God at a particular time and place in human history.

4. DECLINE OF THE CLASS MEETING

Once this is the criterion of evaluation, it becomes quite clear that the decline of the class meeting was due to a neglect of the works of obedience in the weekly catechesis and a growing self-preoccupation with religious experience. This is the very evident concern of the author of the letters in Appendix J, and is reflected by an increasing emphasis on society discipline in Wesley's later sermons and letters—something which can by no means be dismissed as autocratic eccentricity.[62] He saw, more perceptively than most, that however God might apply the fruits of obedient discipleship, the first priority was ensuring that an accountability be exercised for these works of obedience and for the means of grace without which it could not be sustained. Failure to do this would de-tradition Christian discipleship, and render it powerless in the world.

Loss of Accountability

There is much to indicate that this is what happened in nineteenth-century Wesleyan Methodism. The increasing preoccupation with inward piety in the class meeting to the exclusion of practical good works and the means of grace is perhaps most noteworthy in popular Methodist literature, a good example of which is the 1817 pamphlet, *A Description of Class Meetings*, reproduced as Appendix L. And one has only to turn to the following verses from *The Wesleyan Methodist Association Magazine* in 1841 to discern some preoccupations quite removed from accountable discipleship:

> When I first joined Zion's band,
> Who kindly took me by the hand,
> And prayed that I might faithful stand?
> My Class Leader!
>
> Who bade me flee from Satan's wile,
> And shun the world's alluring smile,
> Nor let its charms my soul beguile?
> My Class Leader!
>
> When'er my wandring footsteps stray,
> From Wisdom's sweet and pleasant way,
> Who over me doth weep and pray?
> My Class Leader!
>
> And when with me life's dream is o'er,
> And I shall weep and sigh no more,
> O may we meet on Canaan's shore,
> My Class Leader![63]

It is difficult to avoid the inference that, had the classes been continuing a weekly catechesis which took seriously the accountability for works of obedience and the means of grace as well as the sharing of religious experience, their changing social context would have produced a very different record from the inbred religiosity available to us in this sort of literature.

Effusiveness and Formalism

The corollary of such effusiveness was an empty formalism which rendered many of the class meetings repetitious, and attendance increasingly onerous on the members—as can be inferred from most of the serious nineteenth-century commentary on the classes. By and large they are exhortations to return to ways which were fast being abandoned. An American minister writing at the turn of the twentieth century, for example, strongly commended the class meeting, but could not avoid recalling some extremely ambivalent youthful memories:

> I distinctly remember that some leaders were dull and profitless in their remarks; that some members arose, turned their faces to the wall, and repeated, in a dismal, sanctimonious tone—very different from that used in town meeting or in trading horses—a pious lot of platitudes which meant nothing to them or us. There was the sister who was "but an unprofitable servant," "living at a poor, dying rate," and "meant, by the grace of God, to continue"; the bluff, full-faced farmer who talked like a consumptive about "the waste, howling wilderness of this unfriendly world"; and Simon Go-Softly, who spoke of his poverty as "the dispensation of the Lord to purify him," and that he would patiently bear the Lord's will—the lazy lout! I remember these, and many others like them, whose pet phrases I had heard so often that I could give their testimony verbatim before the meeting began.[64]

Once again, the absence of accountability for works of obedience and the means of grace is noticeable; and attempts to maintain the class meeting without this accountability merely confirmed that they had lost their essential purpose.

Whatever might have been the effect of this for Methodism or for society at large is wholly contingent on this prior deficiency. Indeed, that the social impact of Methodism provides any substance at all for historical investigation is due in the first instance to the faithfulness of the early class members. Christians meeting week by week to give an account of their discipleship will inevitably be aware of what God is doing in the world, and will respond to those gracious initiatives with service which is attuned to the needs of the world in which they live. By the same token, giving an account of their use of the means of grace will ensure that they are attuned to the will of God, and not the exigencies of their particular historical situation.

The Genius of the Class Meeting

The genius of the class meeting catechesis as Wesley prescribed it was the proper synthesis of these two priorities: responsiveness to the immediacy of Christian discipleship in the world, and responsibility to the doctrines and ordinances of the church—spirit and structure, prophetic and priestly ministry, *ecclesiola in ecclesia*, all under the sovereignty of grace. The implications of this for the working of God's salvation in human history are still concealed in an eschatological mystery. And while this may provide much for the social historian to ponder, the task of the Christian is to remain faithful in obedient discipleship until the mystery is fully revealed.

5. THREE POTENTIAL MISUNDERSTANDINGS

1. Personal Growth

All of which is to indicate that the significance we have attributed to the class meeting must be measured against three potential misunderstandings. First of all, personal growth and interpersonal dynamics were a feature of the weekly meetings, but not their purpose. This is an important word for the contemporary church in North America, where small group fellowship can quickly become a means of diverting energies and commitments from the proper task of the church. And whatever such groups might accomplish for persons neglected or discarded by the impersonal structures of the late twentieth-century technological society, all too often they offer an insufficient traditioning of the *evangel*. By stressing the benefits of Christian fellowship, but ignoring the larger questions of social and global justice, they can fail to provide a bedrock for Christian discipleship or to draw on the mainstream of grace. Indeed, as Kurt Back disarmingly concludes in his definitive history of encounter groups, when all is said and done they may prove to have been "nothing more than the American middle class at play."[65] There are strong echoes in these words of the de-traditioned nineteenth-century class meeting.

It must always be asked to what extent the small groups of a church contribute to the essential task of discipleship in the world. Do they really equip Christians to be authentically Christian in a world which, more often than not, is apathetic or hostile to their message? For to be a Christian is not to seek self-fulfillment. It is to receive a direct commission to go into the world, and to join the Risen Christ in the task of proclaiming God's salvation in the power of the Holy Spirit. In a very profound sense, it is to realize the *un*importance of one's own selfhood as long as suffering and oppression remain in a world which rejects the salvation offered in Christ.

This is the demonstrable inference to be drawn from the *comunidades eclesiales de base* of Latin America. To impose their sociopolitical perspectives onto the North American ecclesial consciousness is profoundly to miss the challenge of their message, and to make a rudimentary mistake in contextualization. Their witness rather is that their members are drawn together by grace, and that they sustain one another with a mutual accountability for the privileges and responsibilities of discipleship. It is the grace in their communion which brings the conscientization of their social witness in a context of poverty and oppression. And it is this same accountability which likewise fosters a richness of personal faith—the joy which comes from obedience to the Risen Christ in their midst.[66]

2. Evangelism

The second potential misunderstanding of the class meeting concerns its evangelistic function in early Methodism. However productive it might have been as a method of outreach and ingathering, this was not its initial purpose. The most effective method of evangelism in Wesley's day was in fact field preaching, which appears prominently in early Methodist autobiography as the initial point of contact with those who eventually joined the societies.[67] The class served as a *locus* of evangelism and nurture only because of its prior purpose of sustaining the response to evangelistic outreach by fostering a faithful discipleship through mutual accountability. Those who were drawn into a Christian commitment through the weekly meetings were exposed to the realities of discipleship as the members reported their respective pilgrimages, and the authenticity of this witness lay in their desire—and their need—to watch over one another in love.[68]

The problem with viewing the significance of the class meeting in the light of this particular function is the ecclesiological "blind spot" to which we alluded earlier in the chapter—the changed identity of Methodism from society to church. While the evangelistic message of Wesley and his preachers extended an invitation to all, membership in the societies required a level of commitment which could be exacted by an *ecclesiola*, but not the *ecclesia*. As we have argued, the former by definition is selective, the latter inclusive; and Wesley, by adopting the concept of *ecclesiola IN ecclesia* acknowledged that the purpose of the Methodist societies was to reform the Church of England, not subvert it. The disciplined accountability of the class meeting is precisely why the

societies never became a mass movement in his lifetime, and it was only
after Methodism moved toward the more inclusive and less demanding
form of chapel-oriented membership that numbers dramatically
increased. Most especially was this true in the United States, where the
pattern of outreach adapted to the frontier and forged a very different
ecclesiology.[69]

The significance of the class meeting in this regard is that however
functional the small group format may be for evangelistic purposes
today—and social anthropologists have greatly expanded our understanding of how this can be accomplished[70]—this was not the essential
purpose of the weekly gathering in early Methodism. Indeed, for The
United Methodist Church, the question of *ecclesiola in ecclesia* has now
become inverted: How does an *ecclesia* with the tradition of an *ecclesiola* allow for the deeper conviction of those in its ranks who are ready
to form the new *ecclesiolae*? And how can Wesley's dialectic be traditioned to ensure that they remain *in ecclesia*? The ministry and mission
of an inclusive and pluralistic church, most especially if it is evan-
gelistically oriented, will draw into its ranks the widest range of
adherents. To insist on uniformity of commitment, therefore, is not only
to ignore the work in faith development by contemporary scholars such
as James Fowler.[71] It is to deny the twofold therapy of Wesley's theology: his healing of the forensic split between faith and works;[72] and
his rejection of "that philosophical and theological ineptitude of the
Reformation"—disjunction between nature and grace.[73]

3. *Ecclesiola in Ecclesia*

The third potential misunderstanding brings us back to the issue of
how the class meeting functioned as a form of ecclesial witness to the
world, and the extent to which this proved to be a source of tension with
the Church of England. In terms of contemporary ecclesiology, the
question centers on the extent to which the *ecclesiola* finds its call to
discipleship in the world compatible with its relationship to the *ecclesia*;
and the answer lies in how the role of the institutional church is perceived in the Christian tradition.

The purpose of Protestant ecclesiology has always been the reform of
the church, and in most instances this has included a strong primitivism.
This was certainly the prevailing apologetic of the Anglican theologians
who shaped Wesley's ecclesiology. Yet radical Protestant ecclesiology

has usually gone further, to incorporate some view of the fall of the church; and it is at this point that Wesley must be read very carefully. For in spite of the polemical positions he was often pressed to take, and in spite of the fact that it ultimately proved impossible to hold the societies within the *ecclesia*, his supreme conviction was that the Church of England, with all of its faults and blemishes, was acceptable to God.[74]

The witness which Christians are called to make through the *ecclesiola* will always, of course, create an ecclesiological tension. This is well expressed by Sergio Torres, commenting on the statement concerning the *comunidades eclesiales de base* made at the Conference of the Catholic Bishops (CELAM) held in Puebla, Mexico, in 1979:

> We believe that our theological reflection on the church has not matured with the same speed and profundity that the Spirit of Christ has been poured out in our communities. The life of the churches has moved forward with its own theology. This ecclesiological delay has created no little confusion and some institutional tension within the church. We must create an ecclesiology that gives reason for this joy and this hope that the church is manifesting in the maturation and multiplication of base-level Christian communities.[75]

It is a tension, however, which must be maintained. For if the *ecclesiola* breaks with the *ecclesia*, then it becomes detraditioned and vulnerable to the exigencies of its context. Contemporary examples are not difficult to find: a self-centered piety which masquerades as true religion, disempowering the prophetic witness of churches which once spoke with authority in high places; political liberations which meet the criteria of biblical justice in all but the most crucial—obedience to the Godhead revealed in Jesus the Christ.

The precaution to be observed, therefore, is to view the class meetings, not from the perspective of how they functioned in society and influenced human history, but rather from the perspective of the Christian tradition, taking fully into account what Wesley intended them to be and endeavored to nurture them into being. It is in this respect that his *episkopé* assumes a deeply significant role—and the class meeting likewise. For accountable discipleship requires faith and obedience, neither one without the other. Both are the high privilege of those who have the temerity to proclaim that God has charged them to hand on and live out the message of salvation in Christ through the power of the Holy Spirit.

Such at least was the calling of the early Methodists, who met week by week to work out their salvation by watching over one another in love.

ACCOUNTABLE DISCIPLESHIP

An authentic traditioning of early Methodism should not, indeed cannot, be an abstract study. The final word must therefore be to recommend to present-day congregations the adoption of Covenant Discipleship Groups, described in the companion volume, *Accountable Discipleship* (Discipleship Resources, 1984). These groups are an adaptation of the class meeting, drawing on the criteria of Wesley's *General Rules*, the dynamic of catechesis in the classes, the precedent of a written covenant, and the principles of *ecclesiola in ecclesia*. Affirming on the one hand the need for responsive obedience to the gracious initiatives of the Holy Spirit, and on the other hand the use of the means of grace to sustain an ever-deepening commitment, they are a vocational leaven within the life and work of the church.

It is my hope and prayer that the preceding pages may provide a sense of the accountability to which God called the early Methodists through that particular *ecclesiola* known as the class meeting, so that the call might come today with fresh power and vision for the work which lies ahead.

NOTES

INTRODUCTION

[1] Wayne A. Meeks, *The First Urban Christians: The Social World of the Apostle Paul* (New Haven: Yale University Press, 1983), p. 75.

[2] Ibid., pp. 74-75. For a striking contemporary parallel, see Raymond Fung, *Households of God on China's Soil* (Maryknoll: Orbis Books, 1982).

[3] For example: Norman Cohn, *The Pursuit of the Millenium: Revolutionary Millenarians and Mystical Anarchists of the Middle Ages* (New York: Oxford University Press, 1970); Christopher Hill, *The World Turned Upside Down: Radical Ideas during the English Revolution* (New York: Schocken Books, 1964); E.P. Thompson, *The Making of the English Working Class* (New York: Vintage Books, 1966).

[4] Significant directions are being set for this by scholars in the context of the Third World. See, for example, William Cook, "Historic Patterns in Protestant Grass Roots Communities," *Occasional Essays* (San José, Costa Rica: Latin American Evangelical Center for Pastoral Studies) 9.1 (June 1982):3-40.

[5] So William A. Clebsch, *Christianity in European History* (New York: Oxford University Press, 1979), pp. 3ff.

[6] *The Letters of the Rev. John Wesley, A.M.*, ed. John Telford. Standard Edition, 8 vols. (London: The Epworth Press, 1931), 4:194 (hereafter cited as *Letters*).

[7] *The Journal of the Rev. John Wesley, A.M.*, ed. Nehemiah Curnock. Standard Edition, 8 vols. (London: The Epworth Press, 1909-16) (hereafter cited as *Journal*).

[8] In addition to the Standard Edition of the Letters, two volumes are available in *The Oxford Edition of The Works of John Wesley*, editor-in-chief Frank Baker (hereafter cited as *Oxford*): Volume 25: *Letters I: 1725-39*, ed. Frank Baker (Oxford: at the Clarendon Press, 1980); Volume 26: *Letters II: 1740-1755*, ed. Frank Baker (Oxford: at the Clarendon Press, 1982).

[9] *The Works of John Wesley*, 14 vols. (London: Wesleyan Conference Office, 1872; reprint ed., Grand Rapids, Michigan: Baker Book House, 1979) (hereafter cited as *Works*). This edition is almost identical with the third edition, ed. Thomas Jackson (London, 1829-31). See also *The Standard Sermons of John Wesley*, ed. Edward H. Sugden, 2 vols. (London: Epworth Press, 1921) (hereafter cited as *Sermons*).

[10] "The World Family in History," *London Quarterly and Holborn Review* 177 (1952):207.

[11] *John Wesley*, ed. Albert C. Outler. Library of Protestant Thought (New York: Oxford University Press, 1964), p. vii.

[12] See Albert C. Outler, "The Place of Wesley in the Christian Tradition," in *The Place of Wesley in the Christian Tradition*, ed. Kenneth E. Rowe (Metuchen, N.Y.: The Scarecrow Press, Inc., 1976), p. 18. See also *The Bicentennial Edition of The Works of John Wesley: Volume 1: Sermons 1:1-33*, ed Albert C. Outler (Nashville: Abingdon Press, 1984), pp. 66ff. This will be the definitive edition of Wesley's sermons, with three volumes forthcoming; though to avoid confusion, references below are cited from the standard edition of the *Sermons* and from the *Works*.

[13] *Minutes of the Methodist Conferences, from the first, held in London, by the late Rev.*

John Wesley, A.M., in the year 1744, vol. 1 (London: at the Conference Office, 1812) (hereafter cited as *Minutes*).

14"A Plain Account of the People Called Methodists," *Works,* 8:252.

15Ibid., 8:254.

16Frank Baker, "The People Called Methodists, 3: Polity," in *A History of the Methodist Church in Great Britain,* ed. R.E. Davies and E.G. Rupp, vol. 1 (London: The Epworth Press, 1965), pp. 213-14.

17"The Principles of a Methodist Farther Explained," *Works,* 8:415; *Letters,* 3:182, 201-2; *Oxford,* vol. 11: *The Appeals to Men of Reason and Religion and Certain Related Open Letters,* ed. Gerald R. Cragg (Oxford: at the Clarendon Press, 1975), pp. 122, 318-20, 498.

18Sermon, "The Ministerial Office," *Works,* 7:279. See also Frank Baker, *John Wesley and the Church of England* (Nashville: Abingdon Press, 1970), pp. 284ff.

19Horton Davies, *Worship and Theology in England,* vol. 2: *From Andrewes to Baxter and Fox, 1603-1690* (Princeton: Princeton University Press, 1975), pp. 6-7.

20The concept is implicit in the various sixteenth-century Protestant Confessions, but is nowhere more explicit than in the Westminster Confession of 1646. See Philip Schaff, *Creeds of Christendom,* 3 vols., 4th ed., rev. and enl. (New York: Harper & Brothers, 1877; reprint ed., Grand Rapids, Michigan: Baker Book House, 1983), 3:657-58.

21Not that Wesley regarded the church as all-inclusive. In his discussion of the 19th Article of the Church of England, he makes clear that those members of the church "in whom 'there is one Spirit, one hope, one Lord, one faith'; which have 'one baptism' and 'one Lord and Father of all,'" are those who constitute the Church of England (Sermon, "Of the Church," *Works,* 6:396-97). Nevertheless, this was an emphasis on the visible *ecclesia* as opposed to the invisible *coetus electorum.*

22This concept is usually attributed to the *collegiae pietatis* of Philipp Jakob Spener. See his *Pia Desideria,* translated, edited and with an Introduction by Theodore G. Tappert (Philadelphia: Fortress Press, Seminar Editions, 1964), pp. 89-91. It can also be traced, however, to the early Reformers. Luther, for example, considered forming small groups for those who took their faith seriously, but considered it premature. See Henry Strohl, *La Pensée de la Réforme,* Manuels et Précis de Théologies, vol. 32 (Neuchatel: Delachaux et Niestlé S.E., 1951), pp. 186-87. See also *Common Places of Martin Bucer,* translated and edited by D.F. Wright, The Courtenay Library of Reformation Classics, 4 (Appleford, Berkshire: The Sutton Courtenay Press, 1972), pp. 210-12.

23For more than a century after Wesley it was a mark of Methodist theology not to grasp the significance of this dialectic, as evidenced in English Methodism by an apologetic and even defensive ecclesiological stance. See, for example, A.W. Harrison, "The Church," in *Methodism in the Modern World,* ed. J. Scott Lidgett and Bryan H. Reed (London: The Epworth Press, 1929), pp. 139-65. The same can be said of American Methodist theology after Wesley. In his major survey of the subject, *Theological Transition in American Methodism, 1790-1935* (New York: Abingdon Press, 1965), Robert Chiles finds little if anything on ecclesiology. An appreciation of the Wesleyan dialectic in modern Methodist scholarship is therefore to be welcomed—and noted. See John Deschner, "Methodism," in *A Handbook of Christian Theology,* ed. M. Halverson and A. A. Cohen (New York: Living Age Books, 1958), pp. 232-33. See also Dow Kirkpatrick, ed., *The Doctrine of the Church* (New York: Abingdon Press, 1960).

24"John Wesley's Churchmanship," *London Holborn and Quarterly Review* 185 (1960):210. See also ibid., 210-15, 269-74.

25Frank Baker, *John Wesley and the Church of England,* p. 229. See also pp. 281,283ff.

26"Farther Thoughts on Separation from the Church," *Works*, 13:272-73.

27"But as more Dissenters joined with us, many of whom were much prejudiced against the Church, these, with or without design, were continually infusing their own prejudices into their brethren. I saw this, and gave warning of it from time to time. . . . Nevertheless, the same leaven continued to work in various parts of the kingdom . . . (ibid.).

28Colin Williams, *John Wesley's Theology Today* (Nashville, Abingdon Press, 1960), p. 146.

CHAPTER ONE

1*The Thirty-nine Articles of the Church of England.* Explained with an Introduction by Edgar C.S. Gibson, 2 vols. (London: Methuen & Co. Ltd., 1897), 2:493ff. The definitive study of Wesley's churchmanship is Frank Baker's *John Wesley and the Church of England*, but among shorter studies, that of James H. Rigg is still helpful, *The Churchmanship of John Wesley, and the Relations of Wesleyan Methodism to the Church of England* (London: Wesleyan-Methodist Book-Room, 1886). See also Edgar W. Thompson, *Wesley: Apostolic Man. Some Reflections on Wesley's Consecration of Dr. Thomas Coke* (London: The Epworth Press, 1957).

2As, for example, in his sermon, "Of the Church," *Works*, 6:395-96. See also "An Earnest Appeal to Men of Reason and Religion," *Oxford*, 11:77.

3"Of the Church," *Works*, 6:394-95.

4Ibid., 6:396-97.

5"Farther Thoughts on Separation from the Church," *Works*, 13:272.

6"Reasons Against Separation from the Church of England," *Works*, 13:230-31. This is an abridgement of a lengthier document presented to the crucial 1755 conference. For the full version, see Frank Baker, *John Wesley and the Church of England*, pp. 326ff.

7"An Earnest Appeal," *Oxford*, 11:79-80. See also ibid., pp. 81, 109, 186, 406; and "The Principles of a Methodist Farther Explained," *Works*, 8:444.

8*Letters*, 6:156; 8:139-40.

9Gibson, *Thirty-nine Articles*, 1:230.

10As, for example, at the 1747 Conference: "Q.8. Are the three orders of Bishops, Priests, and Deacons plainly described in the New Testament? A. We think they are, and believe they generally obtained in the churches of the Apostolic age. Q.9. But are you assured, God designed the same plan should obtain in all churches throughout all ages? A. We are not assured of this, because we do not know that it is asserted in Holy Writ" (*John Bennet's Copy of the Minutes of the Conferences of 1744, 1745, 1747 and 1748; with Wesley's Copy of those for 1746*, Publications of The Wesley Historical Society, No.1 [London: Wesley Historical Society, 1896], pp. 47-48). See also *Letters*, 1:285-86; 5:172-73.

11*Journal*, 1:419-20.

12"Reasons against a Separation from the Church of England," *Works*, 13:225; "Farther Thoughts of Separation from the Church," *Works*, 13:272; *Oxford*, 25:593; *Letters*, 7:106.

13*Journal*, 3:390; *Letters*, 2:312-88. Middleton, a fellow of Trinity College, Cambridge, had published in 1748 "A Free Inquiry into the Miraculous Powers, which are supposed to have subsided in the Christian Church, &c."

14*Works*, 14:223-24.

[15]Gerald R. Cragg, *Oxford*, 11:40.

[16]Frank Baker, "John Wesley's Churchmanship," pp. 269-70.

[17]"An Earnest Appeal," *Oxford*, 11:51-55.

[18]For a detailed study of this, see Albert M. Lyles, *Methodism Mocked: The Satiric Reaction to Methodism in the Eighteenth Century* (London: The Epworth Press, 1960).

[19]Gerald R. Cragg, *The Church and the Age of Reason, 1648-1789* (Baltimore, Maryland: Penguin Books, 1960), pp. 157ff.

[20]" An Earnest Appeal," *Oxford*, 11:82.

[21]"A Farther Appeal," *Oxford*, 11:320-21.

[22]*Journal*, 2:335.

[23]"A Farther Appeal," *Oxford*, 11:312.

[24]"A Plain Account of the People Called Methodists," *Works*, 8:248.

[25]Ibid., pp. 249-50.

[26]"A Plain Account," *Works*, 8:254-55. Wesley used the same rationale for the bands: ". . . these are also prudential helps, grounded on reason and experience, in order to apply the general rules given in Scripture according to particular circumstances" (ibid., p.259). See the *34th Article* of the Church of England (Gibson, *Thirty-nine Articles*, 2:716ff.).

[27]"Advice to the People called Methodists," *Works*, 8:354.

[28]*Letters*, 3:9. See also the helpful edition by Michael Hurley, S.J., *John Wesley's Letter to a Roman Catholic* (Nashville: Abingdon, 1968), p. 51.

[29]"Primitive Christianity," *Oxford*, 11:90-94. See also ibid., p. 90n.

[30]*Works*, 8:257. See also his sermon, "Causes of the Inefficacy of Christianity," *Works*, 7:284-85: "However, in some parts, both of England and Ireland, scriptural Christianity is well known [and] is openly and largely declared; and thousands upon thousands continually hear and receive 'the truth as it is in Jesus.' Why is it, then, that even in these parts Christianity has had so little effect? . . . I conceive this: It was a common saying among the Christians in the primitive Church, 'The soul and the body make a man; the spirit and discipline make a Christian'; . . . Now, whatever doctrine is preached, where there is not discipline, it cannot have its full effect upon the hearer."

[31]"A Farther Appeal," *Oxford*, 11:318-19.

[32]"Reasons Against a Separation from the Church," *Works*, 13:226.

[33]Ibid.

[34]"Farther Thoughts on Separation from the Church," *Works*, 13:273-74.

[35]Reginald Kissack, *Church or No Church: A Study of the development of the concept of Church in British Methodism* (London: The Epworth Press, 1964), pp. 59-60: "He had a distaste for Dissent as an almost un-English activity."

[36]Sermon, "On Schism," *Works*, 6:406ff.

[37]*Minutes*, 1:8-9, 57-58, 82. See also the "Large Minutes," *Works*, 8:320-22.

[38]Frank Baker, *John Wesley and the Church of England*, pp. 160-79.

[39]See his letter dated Bristol, September 20, 1788, *Letters*, 8:92. Frank Baker notes that it is difficult to formulate any progression in this regard. "Some of the 'firsts' can easily be assembled: his 'submitting to be more vile' by preaching in the open air at Bristol on 2 April 1739, his summoning of the first annual Conference at the Foundery in London on 25 June 1744, and especially the crucial events of that crucial year of 1784—the signing on 28 February of the Deed Poll which incorporated the Conference as a legal entity, and his ordination of preachers for America on 1 and 2 September. Some admittedly epochal events, however, like his acceptance of Thomas Maxfield as his first

'son in the gospel' can neither be accurately dated nor fully explained" (*John Wesley and the Church of England*, pp. 4-5).

40*Oxford*, 26:206. For the identity of "John Smith," see ibid., p. 138.

41*Irenicum; a Weapon Salve for the Church's Wounds* (London: Mortlock, 2nd ed., 1662), pp. 2-3, 4-5, 106, 124-25.

42*Oxford*, 26:572; *Letters*, 3:182, 201.

43*Bennet Minutes*, pp. 24-25. See also John H.S. Kent, *The Age of Disunity* (London: The Epworth Press, 1966), p. 172.

44*An Enquiry into the Constitution, Discipline, Unity and Worship, of the Primitive Church, That Flourish'd within the first Three Hundred Years after Christ. Faithfully Collected out of the Extant Writings of those Ages. By an Impartial Hand* (London: Printed for J. Wyat, 1713). Cf. *Journal*, 3:232.

45Ibid., Pt. 1, pp. 3, 136ff.; Pt.2, pp. 140-41.

46*Oxford*, 26:174. Earlier in the same letter he continued to affirm the principle of apostolic succession, but by 1756 he had come to a view of the episcopacy which was "both scriptural and apostolical," but not prescribed in scripture as he had once "heartily espoused." Stillingfleet's *Irenicum* had convinced him that it was a non-essential ordinance (*Letters*, 3:182). In 1760, he publicly denied apostolic succession (*Letters*, 4:139-40), and in 1785 referred to it as "a fable which no man ever did or can prove (*Letters*, 7:284).

47*Bennet Minutes*, pp. 39-40. Cf. *Journal*, 2:53.

48"The Principles of a Methodist Farther Explained," *Works*, 8:415. Cf. "A Farther Appeal," *Oxford*, 11:320. See also "On Schism," *Works*, 6:405-6, and *Explanatory Notes upon the New Testament* (London: Bowyer, 1755), I Cor. 11:18.

49*Irenicum*, p. 104.

50"But what is faith? Not an opinion, no more than it is a form of words; not any number of opinions put together, be they ever so true. A string of opinions is no more Christian faith than a string of beads is Christian holiness. It is . . . a power, wrought by the Almighty in an immortal spirit inhabiting an house of clay, to see through that veil into the world of spirits, into things invisible and eternal; a power to discern those things which with eyes of flesh and blood no man hath seen or can see . . . it is a divine evidence or conviction wrought in the heart . . ." "A Letter to the Reverend Dr. Conyers Middleton," *Letters*, 2:381-82. This letter also includes the often-quoted "Away with names! Away with opinions! I care not what you are called . . ." (p. 380). But the real weight of Wesley's argument was *for* a living faith. He published part 6 of this letter as *A Plain Account of Genuine Christianity* (Dublin: Powell, 1753). See also *Works*, 10:1-79; *Oxford*, 11:527-38.

51*Sermons*, 2:126-46.

52*Letters*, 3:202-3.

53"Reasons against a Separation from the Church of England," *Works*, 13:228.

54"A Farther Appeal," *Oxford*, 11:321.

55*Oxford*, 26:206.

56*Oxford*, 25:615-16. Cf. "A Farther Appeal," *Oxford*, 11:295,324.

57*Oxford*, 26:237.

58*Letters*, 4:137.

59A spirit of a somewhat different orientation, however, as H.R. McAdoo has convincingly demonstrated in his distinction between the Anglican and Puritan approaches to piety. As opposed to the piety in the tradition of Bernard of Clairvaux, Anglicanism returned to the patristic principle of edification, resulting in a more restrained devotion.

The liturgical emphases of Anglicanism gave a strong ethical dimension, and a more calm and ordered piety. See *The Structure of Caroline Moral Theology* (London: Longmans, Green and Co., 1949), pp. 138-39. McAdoo expounds this more fully in his definitive study, *The Spirit of Anglicanism: A Survey of Anglican Theological Method in the Seventeenth Century* (New York: Charles Scribner's Sons, 1965).

60For a detailed and illuminating account of Wesley's family background, see John A. Newton, *Susanna Wesley and the Puritan Tradition in Methodism* (London: Epworth Press, 1968). See also Frank Baker, "Wesley's Puritan Ancestry," *London Quarterly and Holborn Review* 187 (1962):180-86.

61*Journal*, 2:268; 5:119ff.

62"In my hours of walking, I read Dr. Calamy's *Abridgment of Mr. Baxter's Life*. What a scene is opened here! In spite of all the prejudices of education, I could not but see that the poor Nonconformists had been used without either justice or mercy; and that many of the Protestant Bishops of King Charles had neither more religion, nor humanity, than the Popish Bishops of Queen Mary" (*Journal*, 4:93).

63*A Christian Library. Consisting of Extracts from and Abridgments of the Choicest Pieces of Practical Divinity, Which Have Been Published in the English Tongue*, 50 vols. (Bristol: W. Pine, 1749-55). This collection is the touchstone for the excellent and well-documented study by Robert C. Monk, *John Wesley: His Puritan Heritage* (New York: Abingdon Press, 1966). See pp. 36ff.

64Perry Miller, *The New England Mind: The Seventeenth Century* (New York: The Macmillan Company, 1939), pp. 4f. See also Owen C. Watkins, *The Puritan Experience: Studies in Spiritual Autobiography* (New York: Schocken Books, 1972), pp. 73ff.

65Ibid., p. 18.

66*The Works of John Whitgift*, edited for The Parker Society by John Ayre. 3 vols. (Cambridge: at the University Press, 1853), 1:171. See also Hugh Martin, *Puritanism and Richard Baxter* (London: SCM Press, 1954), p. 11.

67Leonard J. Trinterud, "The Origins of Puritanism," *Church History* 20 (March, 1951):37-57; Jerald C. Brauer, "Reflections on the Nature of English Puritanism," *Church History* 23.2 (June, 1954):100.

68William Tyndale, *Doctrinal Treatises and Introductions to Different Portions of the Holy Scriptures*, edited for The Parker Society by Henry Walter (Cambridge: at the University Press, 1848), p. 403: "Seek, therefore, in the scripture, as thou readest it, chiefly to say, the law and commandments which God commendeth us to do: and then the mercy promised unto all them that submit themselves unto the law. For all the promises throughout the whole scripture do include a covenant: that is, God bindeth himself to fulfil that mercy unto thee only if thou wilt endeavour thyself to keep his laws; so that no man hath his part in the mercy of God, save he only that loveth his law, and consenteth that it is righteous and good, and fain would do it, and ever mourneth because he now and then breaketh it through informity or doth it not so perfectly as his heart would." See also C.H. Williams, *William Tyndale* (London: Thomas Nelson & Son, 1969), pp. 122-35.

69See, for example, Jean Calvin, *Institutes of the Christian Religion*, ed. John T. McNeill, tr. Ford Lewis Battles. Library of Christian Classics, vols. 20 & 21 (Philadelphia: Westminster Press, 1960), 2:10:1-5,8, where the emphasis is quite different from that of Tyndale, cited above, n.68. See also Leonard Trinterud's essay in *Elizabethan Puritanism*, Library of Protestant Thought (New York: Oxford University Press, 1971), pp. 302-14. After 1585, this was often referred to as the "double covenant": the covenant of works, made with Adam at creation and therefore binding on the whole human race; and after the fall, the covenant of grace, whereby God undertook human redemption, renewing the covenant through Jewish history until its culmination in Christ.

70William Ames, *The Marrow of Theology*, trans. and ed. John D. Eusden (Boston: Pilgrim Press, 1968), pp. 132,149,250.

71Samuel Rutherford, *The Covenant of Life Opened: Or, a Treatise of the Covenant of Grace* (London: Printed for Andrew Crook, 1655), p. 233. See also Gordon S. Wakefield, *Puritan Devotion: its place in the development of Christian Piety* (London: The Epworth Press, 1957), pp. 31-32.

72To assume that Puritanism was an attempt to introduce Calvinism into England against the defenders of officialdom is to misunderstand a very great deal. See Leonard Trinterud, *Elizabethan Puritanism*, p. 303.

73This is the thesis of Geoffrey F. Nuttall's meticulous study, *The Holy Spirit in the Puritan Faith and Experience* (Oxford: Basil Blackwell, 1946). See also John von Rohr, "Covenant and Assurance in Early English Puritanism," *Church History* 34.2 (June 1965):195-203.

74Jerald Brauer, "English Puritanism," p. 102.

75John Dillenberger and Claude Welch, *Protestant Christianity interpreted through its development* (New York: Charles Scribner's Sons, 1958), pp. 104-5.

76John Preston, *The New Covenant, or The Saints Portion. A Treatise unfolding the All-sufficiencie of God, and Mans uprightnes, and the Covenant of Grace* (London: Printed by I.D. for Nicolas Bourne, 1629), 2:228. See also John Preston, *The Breast-plate of Faith and Love. A Treatise Wherein ground and exercise of Faith and Love, as they are set upon Christ their Object, and as they are expressed in Good Workes, es explained* (London: Printed by W.I. for Nicholas Bourne, 1630), 2:155.

77John Preston, *The New Covenant*, 3:148-49.

78John Owen, *Of the Divine Originall, Authority, self-evidencing Light, and Power of the Scriptures* (London: 1659), p. 72.

79Patrick Collinson, *The Elizabethan Puritan Movement* (London: Jonathan Cape, 1967), p. 25.

80A.G. Dickens, *The English Reformation* (New York: Schocken Books, 1964), p. 63.

81Ibid., pp. 236-37.

82See Lowell H. Zuck, ed., *Christianity and Revolution: Radical Christian Testimonies 1520-1650* (Philadelphia: Temple University Press, 1975), passim. See also Hans J. Hillerbrand, "Anabaptism and the Reformation: Another Look," *Church History* 29.4 (December 1960):404-23; and James M. Estes, "Johannes Brenz and the Problem of Ecclesiastical Discipline," *Church History* 41.4 (December 1972):464-79.

83See A.F. Scott Pearson, *Church and State: Political Aspects of Sixteenth Century Puritanism* (Cambridge: at the University Press, 1928), p. 116.

84So the Treatise of Robert Browne (Middelburg, 1582), reproduced in Albert Peel and Leland H. Carlson, ed., *The Writings of Robert Harrison and Robert Browne*, Elizabethan Nonconformist Texts, vol. 2, published for The Sir Halley Stewart Trust (London: George Allen and Unwin, Ltd., 1953), pp. 150-70.

85For perhaps the most complete account of the *classis* movement, see Roland G. Usher, *The Presbyterian Movement in the reign of Queen Elizabeth, as illustrated by the Minute Book of the Dedham Classis* (London: Camden Society, 3rd series, vol. 8, 1905). See also Roland G. Usher, *The Reconstruction of the English Church*, 2 vols. (New York: Appleton and Company, 1910), 1:43ff.; and M.M. Knappen, ed., *Two Elizabethan Puritan Diaries; by Richard Rogers and Samuel Ward* (Chicago: The

American Society of Church History, 1933), pp. 26,66-67,94.

While *classis* was the same word adopted by Wesley for the Methodist class meeting, there is no clear indication that he derived it from early English Puritanism; though it is unlikely that he was unaware of this earlier usage.

[86]See A.F. Scott Pearson, *Thomas Cartwright and Elizabethan Puritanism* (Cambridge: at the University Press, 1925; Leonard Trinterud, ed., *Elizabethan Puritanism*, pp. 235ff.

[87]As, for example, in the 1584 petition of Thomas Sampson. See John Strype, *Annals of the Reformation and Establishment of Religion, and other various occurrences in the Church of England, during Queen Elizabeth's happy reign; &c.*, 4 vols. in 7 (Oxford: at the Clarendon Press, 1824), 3:1:321.

[88]*Oxford*, 26:235. See also Patrick Collinson, *Elizabethan Puritan Movement*, pp. 291f.

[89]Richard Bancroft, *Daungerous Positions and Proceedings, published and practised within this Iland of Brytaine and under pretence of Reformation, and for the Presbyteriall Discipline* (London: Imprinted for John Wolfe, 1593), pp. 120-24.

[90]Strype, *Annals of the Reformation*, 3:1:412.

[91]The Solemn League and Covenant is reproduced in Henry Bettenson, ed., *Documents of the Christian Church*, 2d ed. (London: Oxford University Press, 1963), pp. 286-89.

[92]These are reproduced in Philip Schaff, *The Creeds of Christendom*, 3:600-704.

[93]Ibid., 3:657-58.

[94]Cited in Champlin Burrage, *The Early English Dissenters in the light of recent research*, 2 vols. (Cambridge: at the University Press, 1912; reprint ed., New York: Russell & Russell, 1967), 1:70, 2:13.

[95]Ibid., 1:98-99. See also *The Writings of Harrison and Browne*, pp. 252-56, where the principles are clearly laid out according to the "Calling, Planting and Covenant of the Church" under "one kinde of government" by "covenant" and "condicion."

[96]*The Remains of Edmund Grindal, D.D., Successively Bishop of London, and Archbishop of York and Canterbury*, edited for The Parker Society by William Nicholson (Cambridge: at the University Press, 1843), pp. 201ff.

[97]John Robinson and John Smyth were responsible for bringing Separatism to the north Nottinghamshire area. Both were fellows of Cambridge colleges, and had been ejected for refusing to subscribe to the anti-Puritan measures of King James I in 1603, and for forming gathered churches. They emigrated to Amsterdam in 1608, where Smyth adopted Anabaptist positions. Robinson moved to Leyden, where his congregation thrived, and where his Separatist views tended to modify. See R. Tudur Jones, *Congregationalism in England, 1662-1962* (London: Independent Press, 1962), pp. 20ff.

[98]William Ames, *The Marrow of Theology*, p. 209.

[99]The acknowledged leaders of the group who presented the *Apologeticall Narration* were Philip Nye, Thomas Goodwin, William Bridge, Jeremiah Burroughes, and Sidrach Simpson. It was followed in 1644 by John Cotton's *Keyes of the Kingdom of Heaven*, which greatly influenced John Owen. See R. Tudur Jones, *Congregationalism in England*, p. 28; and Geoffrey Nuttall, *Visible Saints: The Congregational Way 1640-1660* (Oxford: Basil Blackwell, 1957), pp. 8ff.

[100]Philip Schaff, *Creeds of Christendom*, 3:712. The entire *Declaration* is reproduced ibid., pp. 707-29. See also the helpful study by Albert Peel, *The Savoy Declaration of Faith and Order, 1658* (London: Independent Press, 1939).

[101]John Owen, *Of Schisme* (Oxford, 1657), cited in Geoffrey Nuttall, *Visible Saints*, p. 59.

Cf. Calvin, *Institutes*, 1:7:8. See also M.M. Knappen, *Tudor Puritanism: A Chapter in the History of Idealism* (Chicago: The University of Chicago Press, 1939), pp. 354ff.

102Schaff, *Creeds of Christendom*, 3:724-25.

103Cited in Geoffrey Nuttall, *Visible Saints*, p. 112. To implement this discipline, the Independents required some evidence of religious experience prior to admission to the Lord's Supper, whereas Presbyterians required only some profession of faith from a prospective member. Admission to the gathered church of Congregationalism was restricted to those who were worthy, and who were convinced that they were "regenerate and received of God" (ibid.). Edmund Morgan has examined this aspect of Congregationalism in some detail, and suggests that the principle was taken to its most extreme in New England, and thence back to the homeland. See *Visible Saints: The History of a Puritan Idea* (Ithaca: Cornell University Press, 1963). See also Gerald R. Cragg, *Puritanism in the Period of the Great Persecution 1660-1688* (Cambridge: at the University Press, 1957), pp. 167-68.

104See Alexander Gordon, ed., *Freedom After Ejection: A Review (1690-1692) of Presbyterian and Congregational Nonconformity in England and Wales* (Manchester: at the University Press, 1917). It is interesting to note the use of the word *society* as a synonym for *congregation* (for example, p. 44).

105"Thoughts upon Liberty," *Works*, 11:39.

106One of the outstanding Puritan scholars, Baxter's career is typical of the misfortunes which dogged those of moderate and catholic outlook in an age of extremisms. He was committed to church and civil discipline, but opposed to episcopal government; and while this gave him collegiality with Presbyterians and Congregationalists, it also led him to support the Restoration of Charles II. This in turn led to the offer of a bishopric (which he refused); yet he was ejected from his living in 1662 because he could not support the Act of Uniformity with regard to the episcopacy and reform of the Prayer Book. He was persecuted, along with the other ejected ministers, for the next two decades; and in 1685, following the accession of James II, was tried and imprisoned for sedition. Released the following year, he lived to see the Act of Toleration passed in 1689, which gave nonconformist ministers a measure of freedom.

107A. Harold Wood, *Church Unity without Uniformity: A Study of Seventeenth-century English Church Movements and of Richard Baxter's Proposals for a Comprehensive Church* (London: Epworth Press, 1963), p. 23.

108Richard Baxter, *A Treatise of Episcopacy; confuting by Scripture, Reason, and the Churches Testimony, that sort of Diocesan Churches, Prelacy, and Government, Which casteth out The Primitive Church-Species, Episcopacy, Ministry and Discipline, and confoundeth the Christian World by Corruption, Usurpation, Schism, and Persecution* (London: printed for Nevil Simmons, 1681), p. 47.

109*Minutes*, 1:64ff.; "The Large Minutes," *Works*, 8:302. Baxter's guidelines were definitively laid out in his *Gildas Salvianus: The Reformed Pastor: shewing the nature of the pastoral work: especially in private instruction and catechising: with an open confession of our too open sins* (London, 1656), vol. 14 of *The Practical Works of The Rev. Richard Baxter: with a life of the author and a critical examination of his writings, by the Rev. William Orme*, 23 vols. (London: James Duncan, 1830).

110*Reliquiae Baxterianae: Or, Mr. Richard Baxter's Narrative of The Most Memorable Passages of his Life and Times*, Faithfully Publish'd from his own Original Manuscript, by Matthew Sylvester (London, 1696), Appendix 1, p. 10; Appendix 2, p. 24.

111Ibid., 2:14, p. 144; Appendix 3, pp. 59,62-63; Appendix 4, p. 76.

112Ibid., Appendix 4, p. 69. See also A. Harold Wood, *Church Unity*, pp. 33ff.

113Geoffrey Nuttall, *Visible Saints*, p. 70. This entire section on Congregational fellowship and covenant draws heavily on Nuttall's seminal work.

114Ibid., p. 80.

115Ibid., p. 81.

116Cited in Gerald R. Cragg, *Puritanism in the Period of the Great Persecution*, p. 152.

117Joseph Alleine, *An Alarm to Unconverted Sinners (1672)* (Nashville: Publishing House of the M.E. Church, South, 1920), p. viii.

118David Tripp, *The Renewal of the Covenant in the Methodist Tradition* (London: Epworth Press, 1969), p. 192, n.7. "Broadsides" or "Broadsheets" were a popular form of mass communication in the seventeenth and eighteenth centuries. They consisted of a single sheet of newsprint, and were sold cheaply, usually for one penny, in much the same way that special "Stop Press" editions of modern newspapers used to be sold in large cities before the advent of television.

119Richard Alleine, *Vindiciae Pietatis: or, A Vindication of Godlinesse, In the greatest Strictness and Spirituality of it, from the Imputations of Folly and Fancy. Together with Several Directions for the Attaining and Maintaining of a Godly Life* (London: Printed for Peter Parker, 1663).

120For an analysis of the Puritan authors in *A Christian Library*, see Robert C. Monk, *John Wesley: His Puritan Heritage*, pp. 258-62. See also Frank Baker, "The Beginnings of the Methodist Covenant Service," *The London Quarterly and Holborn Review* 180.3 (July 1955):216.

121*Journal*, 4:126. Cf. Richard Alleine, *Vindication*, Third Part, pp. 293-97.

122David Tripp, *Renewal of Covenant*, pp. 35, 55-107.

123Leslie F. Church, *More About the Early Methodist People* (London: The Epworth Press, 1949), pp. 274ff. See also Thomas Jackson, ed., *The Lives of Early Methodist Preachers. Chiefly Written by Themselves*, 4th ed., 6 vols. (London: Wesleyan Conference Office, 1876), 2:111.

124Robert Dickinson, *The Life of the Rev. John Braithwaite* (London: J. Kershaw, 1825), pp. 102-3.

125Cited in Leslie F. Church, *More About the Early Methodist People*, p. 276.

CHAPTER TWO

1The definitive treatment of this theme remains Meyrick H. Carré, *Phases of Thought in England* (Oxford: at the Clarendon Press, 1949), in which the *via media* is given a pedigree long antecedent to the Reformation. See also A.G. Dickens, *The English Reformation*, pp. 59-82.

2See, for example, Neelak S. Tjernagel, *Henry VIII and the Lutherans: A Study in Anglo-Lutheran Relations from 1521-1547* (St. Louis: Concordia Publishing House, 1965), p. 263 & n.

3The Wittenberg Articles of 1536, for example, defined justification by faith according to the Augsburg Confession, but then went into a long elaboration of the necessity for ensuing good works, clearly indicating some compromise on the part of the German theologians in response to the English negotiators. See Neelak S. Tjernagel, *Henry VIII and the Lutherans*, p. 263n.

4Charles Lloyd, ed., *Formularies of Faith put forth by Authority during the reign of Henry VIII* (Oxford: at the Clarendon Press, 1825), p. 209.

[5]Ibid., p. 359.

[6]For a concise but thorough assessment of Cranmer, see G.W. Bromiley, *Thomas Cranmer, Theologian* (London: Lutterworth Press, 1956). Cranmer's own writings are available in two volumes edited for The Parker Society by John Edmund Cox: *Writings and Disputations* (Cambridge: at the University Press, 1844); *Miscellaneous Writings and Letters* (Cambridge: at the University Press, 1846). See also *The Two Liturgies, A.D.1549 and A.D.1552: with other Documents set forth by authority in the reign of King Edward VI*, edited for The Parker Society by Joseph Ketley (Cambridge: at the University Press, 1844); and *The Thirty-nine Articles*, ed. Edgar C. S. Gibson.

[7]*Journal*, 2:101.

[8]*The Doctrine of Salvation, Faith, and Good Works. Extracted from the Homilies of the Church of England* (London: [Strahan] for James Hutton, 1739). For availability of this and other primary Wesleyan sources, see Frank Baker, *A Union Catalogue of the Publications of John and Charles Wesley* (Durham, N.C.: Duke University, 1966).

[9]Barnes' major treatises, including *Onely fayth justifieth before God*, were published in 1531, and represent the most Lutheran position of any contemporary theologian. He was a pivotal figure in the many abortive attempts to reach agreement between the English church and the German Protestant Schmalkaldic League. See the helpful edition of his works by Neelak S. Tjernagel, *The Reformation Essays of Dr. Robert Barnes* (St. Louis: Concordia Publishing House, 1963).

[10]*An Extract of Mr. Richard Baxter's Aphorisms of Justification. Publish'd by John Wesley . . .* (Newcastle upon Tyne: John Gooding, 1745). See also *Minutes* 1ff., 21ff., 32ff.

[11]Richard Baxter, *Aphorisms of Justification* (London: printed for Francis Tyton, 1649), p. 183. In many ways this was an unsatisfactory work, which Baxter did his best to disown and to supplant with further publications on the subject. To what extent he departed from his essential position in the *Aphorisms*, however, is less clear. See C.F. Allison, *The Rise of Moralism: The Proclamation of the Gospel from Hooker to Baxter* (New York: The Seabury Press, 1966), pp. 155-56. Cf. *The Practical Works of The Rev. Richard Baxter*, 1:448.

[12]Ibid., p. 196. Cf. Geoffrey Nuttall, *Richard Baxter and Philip Doddridge: A Study in a Tradition* (London: Oxford University Press, 1951), p. 23.

[13]Baxter, *Aphorisms*, pp. 194,233. Cf. Robert C. Monk, *John Wesley: His Puritan Heritage*, pp. 126ff.

[14]C.F. Allison, *The Rise of Moralism*, pp. 178ff. The importance of Wesley's Anglican heritage in this regard is convincingly demonstrated by Allison's incisive study. Working his way meticulously through the writings of the period, he reaches the significant conclusion that the "concern about immorality and lawlessness, occasionally expressed under Charles I, grew into a spectre of antinomianism which cast a darker and darker shadow over nearly all the theology written well into Restoration times. Seventeenth-century teaching concerning the Gospel cannot be separated from anti-nomianism and the fear of it" (p. 194).

[15]The English Civil War generated in Baxter at an early stage in his career a strong motivation to refute antinomianism. Later in life, he noted that, as a young chaplain, he was concerned about the tendency of soldiers in the army to accept a doctrine of imputed righteousness which seemed to absolve them of ethical responsibility on the grounds that "Christ hath repented and believed for us, and that we must no more question our faith and Repentance, than Christ. This awakened me better to study these points and being young, and not furnished with sufficient reading of the Contro-

versie, and also being where were no libraries, I was put to study only the naked matter in itself. Whereupon I shortly wrote a small book called Aphorisms of Justification. . . ." (*A Treatise of Justifying Righteousness* [London, 1676], cited in C.F. Allison, *The Rise of Moralism*, p. 155).

16See, for example, "The Principles of a Methodist" (1742), *Works*, 8:359-74.

17Albert C. Outler, "The Place of Wesley in the Christian Tradition," pp. 19-22. Frank Baker, *John Wesley and the Church of England*, pp. 7-38. V.H.H. Green, *The Young Mr. Wesley: A Study of John Wesley and Oxford* (New York: St. Martin's Press, 1961); Maximin Piette, *John Wesley in the Evolution of Protestantism* (New York: Sheed & Ward, 1937), pp. 305ff.

18"A Plain Account of Christian Perfection," *Works*, 11:366-67. See also Frank Baker, "John Wesley and the 'Imitatio Christi'," *The London Quarterly and Holborn Review* 166 (1941):74-87.

19*The Rules and Exercises of Holy Living (and) The Rules and Exercises of Holy Dying*, in *The Whole Works of the Right Reverend Jeremy Taylor*, edited by Reginald Heber, revised and corrected by Charles Page Eden, 10 vols. (London: Longman, Brown, Green and Longmans . . . , 1847), 3:37ff.

20Ibid., 3:114.

21Ibid., 3:148.

22"A Short History of the People Called Methodists," *Works*, 13:307.

23Robert F. Wearmouth's research in this regard is vivid in its detail. See *Methodism and the Common People of the Eighteenth Century* (London: The Epworth Press, 1945), pp. 19ff, 77ff. For an insight into the attitudes of the established church, see Basil Willey, *The Eighteenth Century Background: Studies on the Idea of Nature in the Thought of the Period* (London: Chatto & Windus, 1946), pp. 43ff.

24Richard P. Heitzenrater, "John Wesley and the Oxford Methodists, 1725-35," (Ph.D. Dissertation, Duke University, 1972), p. 382. See also *The Elusive Mr. Wesley: John Wesley His Own Biographer*, 2 vols. (Nashville: Abingdon Press, 1984), 1:73f.

25Non-jurors were those clergy whose high view of the church forbade them to take the oath of loyalty to the new monarchs, William and Mary, following the "Bloodless Revolution" of 1688 and the abdication of James II. Many of them suffered considerable hardship as a result of their stand, and their spirited defense of their position in the controversies which ensued gave ample evidence of the loss incurred by the church by their expulsion. See Gerald R. Cragg, *Reason and Authority in the Eighteenth Century* (Cambridge: at the University Press, 1964), pp. 184ff.

26William Law, *A Serious Call to a Devout and Holy Life* (London: Printed for William Innys, 1729), p. 27.

27Ibid., pp. 18-19. Wesley's personal relationship with Law continued for some years, and exposed him further to the High-Churchmanship of the Non-Jurors, which V.H.H. Green has described as "rooted in the patristic writings and traditions broadly represented by Hooker and Laud . . . founded on what its advocated held to be the practice and principles of the primitive and apostolic Church, in themselves the measure of orthodoxy (*The Young Mr. Wesley*, pp. 272,274). See also Frank Baker, *From Wesley to Asbury: Studies in Early American Methodism* (Durham, N.C.: Duke University Press, 1976), pp. 22-23; and *Proceedings of the Wesley Historical Society* 37 (1969-70):78-82.

28"The Duty of Receiving the Lord's Supper," cited in Charles Rogers, "The Concept of Prevenient Grace in the Theology of John Wesley" (Ph.D. Dissertation, Duke University, 1967), p. 118. Rogers' summary of this essay, an unpublished manuscript in the

Colman Collection, is helpful in linking Wesley's Oxford theology to a concept of conditional covenant, something which Wesley touched on only briefly in the sermon he later based on it, "The Duty of Constant Communion," *Works,* 7:147-57.

29John D. Walsh, "Origins of the Evangelical Revival," in *Essays in Modern Church History; in Memory of Norman Sykes,* edited by G.V. Bennett & J.D. Walsh (London: Adam & Charles Black [1966]), p. 142.

30*Journal,* 1:110.

31Ibid., 1:142.

32Ibid., 1:151.

33John Preston, *The New Covenant,* 2:155.

34Martin Schmidt, *John Wesley: A Theological Biography,* 2 vols. (Nashville: Abingdon Press, vol. 1, n.d.; vol. 2, pt. 1, 1972; vol. 2, pt. 2, 1973), 1:161ff.

35Cited ibid.

36Wesley, *Journal,* 1:372.

37Ibid., 1:424.

38Ibid., 1:436, 439-40, 442, 447, 454ff., 459. Wesley readily acknowledged his debt to Böhler, describing his work in England as that which would "never come to an end till heaven and earth pass away" (ibid., pp. 460,471).

39Ibid., 1:465ff. ". . . I felt my heart strangely warmed. I felt I did trust in Christ, Christ alone for salvation; and an assurance was given me that He had taken away *my* sins, even *mine,* and saved *me* from the law of sin and death" (pp. 475-76).

40R. Newton Flew, "Methodism and Catholic Tradition," in *Northern Catholicism: Centenary Studies in the Oxford and Parallel Movements,* edited by N.P. Williams and Charles Harris (London: SPCK, 1933), p. 526.

41"My father did not die unacquainted with the faith of the gospel, of the primitive Christians, or of our first Reformers; the same which, by the grace of God, I preach, and which is just as new as Christianity. What he experienced before, I know not; but I know that during his last illness, which continued eight months, he enjoyed a clear sense of his acceptance with God. I heard him express it more than once, although at that time I understood him not. 'The inward witness, son, the inward witness,' said he to me, 'that is the proof, the strongest proof, of Christianity' " (*Letters,* 2:134-35).

42*Sermons,* 1:263-79. This was preached before the University on January 1, 1733, and was regarded by Wesley as a definitive statement of the principles underlying the Holy Club. Richard Heitzenrater's detailed account of Wesley's preparations and anticipation of its delivery makes this clear ("John Wesley and the Oxford Methodists," pp. 195ff.). It is therefore significant that Wesley included it in the second volume of *Sermons on Several Occasions* (London: Strahan, 1748).

43*Journal,* 1:460,462.

44Umphrey Lee, *The Historical Backgrounds of Early Methodist Enthusiasm* (New York: Columbia University Press, 1931), p. 16.

45In *The Life of God in the Soul of Man* (London: Printed for J. Downing, 1726), Henry Scougal had defined true religion as "an Union of the Soul with God, a real participation of the Divine Nature, the very image of God drawn upon the Soul, or, in the Apostle's phrase, it is Christ formed within us" (p. 4). The book was studied by the Holy Club in August 1732 (Heitzenrater, "Wesley and the Oxford Methodists," p. 518), having been recommended to Wesley by his mother (*WHS Proc.* 18 [1931-32]:171). It was also among his readings in Georgia (*Journal,* 1:167,247-48).

46This fourteenth-century work had been popularized by Martin Luther, who encouraged its publication in printed form. See the new translation, with Introduction and

Commentary, *The Theologia Germanica of Martin Luther* (New York: Paulist Press, 1980). See also Frank Baker, *WHS Proc.* 37 (1969-70):81.

47*Journal*, 1:420; 2:515. In 1764, Wesley listed his objections to the mystics: They lacked a concept of church communion; they held to justification by works; they indulged in unscriptural speculations; they were dark, reserved, and narrow in their outlook. But above all, their language was "both unscriptural and affectedly mysterious. I say affectedly, for this does not necessarily result from the nature of the things spoken of. St. John speaks as high and as deep things as Jacob Behmen. Why then does not Jacob speak as plain as him?" (ibid., 5:46). It was Jakob Böhme to whose writings William Law had been especially attracted as his involvement with German mysticism had intensified. Cf. Harald Lindström, *Wesley and Sanctification: A Study in the Doctrine of Salvation* (Stockholm: Nya Bokförlags Aktiebolaget, 1946; reprint ed., Wilmore, Kentucky: Francis Asbury Publishing Company, Inc. [1980]), pp. 67-68, 161-83.

48This correspondence is reproduced ibid., 8:319-24.

49Nor yet that he abandoned the writings of all the mystics who had influenced him during his formative years. For a detailed assessment of these, see Robert G. Tuttle, Jr., *John Wesley: His Life and Theology* (Grand Rapids, MI: Zondervan Publishing House, 1978), pp. 141ff., 330ff.

50*Sermons*, 1:272ff.

51*Oxford*, 11:46-48. Cf. "The New Birth," *Sermons*, 2:226-243.

52"The Nature of Enthusiasm," *Sermons*, 2:96ff.

53*Journal*, 2:130. Cf. *Oxford*, 11:414,437,443.

54Wesley's difficulties with this doctrine of assurance were of course compounded by the "enthusiasm" of his day, and his concern to take the gospel to precisely the people among whom it was most likely to be manifest. These tensions are very evident in his various statements on the subject, which makes the clarity of his definitive statement in 1767 all the more creditable: "The Witness of the Spirit: Discourse II," *Sermons*, 2:341-59.

55*Journal*, 2:275-76.

56See, for example, the correspondence with his mother, *Oxford*, 25:144-218 passim, but especially pp. 173-76,178-80. Martin Schmidt sees in this correspondence "the unbroken continuation of that rationalist tradition in English thought, which was not interrupted by the convulsion brought by the Reformation" (*John Wesley*, 1:86).

57*Minutes*, 1:24.

58*Sermons*, 1:123f.

59George Bull, *Harmonia Apostolica: Or Two Dissertations; in the Forms of which the Doctrine of St. James on Justification by Works is Explained and Defended: in the latter the Agreement of St. Paul with St. James is clearly shown*, 2nd ed., Library of Anglo-Catholic Theology, vol. 24 (Oxford: John Henry Parker, 1844), p. 4. See also p. 58.

60Ibid., pp. 14ff. See also C.F. Allison, *The Rise of Moralism*, pp. 118-37.

61Ibid., p. 192.

62*The Ecclesiastical Polity and other Works of Richard Hooker; with His Life by Izaak Walton, and Strype's Interpolations, &c.*, edited with an introduction by Benjamin Hanbury, 3 vols. (London: Holdsworth and Ball, 1830), 1:215ff.

63*The Works of Lancelot Andrewes*, edited by J.P. Wilson and J. Bliss, 11 vols. (Oxford: J.H. Parker, 1841-54), 6:21.

64*The Works of the Most Reverend Father in God, William Laud, D.D., Sometime*

Archbishop of Canterbury, edited by W. Scott and J. Bliss, 7 vols. in 9 (Oxford: J.H. Parker, 1847-60), 2:74-75,105-6.

[65] Allison, *Rise of Moralism*, p. 202.

[66] Ibid., pp. 193-94, where it is noted that Taylor's *Holy Living* had reached its 14th edition in the year after the death of Charles II, and *Holy Dying* its 21st edition by 1710. To say nothing, of course, of the impact of Taylor on Wesley himself.

[67] See, for example, William Tyndale's 1527 treatise, "The Obedience of a Christen man, and how Christen rulers ought to governe, wherein also (if thou marke diligently) thou shalt find eyes to perceave the craftie conveyance of all jugglers," in *Doctrinal Treatises*, edited by Henry Walter for The Parker Society (Cambridge: at the University Press, 1848), pp. 127-344. See also Robert Barnes, "A Supplication unto the most gracious Prince Henry VIII," in *The Whole Workes of W. Tyndall, John Frith and Doct, Barnes* (London: John Daye, 1573), pp. 178-205. The subject received a considered apologetic in the "Homily of Obedience," *Homilies* (1899 edition), esp. pp. 109-10. Cf. Cranmer, *Miscellaneous Writings*, p. 116.

[68] Allison, *Rise of Moralism*, p. 196.

[69] *Oxford*, 11:18.

[70] *Homilies* (1899 edition), pp. 23,25,29,33-46,47-62; Gibson, *Thirty-nine Articles*, 1:378-423.

[71] Thus the "Lambeth Articles" of 1595, perhaps the high point of English Calvinism, were contemporaneous with the work of Richard Hooker. See Gibson, *Thirty-nine Articles*, 2:475-76.

[72] For a definitive study of this progression, see Henry R. McAdoo, *Spirit of Anglicanism*.

[73] Gibson, *Thirty-nine Articles*, 2:410.

[74] "The Place of Wesley in the Christian Tradition," pp. 25ff.

[75] "A Farther Appeal," *Oxford*, 11:106,112-13. See also "A Letter to the Rev. Mr. Horne," ibid., p. 451.

[76] Ibid., pp. 106,115.

[77] "Justification by Faith," *Sermons*, 1:119.

[78] "The Great Privilege of Those that are Born of God," *Sermons*, 1:300.

[79] "The New Birth," *Sermons*, 2:227.

[80] John W. Packer, *The Transformation of Anglicanism 1643-1660, with special reference to Henry Hammond* (Manchester: Manchester University Press, 1969), pp. 55ff.

[81] The Synod held at Dort in 1618-19 condemned the Remonstrant, or Arminian, position in strongly Calvinist canons. Jacob Arminius, professor of theology at Leiden, had become the chief figure among the Remonstrants, who countered the Calvinist sub- and supra-lapsarian controversy of the Dutch Reformed Church with a doctrine of grace for all. Yet these issues had already been fought out in England, and at Cambridge in particular. See H.C. Porter, *Reformation and Reaction in Tudor Cambridge* (Cambridge: at the University Press, 1958), p. 409. See also Robert Peters, "John Hales and the Synod of Dort," in *Studies in Church History*, vol. 7, ed. G.J. Cuming and Derek Baker (Cambridge: at the University Press, 1971), p. 288. Hales was one of a brilliant group of young Anglican theologians which included Gilbert Sheldon, George Morley, William Chillingworth, Henry Hammond, John Earle, Sydney Godolphin and Lord Falkland. He visited the Synod, and observed, with a disdain amounting to contempt, the method by which predetermined pronouncements were made on the doctrines which have subsequently become known as the TULIP formulation (total human depravity, unconditional election, limited atonement, the irresistibility of grace, and the perseverance of the elect); and, after listening to a

Remonstrant exposition of John 3:16, there "bid John Calvin goodnight." As one of the participants in a seventeenth-century Anglican disputation put it, "You are mistaken when you think the Doctrine of Universall redemption Arminianisme. It was the Doctrine of the Church of England before Arminius was borne. We learne it out of the old Church-Catechisme" (cited in Packer, *Transformation of Anglicanism*, p. 56).

[82]See his sermon, "Free Grace," preached at Bristol in 1740, *Works*, 7:373-86. Cf. *Journal*, 2:421f., 426ff., 439. See also "Salvation for all—Wesley and Calvinism," in Robert E. Cushman, *Faith Seeking Understanding: Essays Theological and Critical* (Durham, North Carolina: Duke University Press, 1981), p. 64.

[83]"Working out our Own Salvation," *Works*, 6:512. Cf. other sermons, such as "What is Man?" *Works*, 7:228-29; "On Conscience," *Works*, 7:187ff.

[84]Gibson, *Thirty-nine Articles*, 2:378.

[85]*Sermons*, 2:445.

[86]*Journal*, 3:85.

[87]*Minutes*, 1:26. See also Robert E. Cushman, "Salvation for All," pp. 69f.

[88]"Predestination Calmly Considered," *Works*, 10:231-32.

[89]"The Means of Grace," *Sermons*, 1:242ff.; "The Scripture Way of Salvation," *Sermons*, 2:455; "On Attending the Church Service," *Works*, 7:183.

[90]*Minutes*, 1:16-19. Cf. "The Large Minutes," *Works*, 8:323-34.

[91]*Minutes*, 1:5.

[92]Ibid., 1:24.

[93]Gibson, *Thirty-nine Articles*, 2:410.

[94]Albert Outler describes predestination as the "noisy gong" which tended to obscure the more subtle issue of the formal cause of justification. See "The Place of Wesley in the Christian Tradition," p. 25.

[95]The definitive exposition of these, as well as the most lucid articulation of the theological argument, remains Robert E. Cushman's article, "Salvation for All" (above n.82).

[96]See, for example, *Journal*, 5:243-44.

[97]See the "Lambeth Articles" in Gibson, *Thirty-nine Articles*, 2:475f.

[98]As expressed, for example, in the sixth of the "Lambeth Articles," ibid.

[99]Ibid., 2:388ff.

[100]*Sermons*, 2:427f.

[101]Ibid., 2:428.

[102]Ibid., 2:433.

[103]Ibid., 2:438.

[104]"Justification by Faith," *Sermons*, 1:120.

[105]For a more detailed treatment of this point, see my article "Christ Our Righteousness: The Center of Wesley's Evangelistic Message," *Perkins Journal* 37.3 (Spring 1984):34-47.

[106]The second of the "Lambeth Articles," in Gibson, *Thirty-nine Articles*, 2:475. Wesley observed, some forty years after preaching his sermon on "Free Grace" at Bristol (above, n.82.), that he and his brother had been genuinely puzzled at the time by the strong Calvinist reaction. They had assumed they were preaching salvation by grace through faith, but had been accused of preaching salvation by works because they did not simultaneously affirm predestination. Wesley came to realize that the Calvinist position could accommodate "no meduim between salvation by works and salvation by absolute decrees" ("Thoughts on Salvation by Faith," *Works*, 11:493).

Robert E. Cushman notes that this was a decisive difference between Wesley and the Calvinists. "He viewed the process of faith from an empirical vantage point as well as from a speculative one; they from a predominantly scholastic and rationalistic approach" ("Salvation for all," p. 105).

[107]See below, pp. 85ff.

[108]See "A Dialogue between an Antinomian and his Friend," *Works*, 10:266-84. Cf. *Journal* 3:463; *Minutes*, 1:6,24.

While Calvin himself had specifically censured antinomianism as an inference from election, (*Institutes*, 2:7;13-15), a division from orthodox Calvinism in seventeenth-century English Nonconformity had progressed to a high Calvinism in the eighteenth century, laying excessive stress on the doctrine of irresistible grace. See Peter Toon, *The Emergence of Hyper-Calvinism in English Nonconformity 1689-1765* (London: The Olive Tree, 1967), esp. pp. 144ff. Wesley himself was accused of antinomianism at precisely the points at which he appropriated the Puritan tradition, one Anglican criticism being that such teachings came "second or third hand from the Lake of Geneva" instead of from "the fresh springs of primitive antiquity" (George Horne, cited by Gerald R. Cragg, *Oxford*, 11:437). Cf. *Journal*, 2:467-68.

[109]*Wesley and Sanctification*, pp. 74-75.

[110]For example, "The Lord Our Righteousness," *Sermons* 2:420-41; "The Scripture Way of Salvation," *Sermons* 2:442-60; "A Plain Account of Christian Perfection," *Works* 11:366-46.

[111]*Minutes*, 1:96-97.

[112]*Letters*, 5:252.

[113]*Journal*, 5:427.

[114]*Letters*, 5:259. The definitive exponent of the issues in the dispute, however, was John Fletcher. See his *Checks to Antinomianism, in a Series of Letters to Rev. Mr. Shirley and Mr. Hill*, in *The Works of the Rev. John Fletcher*, 9 vols. (London: John Mason, 1859), vols. 1-3. See also John Allan Knight, "Aspects of Wesley's Theology after 1770," *Methodist History* 6.3 (April 1968):33-42.

[115]*Journal*, 3:85.

[116]*Minutes*, 1:29.

[117]"The Righteousness of Faith," *Sermons*, 1:137.

[118]*Minutes*, 1:24.

[119]This was consistently affirmed at the early Conferences. See Wesley's own summary of the minutes in "A Plain Account of Christian Perfection," *Works*, 11:387ff.

[120]Calvin, *Institutes*, 3:17:15.

[121]*Journal*, 2:488ff. See also R. Newton Flew, *The Idea of Perfection in Christian Theology. An Historical Study of the Christian Ideal for the Present Life* (London: Oxford University Press, 1934), pp. 245ff.

[122]"A Plain Account of Christian Perfection," *Works*, 11:393.

[123]Ibid., 11:394.

[124]Ibid., 11:396.

[125]Ibid., 11:426.

[126]*Letters*, 3:212; 5:315,333; 6:116.

[127]"A Plain Account of Christian Perfection," *Works*, 11:381,426,443.

CHAPTER THREE

[1]Wesley dated his adherence to the principle of *ecclesiola in ecclesia* back to 1730. See "The Ministerial Office," *Works*, 7:279.

[2]"A Short History of the people called Methodists," *Works*, 13:307.

[3]Horneck was born in 1641 near Coblentz, and was educated at Heidelberg and Wittenberg. He came to England in 1661, and quickly made an impression at Queen's College, Oxford, with his Old Testament scholarship and his piety. He was ordained into the Church of England, and after a brief return to Germany, remained permanently in England as the preacher at the Savoy. See Richard B. Hone, *Lives of Eminent Christians*, 3 vols. (London: J.W. Parker, 1837-39), 2:287ff. See also the biographical sketch in Anthony Horneck, *Several Sermons upon the Fifth of St. Matthew; being part of Christ's Sermon on the Mount*, 2 vols., 3d ed. (London: Jer. Batley, 1717), 1:viiiff.

[4]Hone suggests (*Lives of Eminent Christians*, 2:322) that a factor in the formation of the religious societies was an attempt to combat the "favour shown to popery in high quarters, and the efforts it was making to regain possession of the public mind." Observing that the meetings were similar to those which "had not been incommon among the old puritans, and were still countenanced by the non-conformists," he proposes that perhaps "the exigencies of the times now recommended them to the notice and adoption of members of the church" (ibid., 2:323).

[5]Josiah Woodward, *An Account of the Rise and Progress of the Religious Societies in the City of London, &c., and of their Endeavours for the Reformation of Manners*, 1st ed., 1698, 5th ed. (London: J. Downing, 1724). A broader historical context is provided by Garnet V. Portus, *Caritas Anglicana; or, An Historical Inquiry into those Religious and Philanthropical Societies that flourished in England between the Years 1678 and 1740* (London: A.R. Mowbray & Co. Ltd., 1912). There is a good chapter in John S. Simon, *John Wesley and the Religious Societies* (London: Epworth Press, 1921), pp. 9-27; and some useful additional research has been added by David Pike, whose Leeds University thesis, "The Religious Societies in the Church of England (1678-1723) and their influence on Early Methodism," has been summarized in *WHS Proc.* 35 (1965-66): 15-20, 32-38.

[6]Woodward, *Account*, p. 134.

[7]Ibid., pp. 136-38.

[8]Ibid., pp. 139-40.

[9]Ibid., pp. 141-47.

[10]Ibid., pp. 82-83.

[11]Ibid., p. 83.

[12]Ibid., p. 133.

[13]Ibid., pp. 121-23.

[14]Ibid.

[15]John S. Simon, *Wesley and the Religious Societies*, p. 23. See also *WHS Proc.* 13 (1922): 169-78.

[16]Woodward, *Account*, pp. 73-74. See also *An Account of the Societies for Reformation of Manners, in London and Westminster, And other Parts of the Kingdom. With A Persuasive to Persons of all Ranks, to be Zealous and Diligent in Promoting the Execution of the Laws against Prophaneness and Debauchery, For the Effecting a National Reformation* (London: Printed for B. Aylmer, 1699), p. 5.

[17]W.K. Lowther Clarke, *A History of the S.P.C.K.* (London: S.P.C.K., 1959), p. 3.

18Woodward, *Account*, pp. 75-76.

19*Journal*, 5:4,5n.,101,154 & n.

20W.O.B. Allen and Edmund McClure, *Two Hundred Years: The History of the Society for Promoting Christian Knowledge, 1698-1898* (London: S.P.C.K., 1898), pp. 87ff. Cf. *WHS Proc.* 35 (1965-66): 15, and Richard P. Heitzenrater, "John Wesley and the Oxford Methodists," pp. 170,245.

21Luke Tyerman, *The Life and Times of the Rev. Samuel Wesley, M.A., Rector of Epworth, and the father of the Revs. John and Charles Wesley, the founders of the Methodists* (London: Simpkin, Marshall & Co., 1866), pp. 220-21. The entire sermon is reproduced in *The Methodist Magazine* 37 (1814): 648-55, 727-36.

22This is included as an appendix to his *The Pious Communicant Rightly Prepar'd* (London: Printed for Charles Harper, 1700).

23Allen & McClure, *S.P.C.K.*, p. 89. The description of a society in Old Rumsey, Kent, cited by Woodward, was apparently the deciding factor for Samuel Wesley. The conditions facing the minister there were very similar to those at Epworth—"the people were very ignorant and irreligious, the place of Divine Worship indecently kept, and the public Service neither understood, nor attended" (*Account*, pp. 54-55).

24Allen & McClure, *S.P.C.K.*, p. 90-92.

25Ibid.

26*Journal*, 3:32-34.

27Ibid., 3:33. See also Frank Baker, *John Wesley and the Church of England*, p. 9, p. 342, n.16.

28*Journal*, 3:33.

29Maldwyn Edwards notes that, in her later years when she took up residence at the Foundery, Mrs. Wesley must have provided the same pastoral concern for the classes which met there. "To all the Methodist society she must have been a mother in God." *Family Circle: A Study of the Epworth Household in Relation to John and Charles Wesley* (London: Epworth Press, 1949), p. 84.

30*WHS Proc.* 35 (1965-66):17-20.

31Thomas Day, for example, one of the original trustees of the City Road Chapel, joined a Methodist society in February 1756, but regarded his membership with some diffidence, complaining about his class assignment, and maintaining ties with three other religious societies in the vicinity of Southwark. Likewise Charles Skelton, one of Wesley's preachers, left Methodism in 1753, and affiliated with a society which met in Globe Alley. See *WHS Proc.* 7 (1910):106-10. See also *Letters*, 3:152; *Journal*, 4:95n.

32*WHS Proc.* 35 (1965-66):19.

33See John Walsh, "Origins of the Evangelical Revival." This article is important for its perspective on the Revival as a whole, in which Wesley played the foremost, but not the only, leadership role. The preaching of George Whitefield, Howell Harris, and the Moravians, made just as forceful an impact on the religious societies. See also *George Whitefield's Journals; A new edition containing fuller material than any hitherto published* (London: The Banner of Truth Trust, 1960), pp. 87-89, 214-17; Garnet V. Portus, *Caritas Anglicana*, pp. 193ff.; and Frederic Platt, *WHS Proc.* 22 (1939-40):155-64.

34"James Hutton's Second Account of the Moravian Work in England, down to the year 1747," *WHS Proc.* 15 (1926):208.

35Allen & McClure, *S.P.C.K.*, p. 127.

36Julia Wedgwood, *John Wesley and the Evangelical Reaction of the Eighteenth Century* (London: Macmillan and Co., 1870), pp. 156-57.

37A concise summary of this period can be found in Clifford W. Towlson, *Moravian and*

Methodist: Relationships and Influences in the Eighteenth Century (London: Epworth Press, 1957), pp. 21ff. See also William George Addison, *The Renewed Church of the United Brethren, 1722-1930* (London: S.P.C.K., 1932), pp. 146ff.

[38] See Matthew Spinka, *John Hus' Concept of the Church* (Princeton, N.J.: Princeton University Press, 1966), pp. 255ff. Hus adopted the ecclesiology of John Wyclif, affirming that belief should not be in the church, but in God alone, the universal church being the mystical body of Christ of which he alone is the head. This effectively opened the way for a royal control of church and state, which later came to political fruition in the Protestant Reformation. See Michael Wilks, "Reformatio Regni: Wyclif and Hus as Leaders of Religious Protest Movements," in *Schism, Heresy and Religious Protest*, Studies in Church History, vol. 9, ed. Derek Baker (Cambridge: at the University Press, 1972), pp. 109-30. For an insight into the connectedness of radical Christianity during the late medieval period, see John Passmore, *The Perfectibility of Man* (New York: Scribner's Sons, 1970), pp. 212ff. See also Norman Cohn, *The Pursuit of the Millenium*, pp. 205ff.

[39] Two early histories of Moravianism remain important resources: David Cranz, *The Ancient and Modern History of the Brethren, or, a Succinct Narrative of the Protestant Church of the United Brethren, or Unitas Fratrum, In the remoter Ages, and particularly in the present Century*, tr. Benjamin La Trobe (London: W. and A. Strahan, 1780); and Henry Rimius, *A Candid Narrative of the Rise and Progress of the Hermhuters, commonly called Moravians, or, Unitas Fratrum; with a short Account of their Doctrines, drawn from their own Writings* (London: Printed for A. Linde, 1753).

Also useful is J.E. Hutton, *A Short History of the Moravian Church* (London: Moravian Publication Office, 1895), and the relevant chapters in J. Taylor Hamilton and Kenneth G. Hamilton, *History of the Moravian Church: The Renewed Unitas Fratrum* (Bethlehem, Pa.: Interprovincial Board of Christian Education, Moravian Church in America, 1967).

The definitive study of early Moravianism, however, is Gillian Lindt Gollin, *Moravians in Two Worlds* (New York: Columbia University Press, 1967). This makes considerable use of materials in Moravian archives at Herrnhut and in the United States, and sheds important new light on the formation of *choirs* and *bands*.

[40] For a biography of one of their most important leaders in this regard, see Matthew Spinka, *John Amos Comenius, That Incomparable Moravian* (Chicago, Illinois: University of Chicago Press, 1943), pp. 50ff. See also A.J. Lewis, *Zinzendorf, The Ecumenical Pioneer: A Study in the Moravian Contribution to Christian Mission and Unity* (Philadelphia: Westminster Press, 1962), pp. 34ff.; and Norman Cohn, *Pursuit of the Millenium*, pp. 156ff.

[41] Spener first published his ideas in the *Pia Desideria* of 1675, the name *Pietist* first being used in ridicule at Frankfurt in 1674. See above, p. 154, n. 22.

[42] Wesley visited Halle in 1738, and was familiar with the work of the Pietists. See *Journal*, 2:58.

[43] Woodward, *Account*, pp. 20ff. See also Allen and McClure, *S.P.C.K.*, pp. 113-14.

[44] Cited in A.J. Lewis, *Zinzendorf*, p. 23.

[45] Christian David's spiritual pilgrimage is poignantly on record in Wesley's *Journal*, 2:28ff.

[46] Cited in Gillian Lindt Gollin, *Moravians in Two Worlds*, pp. 26f. See also Henry Rimius, *Candid Narrative*, p. 21; J.T. & K.G. Hamilton, *History*, pp. 29ff.; and W.G. Addison, *Renewed Church*, pp. 40ff.

[47] In effect, this had to be an *ecclesiola* within the *ecclesia*. Even if Zinzendorf had wished

to renew the *Unitas Fratrum* at that time, the church and state law in Saxony would not
have allowed it. See A.J. Lewis, *Zinzendorf*, p. 52.

48 For details of these two documents, see Gollin, *Moravians in Two Worlds*, pp. 27ff.

49 Rimius, *Candid Narrative*, p. 21.

50 Ibid., pp. 21ff.; Gollin, *Moravians in Two Worlds*, pp. 69ff.; Cranz, *History*, pp. 114ff.

51 Or, *die Banden*. After 1736, they were known as *Kleine Gesellschaften*, little societies.
See W.G. Addison, *Renewed Church*, p. 61.

52 Martin Schmidt, *John Wesley*, 1:231-32.

53 Cited in C.W. Towlson, *Moravian and Methodist*, p. 185.

54 Cited ibid., from Spangenberg's *Leben des Grafen Zinzendorf*.

55 Cited ibid., and in Schmidt, *John Wesley*, 1:231.

56 For Zinzendorf, Christ was the sole means through which a person could hope to
understand God, but by sensation rather than ideas. "He did not break with [dogmatic
formulations] but he laid all the stress on the religious experience which those formularies should explain and guard. . . ." R. Newton Flew, *The Idea of Perfection: An
Historical Study of the Christian Ideal for the Present Life* (London: Oxford University
Press, 1934), p. 343.

57 Gollin, *Moravians in Two Worlds*, p. 68.

58 Ibid., p. 233, n.43.

59 Schmidt, *John Wesley*, 2:1:267.

60 W.G. Addison, *Renewed Church*, p. 44. The key clauses from this agreement affirmed
the Lutheran standards of church membership and the public worship of the Lutheran
church along with the right of the Moravians to retain their ancient constitution.

61 On Comenius, see above, n.40. For a discussion of the relationship between Zinzendorf and the episcopacy, see K.G. Hamilton, "The Office of the Bishop in the Renewed
Moravian Church," *Transactions of the Moravian Historical Society* 16.1 (1953):44.

62 Zinzendorf himself was so expelled in 1736 on a technicality, and set up a second
headquarters at Marienborn, where the first synod of the Renewed Church of the
Unitas Fratrum was held, effectively marking the beginning of the Count's world
travels. See J.T. and K.G. Hamilton, *History*, pp. 60ff.

The Schwenkfelders were followers of Caspar Schwenkfeld (1487-1541), whose
early support for Luther did not survive their differences, notably Schwenkfeld's radical
spiritualizing of the faith as exclusively an inner experience. His followers formed small
societies which continued to exist into the eighteenth century. See Lowell H. Zuck, ed.,
Christianity and Revolution, pp. 107ff.

63 *Journal*, 1:197-205. Cf. "A Short History of the People Called Methodists," *Works*,
13:305-6; *Oxford*, 25:495. See also Frank Baker, *Wesley to Asbury*, pp. 18ff.; and
C.W. Towlson, *Moravian and Methodist*, pp. 35ff.

64 *Journal*, 1:436ff.

65 Cited in Martin Schmidt, *John Wesley*, 1:229.

66 C.W. Towlson, *Moravian and Methodist*, pp. 186ff.

67 The exact nature of this society has been a point of dispute. See Frank Baker,
"Methodist Polity," p. 217. Cf. Martin Schmidt, *John Wesley*, 1:245; John S. Simon,
Wesley and Religious Societies, pp. 198-99.

68 Daniel Benham, *Memoirs of James Hutton; Comprising the Annals of His Life and
Connection with the United Brethren* (London: Hamilton, Adams, and Co., 1856),
pp. 8ff.

69 *Journal*, 1:458-59.

70 *Journal*, 2:3ff. Wesley remained committed to the bands in principle, however, and

was present at the Fetter Lane society meeting September 25, 1738 when additional rules concerning their implementation were approved (*Journal*, 2:77).

[71] Ibid., 2:20ff. Martin Schmidt observes that Wesley's record of the Herrnhut community has not been fully appreciated by Moravian historians (*John Wesley*, 1:286, n.3).

[72] As, for example, in his description of a funeral service, where he noted that even the burial ground was allocated according to sex and marital status (*Journal*, 2:22).

[73] *Oxford*, 25:561.

[74] The letter was not sent. Wesley notes that he held it back to make sure of his judgment in these criticisms (*Journal*, 2:496); though the differences which were to lead to the breach with the Fetter Lane society are already clear.

[75] As, for example, in his division of the bands at Bristol, which was essentially according to the Moravian pattern. See *Oxford*, 25:631ff.

[76] *Oxford*, 25:591.

[77] Luke Tyerman, *The Life and Times of Wesley*, 1:210.

[78] *Journal*, 2:71ff.

[79] See above, p. 41.

[80] "Mon. 2 [April 1739]—At four in the afternoon I submitted to be more vile, and proclaimed in the highways the glad tidings of salvation, speaking from a little eminence in a ground adjoining to the city to about three thousand people" (*Journal*, 2:172).

[81] *Journal*, 2:312.

[82] Ibid.

[83] Ibid., 2:314. Cf. Martin Schmidt, *John Wesley*, 2:1:40ff.

[84] *Journal*, 2:314.

[85] Ibid., 2:315.

[86] *John Wesley*, 2:1:99. "It would be tempting to say with extreme caution that this is another instance of a basic difference between the German and English temperament" (ibid.).

[87] "A Plain Account of the People called Methodists," *Works*, 8:253.

[88] *Journal*, 2:329.

[89] *A Serious Call*, pp. 68-69.

[90] *Minutes*, 1:23; "A Plain Account of Christian Perfection," *Works*, 11:402-3.

[91] *Journal*, 2:370.

[92] *Oxford*, 26:24ff. Cf. "An Answer to The Rev. Mr. Church's Remarks," *Works*, 8:376ff. See also Martin Schmidt, *John Wesley*, 2:1:39ff.

[93] *Journal*, 2:194.

[94] "Principles of a Methodist Farther Explained," *Works*, 8:441. Cf. *Minutes*, 1:39; "An Earnest Appeal," *Oxford*, 11:84-85.

[95] "A Plain Account of the People called Methodists," *Works*, 8:249. Cf. "Thoughts Upon Methodism," *Works*, 13:258-59; "A Short History of the People called Methodists," *Works*, 13:306-8.

[96] *The Nature, Design, and General Rules of the United Societies in London, Bristol, King's-wood, and Newcastle upon Tyne* (Newcastle upon Tyne: John Gooding, 1743), p. 3. See also *Works*, 8:269-71.

[97] This was at the root of his disagreement with the Moravians at Fetter Lane, and of the dispute with George Whitefield and John Cennick at Bristol and Kingswood. Wesley specified that the disciplinary action he took at Kingswood in February 1741 was not for differences of opinion, but for "scoffing at the Word and ministers of God . . . talebearing, back-biting, and evil speaking." The occasion was clearly a challenge of

doctrinal leadership as well as discipline. See *Journal*, 2:421f., 426ff.,430, and above, p. 73, n.82.

[98]*Journal*, 2:353.

[99]This included a rebuke from Isaac Watts, who informed Doddridge that his reported participation in services at Whitefield's Tabernacle had lowered the character of a Dissenting minister. See Geoffrey Nuttall, ed., *Philip Doddridge 1702-51: His contribution to English Religion* (London: Independent Press Ltd., 1951), pp. 25,83,93f. Wesley admired the catholic spirit of Doddridge, and sought his advice for the *Christian Library* (*Journal*, 3:206,244-45,326n.).

[100]"A Plain Account of the People called Methodists," *Works*, 8:250. Cf. "Large Minutes," *Works*, 8:300.

[101]"A Farther Appeal," *Oxford*, 11:306.

[102]*Rules of the United Societies*, p. 5; *Works*, 8:270.

[103]Ibid.

CHAPTER FOUR

[1]*Journal*, 2:197.

[2]Some interesting details gleaned from the London Gazette of 1713 and the poll-books of Bristol have been collated to give some suggestions, but inconclusively. See *WHS Proc.* 3 (1902);64-65; 19 (1934-35):65.

[3]*Journal*, 2:528; "Thoughts upon Methodism," *Works*, 13:259; "A Short History of the People called Methodists," *Works*, 13:310. The word *class* was a derivation of the Latin *classis* (division). See *Journal*, 2:528n. See also above, pp. 27f.

[4]"Thoughts upon Methodism," *Works*, 13:259.

[5]*Journal*, 2:535.

[6]"A Plain Account of the People called Methodists," *Works*, 8:253.

[7]Ibid., 8:254. The minutes of the 1744 Conference indicate that class meetings, in addition to society and band meetings, had already become established as a "prudential means of grace" (*Minutes* 1:18).

[8]"Plain Account," *Works*, 8:256ff.

[9]See also Jonathan Crowther, *A True and Complete Portraiture of Methodism; or the History of the Wesleyan Methodists: including their Rise, Progress, and Present State &c.* (New York: James Eastburn, 1813), p. 229; and George J. Stevenson, *City Road Chapel, London, and its Associations Historical, Biographical, and Memorial* (London: 1872), p. 29.

[10]Leslie F. Church, *The Early Methodist People* (London: Epworth Press, 1948), p. 156.

[11]The best available collection remains Thomas Jackson's *The Lives of Early Methodist Preachers*. Many of these accounts first appeared in the *Arminian Magazine* (1778ff.), which is likewise a goldmine for descriptions of class meeting experiences.

[12]Joseph Nightingale, *A Portraiture of Methodism: being An Impartial View of the Rise, Progress, Doctrines, Discipline, and Manners of the Wesleyan Methodists. In a Series of Letters, Addressed to a Lady* (London: For Longman, Hurst, Rees, and Orme, 1807), p. xi.

[13]Ibid., pp. 185-88. The account includes several hymns under headings cited from the *Methodist Hymn Book*: "Praying for Repentance," "A Mourner convinced of Sin," "A Mourner brought to the Birth," "Rejoicing," "A Believer groaning for full Redemption."

176 Notes for Pages 97–101

Only one of these hymns, "My God, I am thine! What a comfort divine!", is to be found in modern Methodist hymnody.

14 Ibid., pp. 181-89. Cf. Crowther, *Portraiture*, p. 228; William Peirce, *The Ecclesiastical Principles and Polity of the Wesleyan Methodists*, 3d ed., rev. Frederick J. Jobson (London: Wesleyan Conference Office, 1873), pp. 77-78.

15 E.P. Thompson, *English Working Class*, p. 38.

16 *General Rules*, p. 3; cf. *Works*, 8:270. See also "A Plain Account of the People called Methodists," *Works*, 8:253; "The Large Minutes," *Works*, .8:301; "Thoughts upon Methodism," *Works*, 13:259.

17 Wesley's lay preachers were initially styled as *helpers*, and were authorized, in the absence of a minister, to "feed and guide the flock" (*Minutes*, 1:14ff.). At the 1749 Conference, certain preachers were designated *assistants*, to be appointed in circuits to "take charge of the Societies, and the other Preachers therein" (*Minutes*, 1:39ff). For the development of the role of lay preaching in Methodist polity, see Frank Baker, "The People called Methodists: Polity," pp. 230ff.

18 *Letters*, 8:196. See also ibid., 6:293; 7:205; 8:244. The *stewards*, a term we have already noted in the Anglican religious societies (above, pp. 68f., 73), were responsible for the temporal affairs of the Methodist connection. They too were appointed by Wesley or his assistants. Frank Baker, "The People called Methodists: Polity," pp. 226ff.

19 *Journal*, 5:403ff.; *Letters*, 7:385.

20 "A Plain Account of the People called Methodists," *Works*, 8:254-55.

21 *Letters*, 7:227.

22 Ibid., 8:20.

23 Ibid., 7:166.

24 See Wellman J. Warner, *The Wesleyan Movement in the Industrial Revolution* (London: Longmans, Green and Co., 1930), pp. 248-67, where there is an illuminating biographical survey of sixty-three of the first generation of Methodist preachers as listed by William Myles in *A Chronological History of the People called Methodists; from their rise in the year 1729, to their last Conference in 1802*, 3d ed., enlarged (London, 1803), pp. 445-49.

The progression is likewise illustrated throughout Jackson's *Lives*. It continued in the nineteenth century, not only in Wesleyan Methodism, but in the various breakaway movements. See, for example, William W. Stamp, *Historical Notices of Wesleyan Methodism, in Bradford and its vicinity* (London: Mason, 1841), p. 69; W.R. Sunman, *The History of Free Methodism in and about Newcastle-on-Tyne* (Newcastle-on-Tyne: A. Dickson, 1902), p. 202; William Garner, *The Life of The Rev. and Venerable William Clowes, one of the patriarchs of the Primitive Methodist Connexion* (London: William Lister, 1868), pp. 110,112.

25 Jackson, *Lives*, 3:71.

26 Ibid., 3:69-70.

27 Ibid., 3:82. Cf. *Oxford*, 26:430 & n.6.

28 William W. Stamp, *The Orphan-House of Wesley; with notices of early Methodism in Newcastle-upon-Tyne, and its vicinity* (London: John Mason, 1863), pp. 121ff. This account does not date his appointment, but it was possibly during Wesley's visits of 1757 or 1759 (*Journal*, 4:220-22,323-26).

29 Jackson, *Lives*, 5:128. See also Leslie F. Church, *More about the Early Methodist People*, p. 236.

30 Charles L. Goodell, *The Drillmaster of Methodism; principles and methods for the class leader and pastor* (New York: Eaton & Mains, 1902), passim.

[31] Robert Southey, *The Life of Wesley; and the Rise and Progress of Methodism*, 2d. ed., 2 vols. (London: Longman, Hurst, Rees, Orme, and Brown, 1820), 2:211-12.

[32] Nightingale, *Portraiture*, p. 273.

[33] *Journal*, 5:298-99.

[34] E.P. Thompson, *English Working Class*, pp. 370ff.; W.R. Sunman, *Free Methodism in Newcastle-on-Tyne*, pp. 35,102,210; J.J. Graham, *A History of Wesleyan Methodism in Sheffield Park, Sheffield* (Sheffield: Sir W.C. Leng & Co., 1914), pp. 155-56.

[35] *The Wesley Banner and Revival Record* 1 (1849):72-73. Later in the century, John Atkinson surveyed the qualities of a class leader more pragmatically. There were, he suggested, six necessary attributes: a working spirit, blamelessness, common sense, intelligence, sympathy, and enthusiasm (*The Class Leader: his work and how to do it* [New York: Phillips and Hunt, 1882], pp. 22-54). See also John E. Coulson, *The Peasant Preacher: Memorials of Mr. Charles Richardson, A Wesleyan Evangelist, commonly known as the "Lincolnshire Thrasher"; with Sermon Notes and an Itinerary* (London: Hamilton, Adams, and Co., 1865), pp. 40-41,44-45,214-15.

[36] *General Rules*, p. 4; *Works*, 8:269.

[37] Rom. 16:1-2; I Cor. 16:3,10-11; 2 Cor. 8:22-23; Col. 4:7ff. See also C.K. Barrett, *A Commentary on The Second Epistle to the Corinthians* (New York: Harper & Row, 1973), p. 106. The Moravians in England used metal tokens for a time to admit outsiders to their meetings where a serious desire to study their faith was evidenced (*WHS Proc.* 5 [1905-6]:34).

[38] *Journal*, 2:429-30,442ff. See also above, p. 174, n.97.

[39] "A Plain Account of the People called Methodists," *Works*, 8:256-57. Cf. Tyerman, *Wesley*, 1:286.

[40] *Journal*, 3:284-85. This contrasts with a visit to Whitehaven in 1751: "In meeting the classes the next two days, I observed one remarkable circumstance: without an absolute necessity, none of this society ever miss their class. Among near two hundred and forty persons, I met one single exception, and no more" (Ibid., 3:521).

[41] *Minutes*, 1:12,14,40,62ff.,95; *Letters*, 2:300; 4:271-72; 5:345; 6:6,312,359-60; 7:258,274; 8:94,137,147. Cf. Jackson, *Lives*, 4:195; and Robert Dickinson, *The Life of the Rev. John Braithwaite*, p. 192.

[42] *Minutes*, 1:12; Crowther, *Portraiture*, p. 224.

[43] Manuscript letters in the private collection of Dr. Frank Baker, reproduced in full as Appendix J.

[44] *Letters*, 4:194.

[45] *Letters*, 6:208.

[46] *Letters*, 4:273; 8:36,98,197.

[47] Crowther, *Portraiture*, pp. 229-30.

[48] *Journal*, 4:186; 5:83; *Letters*, 4:194,253; 6:208,210,240.

[49] "On Family Religion," *Works*, 7:80-82; "An Answer to The Rev. Mr. Church," *Works*, 8:412-13; "Farther Thoughts on Separation," *Works*, 13:272; *Letters*, 7:224; *Minutes*, 1:57,82.

[50] *Journal of Mr. John Nelson; being an account of God's dealing with his soul from his youth to the forty-second year of his age, and his working by him: Likewise the Oppressions he met with from People of different Denominations*, Written by Himself. With an Introductory Essay by William Reed (London: W. Reed, United Methodist Free Churches' Book Room, 1870), p. 52. See also Jackson, *Lives*, 5:70-71.

[51] *Oxford*, 26:94-95.

[52] *Journal*, 3:276-77. Wesley regarded Hague very highly, as one who "never left his first love, never was weary or faint, but daily grew in grace" (ibid., 3:495).

53A class book of 1820 uses slightly different language: "*Q.* for doubtful; when the true state of the member is not yet discovered. *a.* for one who is a penitent; who is seeking for salvation, but does not profess to enjoy living faith in Christ. *o.* for one who professes to be in a state of justification. *b.* one who meets in band (*A Class Book; containing Directions to Class-Leaders, Rules Forms for Leaders' Weekly Accounts, and The Rules of the Methodist Societies* [London: Printed by T. Cordeux for T. Blanchard, 1820], p. 7). Cf. Appendix I. See also W.J. Townsend, H.B. Workman, and George Eayrs, eds., *A New History of Methodism,* 2 vols. (London: Hodder and Stoughton, 1909), 1:308n.

54*A Collection of Hymns, for the Use of the People called Methodists,* Preface by John Wesley, London, Oct. 20, 1779 (London: Paramore, 1780); see also vol. 7 of the *Oxford Edition of the Works of John Wesley,* ed. Franz Hildebrandt and Oliver Beckerlegge, asst. James Dale (Oxford: at the Clarendon Press, 1983), pp. 77f. Cf. Nightingale, *Portraiture,* pp. 185ff.

55"A Plain account of the People called Methodists," *Works,* 8:254. Cf. Appendix J, p. (6).

56Thomas Martin, *Thoughts on the Nature and Advantages of Class-Meeting, (As Adopted in the Methodist Societies:) Including an Account of the Origin, Authority, and General Oeconomy of that Institution: Intended to Explain and Recommend it, to whomsoever it may concern* (London: Printed at the Conference Office by Thomas Cordeux, 1813).

57This extract from Martin's *Thoughts* appeared in *The Independent Methodist Magazine* I (1826):680-85, and *The Wesleyan Methodist Association Magazine* 4(1841):123-26.

58This is the underlying concern of the writer of the correspondence in Appendix J, who stresses throughout that enquiring into the state of the members' souls is not enough. There must also be a regular accounting for the General Rules of the Societies—not a legalistic catechesis, but a balance between the experience engendered by the weekly meeting and its purpose. It is in this regard that the class meeting also functioned as an important means of Christian instruction. See D. Michael Henderson, "Christian Education: Instructional Theology," in *A Contemporary Wesleyan Theology: Biblical, systematic and Practical,* 2 vols., ed. Charles W. Carter, R. Duane Thompson, and Charles R. Wilson (Grand Rapids, Michigan: Francis Asbury Press, 1983), 2:868f.

59Leslie F. Church, *Early Methodist People,* pp. 149-50.

60"A Plain Account of the People called Methodists," *Works,* 8:257-58.

61Ibid., 8:259. See also *Journal,* 5:85; *Letters,* 4:194,255,272-73; 5:20; 7:166,247,253, 259,301; 8:57.

62See Appendix H.

63*Minutes,* 1:11,12,14; *Letters,* 5:19,312; 6:291,378; 7:47,139,143; 8:57,99. See also the excerpts from Richard Viney's diary, *WHS Proc.* 14 (1923-24):52-53,193; and Stevenson, *City Road Chapel,* pp. 33ff.

64"A Plain Account of the People called Methodists," *Works,* 8:258.

65John Braithwaite noted in 1816, for example, that Saturday evening public band meetings, held in the vestry of the Bradford society, generally had two hundred people present, who spoke "very freely, and with uncommon simplicity" (Robert Dickinson, *John Braithwaite,* p. 489).

66Crowther, *Portraiture,* p. 242. Cf. Nightingale, *Portraiture,* p. 199; and Jackson, *Lives,* 5:159. It is not clear when the *body band* became the means of the weekly visitation of the bands by the preachers, but by the early nineteenth century it seems to have been the general rule. See James Leslie, *An Address to the Weslean [sic] Methodist Preachers and Leaders of Edinburgh. By two members of the Society* (Edinburgh, 1826), pp. 7,10-12; John E. Coulson, *Peasant Preacher,* p. 241. See also W.R. Ward, *Early*

Victorian Methodism: The Correspondence of Jabez Bunting 1830-1858. University of Durham Publications (Oxford: Oxford University Press, 1976), pp. 37,241.

67Jackson, *Lives,* 6:26.

68Nightingale, *Portraiture,* p. 193.

69Crowther, *Portraiture,* p. 238.

70Dickinson, *Braithwaite,* p. 231.

71Ibid., pp. 249ff.

72Cf. ibid., pp. 34-37, 83-85.

73Nightingale, *Portraiture,* pp. 193ff.; Sunman, *Free Methodism in Newcastle-on-Tyne,* p. 29; Leslie, *Address,* pp. 7ff.; Gilbert Murray (Richard Newman Wycherley), *The Methodist Class Meeting* (London: Robert Cully, n.d.), p. 146; William Peirce, *Ecclesiastical Principles,* 3d ed., revised by Frederick J. Jobson (London: Wesleyan Conference Office, 1873), pp. 81ff.; James Rosser, *The History of Wesleyan Methodism in the Isle of Man* (London: J. Mason, 1849), p. 49; John Atkinson, *Class Leader,* p. 208.

74Cited in Nightingale, *Portraiture,* p. 195. Cf. Southey, *Wesley,* 2:112.

75"A Plain Account of the People called Methodists," *Works,* 8:259.

76Ibid. See also "A Second Letter to the Author of the Enthusiasm of Methodists and Papists compar'd," *Oxford,* 11:423-24, where Wesley cites James 5:16 as the New Testament authority for mutual confession in Christian fellowship. For various practices of this in the early church, see Trevor Dearing, *Wesleyan and Tractarian Worship* (London: Epworth Press, 1966), pp. 63f.,74. Cf. William H. Rule, *Wesleyan Methodism regarded as the system of a Christian Church* (London: Aylott & Jones, 1846), pp. 18ff.

77"A Plain Account of the People called Methodists," *Works,* 8:259.

78*Letters,* 3:214. Cf. ibid., 6:14.

79*Journal,* 1:377.

80Ibid., 2:121ff. The best account of the origins and usage of the Lovefeast in Methodism remains Frank Baker, *Methodism and the Lovefeast* (London: Epworth Press, 1957). Some useful insights can also be found in John Bishop, *Methodist Worship in Relation to Free Church Worship* (Scholar Studies Press, Inc., 1975), pp. 88ff. Cf. Crowther, *Portraiture,* pp. 239ff.; Nightingale, *Portraiture,* pp. 201-13.

81"A Plain Account of the People called Methodists," *Works,* 8:258-59; "The Large Minutes," *Works,* 8:307; *Minutes,* 1:12.

82Bishop, *Methodist Worship,* p. 89n.; Church, *More about Early Methodist People,* p.237.

83"A Plain Account of the People called Methodists," *Works,* 8:260.

84Ibid.

85Ibid., 8:261.

86*Minutes,* 1:14-15; *Letters,* 5:198; 6:21; 7:158,291,304,392; 8:175.

87Note Wesley's description of a select society meeting at Newcastle upon Tyne in 1749: "Such a flame broke out as was never there before. We felt such a love to each other as we could not express; such a spirit of supplication, and such a glad acquiescence in all the providence of God, and confidence that He would withhold from us no good thing" (*Journal,* 3:441). Cf. *Letters,* 7:253; 8:254. See also Jackson, *Lives,* 6:57,183; and Myles, *History,* pp. 32-34.

88"A Plain Account of the People called Methodists," *Works,* 8:259-60; *Minutes,* 1:14; Crowther, *Portraiture,* p. 224.

89The phrase "in band" became common usage in describing a band member as opposed to one who met only in class. See, for example, *Journal,* 2:400.

[90]*Minutes*, 1:5. See also above, p. 57.
[91]"A Plain Account of Christian Perfection," *Works*, 11:401-2. The personal testimonies of many of Wesley's preachers are a further evidence of this, their language invariably being that of surrender, the submission of the will to the grace of God. See, for example, Jackson, *Lives*, 5:235-36; 6:216-17; Coulson, *Peasant Preacher*, p. 38; Stevenson, *City Road Chapel*, pp. 531-32; Dickinson, *Braithwaite*, pp. 145,317-18,401-5.
[92]"A Plain Account of Christian Perfection," *Works*, 11:402-3.
[93]Ibid., 11:395-96.
[94]*Letters*, 8:254.
[95]Michael Hill and Bryan Turner, "John Wesley and the Origin and Decline of Ascetic Devotion," in *A Sociology Yearbook of Religion in Britain—4*, ed. Michael Hill (London: SCM Press, 1971), pp. 110ff.

CHAPTER FIVE

[1]Victor Turner, *The Ritual Process: Structure and Anti-Structure* (Chicago: Aldine Publishing Co., 1969; reprint ed. Ithaca, N.Y.: Cornell University Press, 1977), pp. 131-65.
[2]Ibid., p. 132.
[3]Ibid., pp. 139-40.
[4]W.C. Schutz, *FIRO: A Three-Dimensional Theory of Interpersonal Behavior* (New York: Holt, Rinehart and Winston, 1958).
[5]Warren G. Bennis, Edgar H. Schein, David E. Berlew, and Fred I. Steele, *Interpersonal Dynamics: Essays and Readings on Human Interaction*, 2d ed. (Holmewood, Illinois: The Dorsey Press, 1968), p. 16.
[6]Kurt W. Back, *Beyond Words: The Story of Sensitivity Training and the Encounter Movement* (Baltimore, Md.: Penguin Books Inc., 1973), pp. 103ff.
[7]Carl R. Rogers, *Carl Rogers on Encounter Groups* (New York: Harper & Row, 1970), pp. 122-25. See also the important study by Thomas C. Oden, *The Intensive Group Experience: The New Pietism* (Philadelphia: Westminster Press, 1972), and especially pp. 69-77, where contemporary group dynamics are contrasted with the early Methodist class meeting and other small groups in the history of Pietism.
[8]Carl R. Rogers, *Encounter Groups*, p. 116. Cf. pp. 70-71.
[9]Kurt W. Back, *Beyond Words*, pp. 77-78.
[10]Herbert Butterfield, "England in the Eighteenth Century," in *A History of the Methodist Church in Great Britain, Vol. 1*, pp. 23ff.
[11]Gerald R. Cragg, *The Church and the Age of Reason, 1648-1789* (Baltimore, Md.: Penguin Books, 1960), p. 234.
[12]Peter Matthias, *The First Industrial Nation: An Economic History of Britain 1700-1914*, 2d ed. (New York: Methuen, 1983), pp. 52-61; E.J. Hobsbawm, *Identity and Empire: The Making of Modern English Society. Vol. 2: 1750 to the Present Day* (New York: Pantheon Books, 1968), pp. 20,24ff. See also W.E. Tate, *The English Village Community and the Enclosure Movements* (London: Gollancz, 1967).
[13]J.L. and Barbara Hammond, *The Village Labourer* (London: Longmans, Green & Co. Ltd., 1911; repr. ed. Guild Books, 2 vols., 1948), 1:14,124ff.
[14]Peter Laslett, *The World We Have Lost: England Before the Industrial Age* (New York: Charles Scribner's Sons, 1965), p. 18. Cf. J.L. and Barbara Hammond, *The Town*

Labourer (1760-1832) (London: Longmans, Green and Co. Ltd., 1917; reprint ed. Guild Books, 2 vols., 1949), 1:53ff.

[15]Robert F. Wearmouth, *Methodism and the Common People*, pp. 19ff., 77ff. See also George Rudé, *The Crowd in History, 1730-1848* (New York: John Wiley and Sons, 1964), and *Paris and London in the Eighteenth Century: Studies in Popular Protest* (New York: The Viking Press, 1973), Cf. Hammonds, *Town Labourer*, 1:69ff.

[16]Wearmouth, *Methodism and the Common People*, p. 202.

[17]The figures are taken from G. Talbot Griffith, *Problems of the Age of Malthus*, 2d ed. (London: Frank Cass & Company, 1967), p. 18, and correlated with evidence presented by J.D. Chambers, *Population, Economy, and Society in Pre-Industrial England*, ed. W.A. Armstrong (London: Oxford University Press, 1972), pp. 107-27. Cf. John Wesley's own estimate of the population which, contrary to official figures at the time, comes much closer to Griffith's calculations (*Journal*, 6:127; "A Calm Address to the Inhabitants of England," *Works*, 11:142-43).

[18]These figures are taken from the *Minutes*, adjusted to exclude the membership of societies in Scotland, Ireland, America and the Isle of Man. 1766 was the first year they were published.

[19]*Arminian Magazine* 1 (1778): 543; 2(1779):25f.,80,184,242,297f. & passim.

[20]For example, almost five hundred anti-Methodist pamphlets were published between 1738 and 1791. See Donald H. Kirkham, "Pamphlet Opposition to the Rise of Methodism," (Duke University PhD. Dissertation, 1973). A major factor in the decision to publish the *Arminian Magazine* was the perceived need for a Methodist polemical outlet.

[21]Wearmouth, *Methodism and the Common People*, p. 182. See also the helpful chart in Gloster S. Udy, *Key to Change* (Sydney, Australia, 1962), p. 90. Udy's study, which has not received the attention it deserves, is a major contribution to the sociological understanding of the class meeting, then and now.

[22]Kurt Lewin, *Field Theory in Social Science* (New York: Harper, 1951).

[23]It is noteworthy, given contemporary stereotypes, that as often as not these conversions took place in private some time afterwards. See, for example, Jacob Hallas Drew, *The Life, Character, and Literary Labours of Samuel Drew, A.M., by his elder son* (London: Longman, Rees, Orme, Brown, Green & Longman, 1934), pp. 72ff.; *A Memoir of Mr. William Carvosso, Sixty Years a Class Leader in the Wesleyan Methodist Connection*, from the 10th edition (New York: Lane & Scott, 1849), pp. 32ff.; *Memoir of The Rev. Joseph Entwhistle, Fifty-four Years a Wesleyan Minister*, by his son (Bristol, 1848), pp. 10f. See also Jackson, *Lives*, 3:309, 6:274-75; Dickinson, *Braithwaite*, pp. 13ff.; *Methodist Magazine*, 21:3ff.,16ff.,53ff.,123 & passim. Cf. William B. Lewis, "The Conduct and Nature of the Methodist Class Meeting," in *Spiritual Renewal for Methodism: A Discussion of the Early Methodist Class Meeting and the Values Inherent in Personal Groups Today*, ed. Samuel Emerick (Nashville: Methodist Evangelistic Materials, 1958), p. 25.

[24]And especially the sacrament, as in the case of Peter Jaco, one of the earliest of Wesley's assistants (Jackson, *Lives*, 1:262).

[25]The directions for study in this area were set by Kurt W. Back in "Influence through Social Communication," *Journal of Abnormal and Social Psychology* 46 (1951):9-23.

[26]Leon Festinger and Elliot Aaronson, "Arousal and Reduction of Dissonance in Social Contexts," in *Group Dynamics: Research and Theory*, 3d ed., edited by Dorwin Cartwright and Alvin Zander (Evanston, Illinois: Row, Peterson & Company, 1968), p. 125. See also Leon Festinger, *A Theory of Cognitive Dissonance* (Evanston, Illinois:

Row, Peterson and Company, 1957). The theory is the basis of a detailed investigation by Thorvald Källstad, *John Wesley and the Bible: A Psychological Study* (Stockholm: Nya Bokförlags Aktiebolaget, 1974).

[27]See Alex Bavelas, "Communication Patterns in Task-Oriented Groups," in Cartwright and Zander, *Group Dynamics*, pp. 503-11.

[28]Ernst Troeltsch, *The Social Teaching of the Christian Churches*, 2 vols., reprint ed. (Chicago: University of Chicago Press, 1976), 2:461-62. The work of Bryan R. Wilson is important in the development of this concept. See "Analysis of Sect Development" in *Patterns of Sectarianism: Organization and Ideology in Social and Religious Movements*, ed. Bryan R. Wilson (London: Heinemann, 1967), pp. 24-45. See also his *Religion in a Secular Society* (Baltimore, Md.: Penguin Books, 1966).

[29]Ibid., 2:723.

[30]*John Wesley's Letter to a Roman Catholic*, ed. Michael Hurley (Nashville: Abingdon, Press, 1968), p. 28.

[31]I have addressed this issue in "Professing the Call to Serve: Vocation, Competence, and Identity in the Ministerial Office," *Quarterly Review* 2.1 (Spring 1982):27-42.

[32]On this see John C. Bowmer, *Pastor and People: A Study of Church and ministry in Wesleyan Methodism from the death of John Wesley (1791) to the death of Jabez Bunting (1858)* (London: Epworth Press, 1975), pp. 163ff., 198ff. See also the helpful chart provided by Robert Currie, *Methodism Divided: A Study in the Sociology of Ecumenicalism* (London: Faber & Faber, 1968), p. 54, indicating the various divisions and unions which led to the Methodist Church of 1932.

[33]So Albert C. Outler, "Do Methodists have a Doctrine of the Church?" in *The Doctrine of the Church*, ed. Dow Kirkpatrick (Nashville: Abingdon Press, 1964), pp. 20ff.

[34]As, for example, on the issue of slavery in the United States. See "Orange Scott, Luther Lee, and the Wesleyan Methodists," in Donald W. Dayton, *Discovering an Evangelical Heritage* (New York: Harper & Row, 1976), pp. 73-84. In England the challenge came most especially from the Kilhamites, or New Connexion, and from the Primitive Methodists. See E.J. Hobsbawm, *Labouring Men: Studies in the History of Labour* (New York: Basic Books, Inc., 1964), pp. 25ff.; E.P. Thompson, *English Working Class*, pp. 390ff.

[35]Henry Rack, "The Decline of the Class-Meeting and the Problems of Church-Membership in Nineteenth-Century Wesleyanism," *WHS Proc.* 39 (1973-74):12-21. The decline of the class meeting in the United States, at once more swift and pervasive, is a study in itself. The factors were the social development of early American Methodism, which changed its focus in the nineteenth century to rural and frontier evangelism, the topography of which was more conducive to the camp meeting than that of the class, and also the move towards a parish-oriented form of pastorate, rather than the circuit system which relied more heavily on the class leader. American exhortations to retain the class meeting indicate that this office had come to be regarded primarily as that of sub-pastor—a subtle change of emphasis, but profoundly different from its original purpose and function. See John Miley, *A Treatise on Class Meetings* (Cincinnati: The Methodist Book Concern, 1851; L. Rosser, *Class Meetings: Embracing their Origin, Nature, Obligation and Benefits* (Richmond: Published by the Author, 1855). See also Charles W. Ferguson, *Methodists and the Making of America: Organizing to Beat the Devil*, 2d. ed. (Austin, Texas: Eakin Press, 1983), pp. 69-77, 149f.; Frank Baker, *Wesley to Asbury*, pp. 76,104; J. Artley Leatherman, "The Decline of the Class Meeting," in Samuel Emerick, ed., *Spiritual Renewal*, pp. 44f.

[36]Ibid., pp. 14-15. See also Robert Currie, *Methodism Divided*, pp. 125ff., where the

decline of the class meeting is linked to a growing respectability among Methodists and a move away from experiential ritual towards a more formalized worship. Cf. Goodell, *Drillmaster of Methodism*, pp. 75ff.

[37]Rack, "Decline of Class Meeting," p. 21.

[38]William W. Dean, "The Methodist Class Meeting: The Significance of its Decline," *Proceedings of the Wesley Historical Society* 53.3 (December 1981):41-48.

[39]Ibid., p. 43.

[40]Ibid., p. 48.

[41]Elie Halévy, *A History of the English People in the Nineteenth Century*, vol. 1, tr. and ed. E.I. Watkin and D.A. Barker, intr. by R.B. McCallum (New York: Barnes & Noble, 1961).

[42]Elie Haléy, *The Birth of Methodism in England*, tr. and intr. Bernard Semmel (Chicago: University of Chicago Press, 1971).

[43]Ibid. pp. 8ff.

[44]Ibid., p. 33.

[45]Ibid., p. 76.

[46]Bernard Semmel, *The Methodist Revolution* (New York: Basic Books, 1973), p. 5.

[47]Ibid., p. 198.

[48]Cited in Robert F. Wearmouth, *Methodism and the Working-Class Movements of England 1800-1850* (London: The Epworth Press, 1937), pp. 95-96. In some societies, class tickets were adopted (ibid., p. 99).

[49]Cited ibid., p.' 119.

[50]Cited ibid., p. 146.

[51]E.P. Thompson, *English Working Class*, pp. 352ff.

[52]See W.R. Ward, *Religion and Society in England 1790-1850* (New York: Schocken Books, 1973), pp. 35ff.,75ff.,236ff. See also the important earlier study by E.R. Taylor, *Methodism and Politics 1791-1851* (Cambridge: at the University Press, 1935). Robert Currie, *Methodism Divided*, remains the best documented survey of these developments.

[53]E.P. Thompson, *English Working Class*, pp. 388ff.

[54]See, however, the significant contribution of Robert Moore, *Pit-Men, Preachers and Politics: The Effects of Methodism in a Durham Mining Community* (Cambridge: Cambridge University Press, 1974). Taking issue with Thompson, Wearmouth, and the Halévy thesis in general ("Halévy seems to assume that the working class is a bovine mass without its own leadership and ideas." p. 6), Moore provides a historiographical rationale for a wealth of meticulous research.

What remains a *desideratum* is a response from the Christian tradition to the passion of E.P. Thompson in narratives such as the following: " [A Minister of Cragg Dale] related the story of a boy whom he had recently interred who had been found standing asleep with his arms full of wool and had been beaten awake. This day he had worked seventeen hours; he was carried home by his father, was unable to eat his supper, awoke at 4 a.m. the next morning and asked his brothers if they could see the lights of the mill as he was afraid of being late, and then died. (His younger brother, aged nine, had died previously: the father was 'sober and industrious', a Sunday School teacher)" (*English Working Class*, p. 347).

[55]Howard A. Snyder, *The Radical Wesley & Patterns for Church Renewal* (Downers Grove, Illinois: InterVarsity Press, 1980), p. 111.

[56]Ibid., p. 114.

[57]Ibid., pp. 150ff.

58Ernesto Cardenal, *The Gospel in Solentiname*, 4 vols. (Maryknoll: Orbis Books, 1976-82); *Sojourners Magazine*, ed. Jim Wallis. Published monthly by *Sojourners*, 1321 Otis Street N.E., Washington D.C. 20017; *the Other Side*, ed. Mark Olson and John F. Alexander, published monthly by *Jubilee, Inc.*, 300 West Apsley Street, Philadelphia, Pennsylvania 19144. See also Jim Wallis, *The Call to Conversion: Recovering the Gospel for These Times* (San Francisco: Harper & Row, 1981); Alfred C. Krass: *Evangelizing Neo-Pagan North America* (Scottdale, Pa.: Herald Press, 1982).

59Sergio Torres and John Eagleson, ed., *The Challenge of Basic Christian Communities* (Maryknoll: Orbis Books, 1981); Alvaro Barreiro, *Basic Ecclesial Communities: The Evangelization of the Poor* (Maryknoll: Orbis Books, 1982). See also Michel Bavarel, *New Communities, New Ministries: The Church Resurgent in Africa, Asia and Latin America* (Orbis Books, 1983); Joseph G. Healey, *A Fifth Gospel: The Experience of Black Christian Values* (Orbis Books, 1981); James G. O'Halloran, *Living Cells: Developing Small Christian Community* (Orbis Books, 1984); Rosemary Radford Ruether, "'Basic Communities': Renewal at the Roots," *Christianity and Crisis* 41.14 (September 21, 1981).

60Wellman J. Warner, *Wesleyan Movement in Industrial Revolution*, pp. 79ff., 166ff., 208ff.

61So E.J. Hobsbawm, *Labouring Men*, pp. 23-33; J.D. Walsh, "Elie Halévy and the Birth of Methodism," *Transactions of the Royal Historical Society*, Fifth Series, 25 (1975):20; Robert Moore, *Pit-Men, Preachers & Politics*, pp. 8ff.

62Such an interpretation of Wesley's *episkopé*—as, for example, in Robert Currie, *Methodism Divided*, pp. 22ff.—is open to serious question. Cf. *Letters*, 4:194; 6:208,210,240; 8:36,98,197.

63The entire poem is reproduced as Appendix M.

64Charles L. Goodell, *Drillmaster of Methodism*, pp. 139-40.

65Kurt W. Back, *Beyond Words*, p. xxi.

66So Mortimer Arias, *Announcing the Reign of God: Evangelization and the Subversive Memory of Jesus* (Philadelphia: Fortress Press, 1984), pp. 102,106,108.

67*Arminian Magazine*, 1:542, 2:418, 3:374-75 & passim; Jackson, *Lives*, 1:16,187-88, 2:241,297,4:171.

68This emerges vividly from the personal accounts of those who were introduced to the faith in this way, even as children. See, for example, Thornley Smith, *Memoir of the Rev. John Wesley Etheridge* (London: Hodder & Stoughton, 1871), p. 8: "My mother, who was a saint, took me when a child along with her to the class meeting, where the earliest sound impressions I ever felt came upon my heart."

69Theodore L. Agnew, "Methodism on the Frontier," in *The History of American Methodism*, ed. Emory Stevens Bucke, 3 vols. (Nashville: Abingdon Press, 1964), 1:541ff.

70In particular the Church Growth School. One of the best interpretative studies of this approach is George G. Hunter, *The Contagious Congregation* (Nashville: Abingdon Press, 1979).

71James W. Fowler, *Stages of Faith: The Psychology of Human Development and the Quest for Meaning* (San Francisco: Harper & Row, 1981).

72Theodore Runyon, "Wesley and the Theologies of Liberation," in *Sanctification and Liberation: Liberation Theologies in Light of the Wesleyan Tradition*, ed. Theodore Runyon (Nashville: Abingdon Press, 1981), pp. 27,32-33.

[73]Robert E. Cushman, "Salvation for All—John Wesley and Calvinism," in *Faith Seeking Understanding*, p. 74.

[74]Cf. Howard A. Snyder, *The Radical Wesley*, pp. 80ff., 121ff., where Wesley's view of the church as fallen is argued in some detail from his writings. The weight of evidence for Wesley's ecclesiology, however, quite apart from the many instances where he affirms the visible church (see above, pp. 9ff., 32ff.), remains the pattern of his ministry; and clearly this was "reaching out to all," whether or not the church measured up to the task. His mission was to take the gospel "where none else will go," and the state of the church was therefore of secondary concern. The distinction is a fine one, but in the final analysis Wesley was more churchman than radical. He had a basic mistrust of Nonconformity as an ecclesial distraction from the saving of souls.

[75]Sergio Torres and John Eagleson, ed., *Challenge of Basic Christian Communities*, p. 8.

APPENDICES

Appendix A

DR. HORNECK'S RULES FOR RELIGIOUS SOCIETIES

I. All that enter into such a Society, shall resolve upon an holy and serious life.

II. No Person shall be admitted into this Society, till he arrive at the Age of Sixteen, and hath been first confirmed by the Bishop, and solemnly taken upon himself his Baptismal Vow.

III. They [shall] chuse a Minister of the Church of *England* to direct them.

IV. They shall not be allowed, in their meetings, to discourse of any controverted Point of Divinity.

V. Neither shall they discourse of the Government of Church or State.

VI. In their meetings they [shall] use no Prayers, but those of the Church, such as the Litany and Collects, and other prescribed Prayers; but still they shall not use any that peculiarly belongs to the Minister, as the Absolution.

VII. The Minister whom they chuse, shall direct what practical Divinity shall be read as these meetings.

VIII. They may have liberty, after Prayer, and Reading, to sing a Psalm.

IX. After all is done, if there be Time left, they may discourse each other about their spiritual Concerns, but this shall not be a standing Exercise, which any shall be obliged to attend unto.

X. One Day in the Week [shall] be appointed for this meeting, for such as cannot come on the Lord's Day; and he that absents himself without Cause, shall pay Three-pence to the Box.

XI. Every Time they meet, every one shall give Six-pence to the Box.

XII. On a certain Day in the Year, *viz. Whitsun-Tuesday*, two Stewards shall be chosen, and a moderate Dinner provided, and a Sermon preached, and the Money distributed (necessary Charges deducted) to the Poor.

XIII. A Book shall be bought, in which these Orders shall be written.

XIV. None shall be admitted into this Society without the Consent of the Minister, who presides over it; and no Apprentice shall be capable of being chosen.

XV. If any Case of Conscience [shall] arise, it shall be brought before the Minister.

XVI. If any member think fit to leave the Society, he shall pay Five Shillings to the Stock.

XVII. The major Part of the Society [shall] conclude the rest.

XVIII. The following Rules are more especially to be commended to the Members of this Society, *viz.* To love one another: When reviled, not to revile again: To speak Evil of no Man: To wrong no Man: To pray, if possible, Seven Times a Day: To keep close to the Church of *England*: To transact all things peaceably and gently: To be helpful to each other: To use themselves to holy Thoughts in their coming in and going out: To examine themselves every Night: To give every one their due: To obey Superiors, both Spiritual and Temporal.

Reproduced from Anthony Horneck, *Several Sermons upon the Fifth of St. Matthew; Being Part of Christ's Sermon on the Mount. To which is added, The Life of the Author, by Richard, late Lord Bishop of Bath and Wells*, 2 vols., 3d ed. (London: Jer. Batley, 1717), pp. viii-x.

Appendix B

A SPECIMEN OF THE ORDERS OF THE RELIGIOUS SOCIETIES COPIED OUT OF THAT AT POPLER

I.

THAT the sole *Design* of this *Society* being to promote real Holiness of Heart and Life: It is absolutely necessary that the Persons who enter into it, do seriously resolve, by the Grace of God, to apply themselves to all means proper to accomplish these blessed Ends. Trusting in the divine Power and gracious Conduct of the holy Spirit, thro' our Lord Jesus Christ, to excite, advance, and perfect all Good in us.

II.

THAT in order to their being of *one Heart and one Mind* in this Design, every Member of this *Society* shall own and manifest himself to be of the Church of England, and frequent the *Liturgy*, and other publick Exercises of the same. And that they be careful withal to express due Christian *Charity, Candor* and *Moderation* towards all such Dissenters as are of good Conversation.

III.

THAT the Members of this *Society* shall meet together one Evening in the Week at a convenient Place, in order to encourage each other in *practical Holiness*, by discoursing on such Subjects, as tend thereunto; observing the holy Scriptures as their Rule; and praying to God for his Grace and Blessing.

AND to this Assembly any serious Person, known to any of the *Society*, may be admitted, upon Request.

IV.

THAT at such *Meetings* they decline all Disputes about Controversial Points, and all unnecessary Discourse about State-Affairs, or the Concerns of Trade and worldly Things: And that the whole Bent of the Discourse be to *glorifie God, and edifie one another in love.*

V.

THAT it be left to every Person's Discretion to contribute at every *Weekly Meeting*, what he thinks fit towards a *Publick Stock* for pious and charitable Uses; especially for putting poor Children to School: And the Money thus collected shall be kept by the two *Stewards* of the *Society*, who shall be chosen by majority of Votes once a Year, or oftener, to be disposed of by the Consent of the major part of the *Society*, for the Uses above-mentioned. And the said *Stewards* shall keep a faithful *Register* of what is thus collected and distributed, to be perused by any Member of the *Society*, at his Request.

VI.

THAT any respective Member may recommend any Object of Charity to the *Stewards*, who shall (with the Consent of the rest) give out of the *Common Stock*, according as the Occasion requires. And in a Case of extraordinary Necessity, every particular Person shall be desired to contribute farther, as he shall think fit.

VII.

THAT every one that absents himself four Meetings together, (without giving a satisfactory Account to the *Stewards*) shall be look'd upon as disaffected to the *Society*.

VIII.

THAT none shall be admitted into this *Society*, without giving due Notice thereof to the *Stewards*, who shall acquaint the whole *Society* therewith. And after due Enquiry into their Religious *Purposes*, and *manner of Life*, the Stewards may admit them, if the major part of the Society allows of it, and not otherwise. And with the like joint Consent, they may *exclude* any Member proved guilty of any Mis-behaviour, after due Admonition, unless he gives sufficient Testimony of his Repentance and Amendment, before the whole *Society*.

IX.

IT is hereby recommended to every Person concerned in this Society, to consider the dangerous Snares of Gaming; and the open Scandal of being concerned in those Games which are used in Publick Houses; and that it is the safest and most commendable way, to decline them wholly; shunning all unnecessary resort to such Houses and Taverns, and wholly avoiding lewd *Play-Houses*.

X.

THAT whereas the following Duties have been to [sic] much neglected, to the Scandal and Reproach of our holy Religion, they do resolve, by the Grace of God, to make it their serious Endeavour,

1. TO be *Just* in all their Dealings, even to an exemplary Strictness. As *1 Thess.* 4.6.

2. TO *pray* many times every Day: Remembring our continual Dependance upon God, both for Spiritual and Temporal things, *1 Thess.* 5.17.

3. TO partake of the *Lord's-Supper* at least once a Month, if not prevented by a reasonable Impediment, *I Cor.* 11.26. *Luke* 22.19.

4. TO practise the *profoundest Meekness and Humility, Mat.* 11.29.

5. TO watch against *Censuring* others, *Mat.* 7.1.

6. TO accustom themselves to *holy Thoughts* in all Places, *Psal.* 139.23.

7. TO be helpful one to another, *I Cor.* 12.25.

8. TO exercise Tenderness, Patience, and Compassion towards all Men, *Tit.* 3.2.

9. TO make Reflections on themselves when they read the *holy Bible*, or other good *Books*, and when they hear Sermons, *I Cor.* 10.11.

10. TO shun all foreseen *Occasions* of *Evil*: As evil Company, known Temptations, &c. *1 Thess.* 5.22.

11. TO think often on the different Estates of the *Glorified*, and the *Damned*, in the *unchangeable Eternity*, to which we are hastening. *Luke* 16.25.

12. TO *examine* themselves every Night, what *Good* or *Evil* they have done in the Day past, *2 Cor.* 13.5.

13. TO keep a *private Fast* once a Month, (especially near their Approach to the *Lord's Table*,) if at their own Disposal, or to Fast from some Meals when they may conveniently, *Mat.* 6.16, *Luke* 5.35.

14. TO mortifie the Flesh, with its Affections and Lusts, *Gal.* 5.19,24.

15. TO advance in *heavenly Mindedness*, and in all *Grace*, *1 Pet.* 3.8.

16. TO shun *spiritual Pride*, and the Effects of it; as Railing, Anger, Peevishness, and Impatience of Contradiction, and the like.

17. TO pray for the *whole Society* in their private *Prayers*, *Jam.* 5.16.

18. TO read pious Books often for their Edification, but especially the *holy Bible*; and herein particularly, *Joh.* 5.39. *Mat.* 5,6,7, Chap. *Luke* 15,16. Ch. *Rom.* 12,13 Chap. *Eph.* 5,6. Chap. *1 Thess.* 5. Chap. *Rev.* 1,2,3,21,22. Chapters.

And in the *Old Testament, Levit.* 26, Ch. *Deut.* 28. Ch. *Isa.* 53. Ch. *Ezek.* 36. Chap.

19. TO be continually mindful of the great Obligation of this special *Profession of Religion*; and to walk so circumspectly, that none may be offended or discouraged from it by what they see in them; nor occasion given to any to speak reproachfully of it.

20. TO shun all manner of Affectation and Moroseness, and be of a civil and obliging Deportment to all Men.

XI.

THAT they often consider (with an awful Dread of God's Wrath) the sad *Height* to which the Sins of many are advanced in this our Nation; and the bleeding *Divisions* thereof in *Church* and *State*. And that every Member be ready to do, what upon consulting with each other shall be thought adviseable, towards the Punishment of *publick Profaneness*, according to the good Laws of our Land, required to be put in Execution by the *Queen's* and the late *King's* special Order. And to do what befits them in their Stations, in order to the cementing of our Divisions.

XII.

THAT each Member shall encourage the *Catechizing* of young and ignorant People in their respective Families, according to their Stations and Abilities: And shall observe all manner of Religious *Family-Duties*.

XIII.

THAT the major Part of the Society shall have power to make a new *Order* to bind the whole, when need requires; if it be approved by three pious and learned *Ministers* of the *Church of England*, nominated by the whole Society.

XIV.

THAT these *Orders* shall be read over at least Four times in the Year, by one of the *Stewards*; and that with such Deliberation, that each Member may have time to examine himself by them, or to speak his Mind in any thing relating to them.

XV.

LASTLY, That every Member of this Society shall (after mature Deliberation, and due Trial) express his *Approbation* of these Orders, and his *Resolution* to endeavour to live up to them. In order to which, he shall constantly keep a Copy of *them by him*.

The End of the Orders

Reproduced from Josiah Woodward, *An Account of the Rise and Progress of the Religious Societies in the City of London, &c. And of their Endeavours for Reformation of Manners*, 5th ed. (London: Printed and Sold by J. Downing, 1724), pp. 111-18.

Appendix C

AN EXTRACT FROM SAMUEL WESLEY'S ACCOUNT OF THE RELIGIOUS SOCIETY BEGUN IN EPWORTH, IN THE ISLE OF AXHOLM LINCOLNSHIRE, FEB: 1, AN: DOM: 1701-2

I. Every week at set hours, when 2, 3, or more do meet together for this Intent, First to pray to God; Secondly, to read the Holy Scriptures, and discourse upon Religious Matters for their mutual Edification; And Thirdly, to deliberate about the Edification of our neighbour, and the promoting it.

II. Those that do thus meet together, are above all things sollicitous about the Salvation of their neighbour, yea they make it their business to be Christians not only in name but in deed: Least they should strive rashly to pull out the Mote from the Eies of others, not observing the Beam in their own; and lest while they preach to others themselves should become castaways.

III. For this Reason they do not admit every body promiscuously, but if any one desires to be of their Society, it must be done by the Consent of all; and therefore his Piety ought to be known to all, lest a little Leven should spoil the whole Lump, For they take it for Granted that things will then fall out well, when each of them shall be of that mind, as that it may be affirm'd upon good Grounds that *This is Emanuel that dwells through Faith, of the power of God, in the Heart of every One, as in his Temple.*

IIII. Nor do they allow that the number of their members should encrease too much, lest this Religious design should fall with its own weight, or at least be marr'd. Therefore when they have twelve Members they admitt no more. But if God shall stir up more, two shall desire the same Edification with them, they seperate [sic] two Members from them, to form a new Society with those that desire it, till that also grow's up to the number of Twelve, and so another new Society be form'd out of it.

V. A Society or two being now set up; they think it may be practicable to take in such persons only, in whom there may be hopes, that by such a pious Conversation, they may be brought to a real and serious denying of the World, yet not to admitt above 2 or 3 at the most of such Members, of whose solid piety they are not yet sufficiently appris'd, lest by any unwary Charity towards all it may happen by degrees, that Darkness might begin to get ground.

VI. But if they, of whose Conversion to God there may be hopes, shall not blush to devote themselves to Vice and Wickedness and thereby become a scandal to their neighbour: they are no longer look'd as a part of the Society lest those who are sincere should be drawn to partake either of the Vice or of the Scandal.

VII. All Debates about the Corruption of Manners which have crept into the Church, of Amending or Reforming the Church point of Manners, is reffer'd to the first Society. The other Societies are contented with their own Edification and if any one knows what will tend to the publick Edification, he discover's it to the first Society, or at least to some member of the first Society, that so it may be consider'd by all the Members thereof, how it does conduce towards the common design, and may be reduced into practice.

VIII. But this first Society does in no wise assume any prerogative to it self: but the Debating about the publick Edification is for this Reason; least one Society should hinder another, and because all are not fitt to be Counsellors. Hence it is that this Society is obliged to be carefull to take in such Members alone, as are able to help the Church by their Wisdom and good advices.

VIIII. They do not take in any Women into these Societies, in order to avoid scandal and all other abuses the more easily, to which promiscuous meetings cannot but be liable. Women may hear their Husbands at Home, and Girls their parents: for tis a duty incumbent upon every Member of these Societies, next to his own soul to be chiefly solicitous for those of his Family. And if there be any one who is a Master of a Family, yet by his grace Conversation he may be very beneficial to those amongst whom he lives, tis very necessary that by living Examples men may see what a true Christian is, who still is very hard to meet with.

X. They carry on a Subscription in every Society, towards which every Member contributes each Meeting, according to his Charity and

Ability. The money so Collected is to be expended no other way than in promoting the Designs of the Societies, or for Reforming the Church.

XI. Their first care is to set Schools for the Poor, wherein Children (or if need be, Adult Persons,) may be instructed in the Fundamentals of Christianity by men of known and approv'd Piety.

XII. Their second design is to procure little Practical Treatises from Holland, England, and Germany, &c. to translate them into the Vulgar Tounge, print them, and so to give or lend them to those who are less solicitous of their own and others Edification.

XIII. The Third is to establish a Correspondence with such Societies in England, Germany, &c. that so they may mutually Edify one another: especially since they have learn'd that by keeping up a Correspondence, as they gain knowledge and experience in Edifying the whole Church: so their wholesome advices will thereby be forwarded, and the better reduced to practise.

XIIII. The Fourth is to take Care of the Sick and other Poor, and to afford them Spiritual as well as Corporal Helps. When their Stock is sufficiently large to carry on these pious Designs, they deliberate of some other proper method of disposing of that which remains. The means will not fail to be present, if all things shall be done of God, in God, and thro' God.

Reproduced from W.O.B. Allen and Edmund McClure, *Two Hundred Years: The History of The Society for Promoting Christian Knowledge, 1698-1898* (London: S.P.C.K., 1898), pp. 89-93.

Appendix D

ORDERS OF A RELIGIOUS SOCIETY MEETING IN FETTER LANE

In Obedience to the Command of God by St. James, and by the Advice of Peter Boehler, *May 1, 1738, it was agreed,*

1. That they will meet together once in a Week to confess their Faults one to another, and to pray for one another that they may be healed.

2. That any others, of whose Sincerity they are well assured, may, if they desire it, meet with them for that Purpose. And, *May 29*, it was agreed,

3. That the Persons desirous to meet together for that Purpose, be divided into several Bands, or little Societies.

4. That none of these consist of fewer than five, or more than ten Persons.

5. That some Person in each Band be desired to interrogate the rest in order, who may be called the Leader of that Band. And on *Monday, September 26*, it was agreed,

6. That each Band meet twice in a Week, once on *Monday* Evenings, the second Time when it is most convenient for each Band.

7. That every Person come punctually at the Hour appointed, without some extraordinary Reason.

8. That those that are present begin exactly at the Hours.

9. That every Meeting be begun and ended with Singing and Prayer.

10. That every one in order speak as freely, plainly and concisely as he can, the real State of his Heart, with his several Temptations and Deliverances, since the last Time of meeting.

11. That all Bands have a Conference at eight every *Wednesday* Evening, begun and ended with Singing and Prayer.

12. That at nine of the Clock the Names of the Members be called over, and the Absenters set down.

13. That Notice of any extraordinary Meeting be given on the *Wednesday* Night preceding such Meeting.

14. That exactly at ten, if the Business of the Night be not finished, a short concluding Prayer be used, that those may go who are in haste, but that all depart the Room by half an Hour after ten.

15. That whosoever speaks in this Conference stand up, and that none else speak till he is set down.

16. That nothing which is mentioned in this Conference be by any Means mentioned out of it.

17. That every Member of this Society, who is a Member of any other, prefer the meeting with this, and with his particular Band, before the meeting with any other Society or Company whatsoever.

18. That if any Person absent himself without some extraordinary Reason, either from his Band, or from any Meeting of the whole Society, he be first privately admonished; and if he be absent again, reproved before the Whole Society.

19. That any Person who desire, or designs to take any Journey, shall first, if it be possible, have the Approbation of the Bands.

20. That all our Members who are in Clubs, be desired to withdraw their Names, as being Meetings nowise conducing to the Glory of God.

21. That any who desire to be admitted into this Society, be asked, What are your Reasons for desiring this? Will you be entirely open, using no kind of Reserve, least of all, in the Case of Love or Courtship? Will you strive against the Desire of ruling, of being first in your Company, or having your own Way? Will you submit to be placed in what Band the Leaders shall choose for you? Have you any Objections to any of our Orders? The Orders may then be read to them.

22. That those who answer these Questions in the Affirmative, be proposed every fourth *Wednesday*.

23. That every one then present speak clearly and fully whatever Objection he has to any Person proposed to be a Member.

24. That those against whom any reasonable Objection appears, be acquainted with that Objection, and the admitting them upon Trial postponed till that Objection is removed.

25. That those against whom no reasonable Objection appears or remains, be, in order for their Trial, formed into distinct Bands, and some Person agreed on to assist them.

26. That if no new Objection then appear, they be, after two Month's Trial, admitted into the Society.

27. That every fourth *Saturday* be observed as a Day of general Intercession, which may continue from twelve to two, from three to five, and from six to eight.

28. That on Sunday Se'en-night following be a general Love-Feast, from seven till ten in the Evening.

29. That in order to a continual Intercession, every Member of this Society choose some Hour, either of the Day or Night, to spend in Prayer chiefly for his Brethren.

30. That in order to a continual Fast, three of the Members of this

Society Fast every Day (as their Health permits), Sundays and Holidays excepted, and spend as much as they can of that Day, in Retirement from Business, and Prayer.

31. That each Person give Notice to the Leader of his Band how much he is willing to subscribe towards the general Charge of the Bands, and that each Person's Money be paid into the Leader of his Band once a Month at farthest.

32. That no particular Person be allowed to act in any Thing contrary to any Order of this Society, but that every one, without Distinction, submit to the Determination of his Brethren; and that if any Person or Persons do not, after being thrice admonished, conform to the Society, they be not esteemed any longer as Members.

33. That any Person whom the whole Society shall approve, may be accounted a correspondent Member, and as such, may be admitted at our general Meetings, provided he correspond with the Society once in a Month at least.

Reproduced from Daniel Benham, *Memoirs of James Hutton; Comprising the Annals of His Life and Connection with the United Brethren* (London: Hamilton, Adams, and Co., 1856), pp. 29-32.

Appendix E

RULES OF THE BAND SOCIETIES DRAWN UP DECEMBER 25, 1738

The design of our meeting is, to obey that command of God, "Confess your faults one to another, and pray one for another, that ye may be healed."

To this end, we intend, —

1. To meet once a week, at the least.
2. To come punctually at the hour appointed, without some extraordinary reason.
3. To begin (those of us who are present) exactly at the hour, with singing or prayer.
4. To speak each of us in order, freely and plainly, the true state of our souls, with the faults we have committed in thought, word, or deed, and the temptations we have felt, since our last meeting.
5. To end every meeting with prayer, suited to the state of each person present.
6. To desire some person among us to speak his own state first, and then to ask the rest, in order, as many and as searching questions as may be, concerning their state, sins, and temptations.

Some of the questions proposed to every one before he is admitted among us may be to this effect: —

1. Have you the forgiveness of your sins?
2. Have you peace with God, through our Lord Jesus Christ?
3. Have you the witness of God's Spirit with your spirit, that you are a child of God?
4. Is the love of God shed abroad in your heart?
5. Has no sin, inward or outward, dominion over you?
6. Do you desire to be told of your faults?
7. Do you desire to be told of your faults, and that plain and home?
8. Do you desire that every one of us should tell you, from time to time, whatsoever is in his heart concerning you?
9. Consider! Do you desire that we should tell you whatsoever we think, whatsoever we fear, whatsoever we hear, concerning you?
10. Do you desire that, in doing this, we should come as close as

possible, that we should cut to the quick, and search your heart to the bottom?

11. Is it your desire and design to be on this, and all other occasions, entirely open, so as to speak everything that is in your heart without exception, without disguise, and without reserve?

Any of the preceding questions may be asked as often as occasion offers; the [five]* following at every meeting: —

1. What known sins have you committed since our last meeting?
2. What temptations have you met with?
3. How were you delivered?
4. What have you thought, said, or done, of which you doubt whether it be sin or not?
[5. Have you nothing you desire to keep secret?]*

*The fifth question does not appear in editions of the rules after 1779-80. See Frank Baker, *Union Catalogue*, p. 55, #57.

Reproduced from *The Works of John Wesley*, 14 vols. (London: Wesleyan Conference Office, 1872; reprint ed., Grand Rapids, Michigan: Baker Book House, 1979), 8:272-73.

DIRECTIONS GIVEN TO THE BAND-SOCIETIES DECEMBER 25, 1744

You are supposed to have the faith that "overcometh the world." To you, therefore, it is not grievous, —

I. Carefully to abstain from doing evil; in particular, —

1. Neither to buy nor sell anything at all in the Lord's day.
2. To taste no spirituous liquor, no dram of any kind, unless prescribed by a Physician.
3. To be at a word both in buying and selling.
4. To pawn nothing, no, not to save life.
5. Not to mention the fault of any behind his back, and to stop those short that do.
6. To wear no needless ornaments, such as rings, ear-rings, necklaces, lace, ruffles.
7. To use no needless self-indulgence, such as taking snuff or tobacco, unless prescribed by a Physician.

II. Zealously to maintain good works; in particular,—

1. To give alms of such things as you possess, and that to the uttermost of your power.

2. To reprove all that sin in your sight, and that in love and meekness of wisdom.

3. To be patterns of diligence and frugality, of self-denial, and taking up the cross daily.

III. Constantly to attend on all the ordinances of God; in particular,—

1. To be at church and at the Lord's table every week, and at every public meeting of the Bands.

2. To attend the ministry of the word every morning, unless distance, business, or sickness prevent.

3. To use private prayer every day; and family prayer, if you are at the head of a family.

4. To read the Scriptures, and meditate therein, at every vacant hour. And,—

5. To observe, as days of fasting or abstinence, all Fridays in the year.

Reproduced from *The Works of John Wesley*, 8:273-74.

Appendix F

THE

NATURE, DESIGN,

AND

GENERAL RULES,

OF THE

United Societies,

IN

London, Bristol, King's-wood,
and *Newcastle upon Tyne.*

NEWCASTLE UPON TYNE,
Printed by JOHN GOODING, on the *Side.*
[Price One Penny.]

MDCCXLIII.

R U L E S, & c.
O F T H E
UNITED SOCIETIES

1. IN the latter End of the Year 1739, eight or ten Persons came to me in *London*, who appeared to be deeply convinced of Sin, and earnestly groaning for Redemption. They desired (as did two or three more the next Day) that I would spend some Time with them in Prayer, and advise them how to flee from the Wrath to come; which they saw continually hanging over their Heads. That we might have more Time for this great Work, I appointed a Day when they might all come together, which from thenceforward they did every Week, namely on *Thursday*, in the Evening. To these, and as many more as desired to join with them, (for their Number increased daily) I gave those Advices from Time to Time which I judged most needful for them; and we always concluded our Meeting with Prayer suited to their several Necessities.

2. This was the Rise of the UNITED SOCIETY, first at *London,* and then in other Places. Such a Society is no other than *"a Company of Men* having the Form, and seeking the Power of *Godliness, united in order to pray together, to receive the Word of Exhortation, and to watch over one another in Love, that they may help each other to work out their Salvation."*

3. That it may the more easily be discern'd, whether they are indeed working out their own Salvation, each Society is divided into smaller Companies, called Classes, according to their respective Places of abode. There are about twelve Persons in every Class; one of whom is stiled *The Leader*. It is his Business
I. To see each Person in his Class, once a Week at the least; in order
To receive what they are willing to give, toward the Relief of the Poor;
To enquire how their Souls prosper?
To advise, reprove, comfort or exhort, as Occasion may require.
II. To meet the Minister and the Stewards of the Society once a Week; in order
To pay in to the Stewards what they have receiv'd of their several Classes in the Week preceeding;
To shew their Account of what each Person has contributed; And
To inform the Minister of any that are sick, or of any that walk disorderly, and will not be reproved.

4. There is one only Condition previously required, in those who desire Admission into these Societies, *a Desire to flee from the Wrath to come, to be saved from their Sins:* But, wherever this is really fix'd in the Soul, it will be shewn by its Fruits. It is therefore expected of all who continue therein, that they should continue to evidence their Desire of Salvation,

First, By doing no Harm, by avoiding Evil in every kind; especially, that which is most generally practised. Such is

The taking the Name of God in vain;

The profaning the Day of the Lord, either by doing ordinary Work thereon, or by buying or selling:

Drunkenness, *Buying or selling Spirituous Liquors*; or *drinking them* (unless in Cases of extreme Necessity:)

Fighting, Quarreling, Brawling; *Going to Law,* Returning Evil for Evil, or Railing for Railing: The *using many Words* in buying or selling.

The *buying or selling uncustomed Goods:*

The *giving or taking Things on Usury:*

Uncharitable or *unprofitable* Conversation:

Doing to others as we would not they should do unto us:

Doing what we know is not for the Glory of God: As

The *putting on of Gold or costly Apparel.*

The *taking such Diversions* as cannot be used in the Name of the Lord Jesus:

The *Singing* those *Songs,* or *reading* those *Books,* which do not tend to the Knowledge or Love of God:

Softness, and needless Self-indulgence:

Laying up Treasures upon Earth.

5. It is expected of all who continue in these Societies, that they should continue to evidence their Desire of Salvation,

Secondly, By doing Good, by being in every kind, merciful after their Power; as they have Opportunity, doing Good of every possible sort, and as far as is possible, to all Men:

To their Bodies, of the Ability which God giveth, by giving Food to the Hungry, by cloathing the Naked, by visiting or helping them that are Sick, or in Prison:

To their Souls, by instructing, *reproving* or exhorting all we have any Intercourse with: Trampling under Foot that Enthusiastick Doctrine of Devils, that "we are not to do Good," unless *our Heart be free to it."*

By doing Good especially to them that are of the Houshold of Faith, or groaning so to be: Employing them preferably to others, buying one of another, helping each other in Business; and that so much the more, because the World will love its own, and them only.

By all possible *Diligence and Frugality*, that the Gospel be not blamed:

By running with Patience the Race that is set before them; *denying themselves, and taking up their Cross daily*; submitting to bear the Reproach of Christ, to be as the Filth and Off-scouring of the World; and looking that Men should *say all manner of Evil of them falsely, for their Lord's sake:*

6. It is expected of all who desire to continue in these Societies, that they should continue to evidence their Desire of Salvation,

Thirdly, by attending upon all the Ordinances of God: Such are
The publick Worship of God;
The Ministry of the Word, either read or expounded;
The Supper of the Lord;
Private Prayer;
Searching the Scriptures; and
Fasting, or Abstinence.

7. These are the General Rules of our Societies; all which we are taught of God to observe, even in his written Word, the only Rule, and the sufficient Rule both of our Faith and Practice: And all these we know his Spirit writes on every truly awaken'd Heart. If there be any among us who observe them not, who habitually break any one of them, let it be made known unto him who watches over that Soul, as one that must give Account. I will admonish him of the Error of his Ways: I will bear with him for a Season. But if he then repent not, he hath no more Place among us. We have deliver'd our own souls.

JOHN WESLEY

Feb. 23. 1742-3.

Reproduced from the first edition, 1743.

Appendix G

THE CLASS LISTS OF THE BINGLEY SOCIETY, 1763

CLASS, No. 1.

Thomas Middlesbrough,	Farmer,	Castlefield. Leader.
John Wildman,	Plasterer,	Bingley.
Benjamin Wilkinson,	Husbandman,	Micklewood.
John Gott,	Cordwainer,	Bingley.
James Farrah,	Old man,	"
Sarah Moor,	Spinner,	Woodside.
John Gott,	Stuff maker,	Bingley.

CLASS, No. 2.

John Curtiss,	Stuff maker,	Bingley, Leader.
Martha Curtiss,	"	"
Wm. Maud,	Husbandman,	"
Wm. Whitley,	Tailor,	"
James Whitley,	"	"
John Whitaker,	Stuff maker,	Harden.
Mary Whitaker,	"	"
William Haughton,	Weaver,	Micklewood.
Sarah Harrison,	Spinner,	Bingley.
Thos. Patrick,	Weaver,	"
Robt Watson,	Gentleman,	Beck.
Ann Dobson,	Glazier,	"
Abraham Hartley,	Labourer,	Common.

CLASS, No. 3.

David Binns,	Weaver,	Harden Brow, Leader.
Joseph Brown,	Cordwainer,	"
John Jackson,	Weaver,	"
Christian Townend,	"	"
Abrm. Mitchell,	Woolcomber,	"
Grace _____	Spinner,	(There is no place of resi-
Eliz. Wood,	Servant,	dence indicated for these
Robt. Walsh,	Weaver,	last seven members. Pre-
Mary Middlesbrough,	Yeoman,	sumably they all lived in or
Hanh. Wild,	Spinner,	around Harden Brow.)
John Walker,	Shop-keeper,	
John Whitley,	Farmer,	

Reproduced from John Ward, *Historical Sketches of the Rise and Progress of Methodism in Bingley* (Bingley: John Harrison and Son, 1863), pp. 22-23.

Appendix H

CLASS TICKETS

Class Tickets have been exhaustively documented in the *Proceedings of the Wesley Historical Society* (31 [1957-58]: 2-9, 34-8, 70-3; 32 [1959-60]: 34-7, 48-51, 78-80). They usually measured between two by one-and-a-half inches and three-and-a-half by two-and-a-half, though occasionally they were as large as four by two inches. No fewer than thirty-eight different types were issued between 1742 and 1765, initially distinguished each quarter by a different emblem, or ornamental device, but in 1749 by texts of scripture. Picture-tickets finally disappeared in 1764. In 1760, the letters of the alphabet were used in sequence to date the tickets, beginning in August with the letter A, and from November 1763 for the band tickets. The sequence was not always unbroken, but each ticket also carried the date of issue, and the signature of Wesley or one of his assistants.

The original tickets issued in 1741 were for the bands, and it is uncertain whether any distinction was made between these and the class tickets issued until 1750. For a number of years thereafter, there were distinctive band tickets; but these were assimilated in due course with class tickets, when they were distinguished by a different passage of scripture and the addition of the word *band* or the letter *b*. The band ticket was, of course, an indication of a more advanced spiritual state, and until 1758 was the only means of admission to a lovefeast. At the Conference of that year, however, Wesley permitted admission of other society members to lovefeasts once a year, and the production of a current class ticket soon became sufficient for admission to a lovefeast anywhere (*WHS Proc.*, 4 [1904] Supplement, p. 72).

Wesley was concerned throughout his ministry not to have class tickets devalued. They were not to be issued to persons who were not *awakened*; they were not to be issued to children; and there is a delightful anecdote of Wesley himself being refused admission to a lovefeast because he could not display a class ticket to the steward (Frank Baker, *Methodism and the Lovefeast*, p. 35).

The examples on the following pages are reproduced from tickets in the private collection of Dr. Frank Baker.

The first illustration is an example of the early pictorial tickets. Among the later examples, note that the letter *b* has been written on to the ticket for December, 1811, and crossed out on the one for June, 1819. The distinction between class and band tickets was maintained, even when supplies ran out.

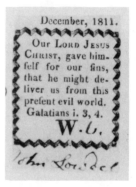

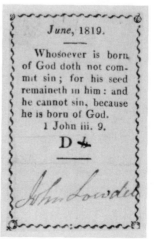

If Wesley or his assistants had to cut individual tickets from series such as these, it does much to explain the irregular shape of many early samples.

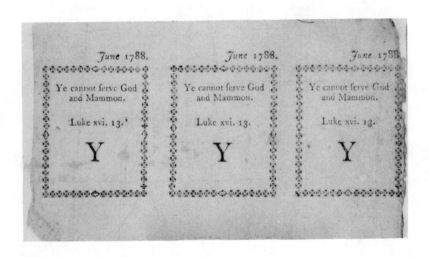

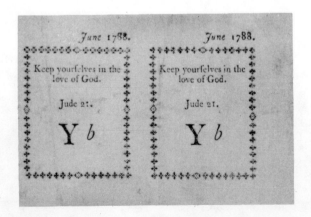

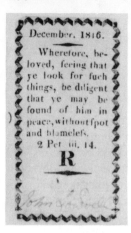

Class tickets often varied from place to place, as illustrated by the examples shown here for December, 1816. The ticket for March, 1833 illustrates the format which became normative during the nineteenth century and into the twentieth.

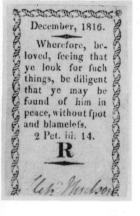

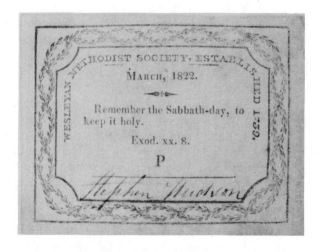

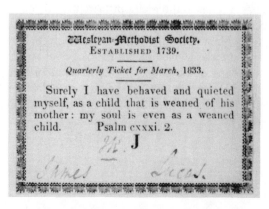

Appendix I

CLASS PAPERS

According to George J. Stevenson (*City Road Chapel*, p. 257), class papers were first used following the 1749 Conference. This was perhaps in response to Wesley's ten-point enumeration of duties which the assistants had been neglecting, including the provision of accurate society lists. The papers were later replaced by class books, though both were in use for a time. Their values as a source of membership information is indicated by the events of 1797, when they were immediately demanded from the Kilhamite seceders.

Papers from the eighteenth century provided some interesting examples of the signs used to denote the members' spiritual states. In addition to **a** (awakened), **?** (doubtful), **.** (justified), and **:** (perfected in love), a paper from Newlands, near Newcastle upon Tyne, dated approximately 1750, shows the notation 7/8 beside the name of John Brewer, a farmer; and in a class list of the Conisholme society, dated 1781, the sign **.** appears no less than twenty-five times (*WHS Proc.*, 12 [1919-20]; 75-77; 13 [1921-22]:69-70).

Among the class papers in the Methodist Archives at The John Rylands Library, Manchester University, is one which has been carefully folded and bound, so that the leader might carry it around. There is another with a simple but powerful note from the minister: "Bro. Stephenson, feed the sheep of the church, for which Jesus shed his precious blood." And in the class book of Henry Pearce, from Redruth, Cornwall, we have much illuminating data about the social life of a class in the 1790s, including the purchase of ale for the quarterly meetings!

The examples on the following pages are reproduced from originals in the personal collection of Dr. Frank Baker, dated 1806 and 1830. The former matches a series in the Methodist Archives dated October 1808 through December 1811. John Marsden led a class which met at Ancoats Street in Manchester on Sunday afternoons at "½ past 2," and Jane Marsden led a class which met at Brook Street on Thursday night at "8 o'clock." Many of the papers in this series record an entry in the column for spiritual state, though on the paper overleaf for 1806 it was used only to indicate that a member was meeting band, and in general was not used at all.

(Actual dimensions: 11"x7")

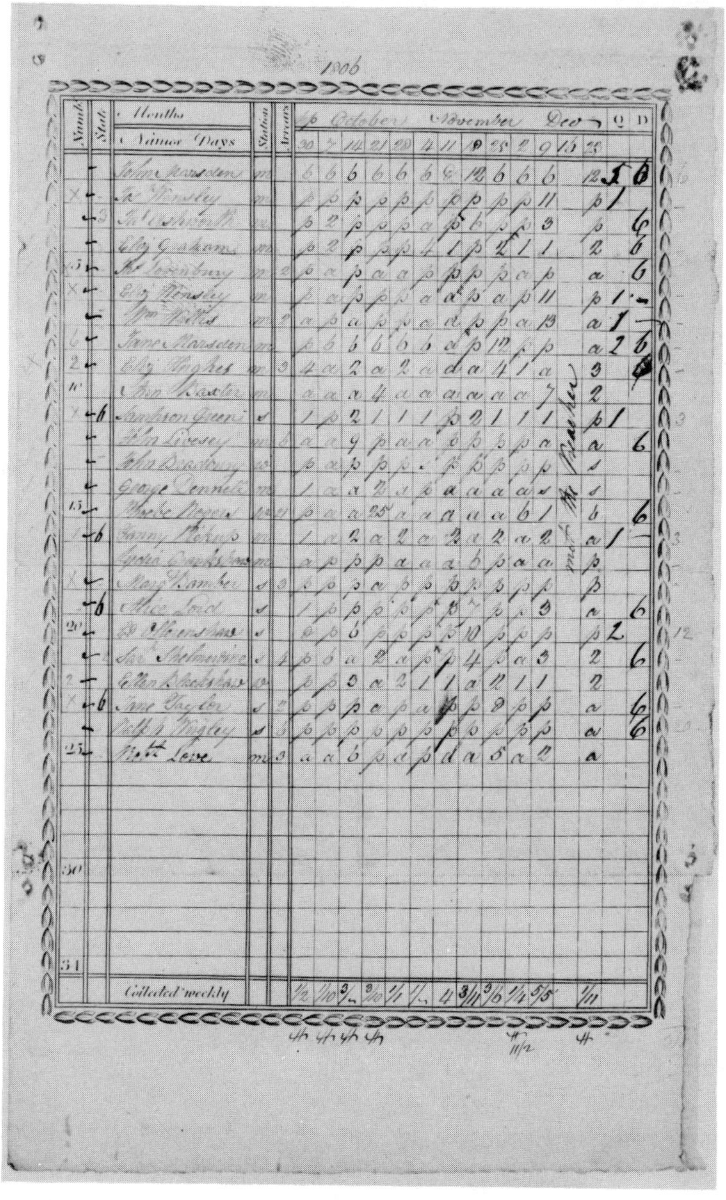

1806

Numb.	Stat.	Months / Names Days	Station	Arrears	Sep 30	Oct 7	14	21	28	Nov 4	11	18	25	Dec 2	9	16	23	Q	D
		John Marsden	m		6	6	6	6	6	6	6	12	6	6	6		12	5	6
X		Jo Wensley	m		p	p	p	p	p	p	p	p	p	p	11		p	1	
	3	Jn Ashworth	m		p	2	p	p	p	a	p	6	p	p	3		p		6
		Eliz Graham	m		p	2	p	p	p	4	1	p	2	1	1		2		6
5		Jn Lowenbury	m	2	p	a	p	a	a	p	p	p	p	a	p		a		6
X		Eliz Wensley	m		p	a	p	p	p	a	d	p	a	p	11		p	1	
		Wm Willis	m	2	a	p	a	p	p	a	d	p	p	a	13		a	1	
6		Jane Marsden	m		p	6	6	6	6	6	d	p	12	p	p		a	2	6
2		Eliz Hughes	m	3	4	a	2	a	2	a	d	a	4	1	a		3		
10		Ann Baxter	m		a	a	a	4	a	a	a	a	a	a	7		2		
X	6	Sampson Green	s		1	p	2	1	1	1	p	2	1	1	1		p	1	
		Jn Livesey	m	6	a	a	9	p	a	a	p	p	p	p	a		a		6
		John Brad[illegible]	m		p	a	p	p	p	.	p	p	p	p	p		s		
		George Bennett	m		1	a	a	2	s	p	a	a	a	a	s		s		
15		Phoebe Rogers	m	1	p	a	a	25	a	a	a	a	a	6	1		6		6
	6	Fanny [illegible]	m		1	a	2	a	2	a	2	a	2	a	2		a	1	
		Lydia Crankshaw	m		a	p	p	p	a	a	a	6	p	a	a		p		
X		Mary Lamber	s	3	6	p	3	a	p	6	p	p	3	p	p		p		
	6	Alice Lord	s		1	p	p	p	p	p	p	7	p	p	3		a		6
20		Jo Ollerenshaw	s		6	p	6	p	p	p	p	10	p	p	p		p	2	
		Sar Shelmerdine	s	4	p	6	a	2	a	p	p	4	p	a	3		2		6
2		Ellen Blackshaw	s		p	p	3	a	2	1	1	a	12	1	1		2		
X	6	Jane Taylor	s	2	p	p	p	a	p	a	p	p	8	p	p		a		6
		Ralph Wrigley	s	3	p	p	p	p	p	p	p	p	p	p	p		a		6
25		Matt Love	m	3	a	a	6	p	a	p	d	a	5	a	12		a		
30																			
31																			
		Collected weekly			1/2	1/10	3/-	3/10	1/1	1/-	4	3/11	3/6	1/4	5/5		1/11		

Mr Barker

(Actual dimensions: 11"x7")

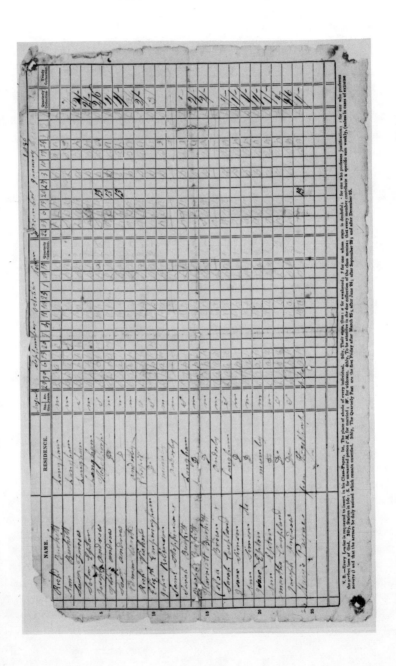

Appendix J

SOME CORRESPONDENCE ON CLASS MEETINGS

The following letters are reproduced from a manuscript dated 1790 in the possession of Dr. Frank Baker. It is not known who wrote them, nor to whom they were written, but they present a thorough description of the class meeting, and a contemporary evaluation of its function within Methodism.

My dr. Sr.

In one of our late interviews you proposed a question which induced me to commit some thoughts to paper that for sometime past have occupied my mind—when you enquired "By what means vital Religion might be increased amongst us? It determined me to employ my 1st leisure in suggesting to you two subjects which seem closely connected with the increase of holiness amongst the present race of Methodists & also the promoting it in future Generations. If these letters contain any thing you judge useful to this end your candour will forgive both the attempt and its imperfections. You will permit me to write without retraint, fully satisfied that I am conversing with one who will not hastily impute improper motives to me—tho' in some instances my expressions may be ungaurded [sic].

My 1st reflections are confined to the means of increasing the purity of Religion amongst the present Race of Methodists. Whatever priviledges we possess—included in the faithful Preaching—Holy Lives—& fervent prayer—it is certain we need an increase of each & all of these—& more faithful Preaching—holy living—& fervent prayer would increase our purity as a Body—but omitting any thing further of this general nature let us confine our thoughts to come particulars. Is there not reason to suppose that a more faithful discharge of the Offices in each part of our Body would be a great means of promoting its prosperity? It is in this view the subject most forcibly strikes me—on the Exercise of discipline in our Societies—depends, as far as means are so argued upon, their prosperity. The Exercise of discipline depends on the Judgment & Integrity of Those who are entrusted with it. If they betray that trust Corruption must ensue.

The Rules of our Societies—which every member professes to walk by, embrace the important Branches of our duty toward God, our neighbour & ourselves. Perhaps they are fully adequate to the end designed in their formation. They are the rule of our discipline. Our members ought to walk by them. Whilst they do we shall be "an holy people." One design of our Classes is to discover how far these Rules are kept. Class leaders are appointed to watch over a small number of Individuals—to know how their Souls prosper—to observe their outward deportment—to unite them with each other & the body at large in spreading scriptural christianity. The Class Leader is required to unite with his Brethern [sic] & the preachers in each Society for these purposes.

Now it follows as far as Class Leaders are materially deficient in enquiring into the State of their People's minds—of observing their outward conduct—uniting with them in promoting the Cause of Christianity—or with their Brethern & the Preachers in watching over the affairs of the Society—They betray their trust—Discipline is relaxed—& Corruption follows.

How then shall the office of a Class Leader be faithfully discharged since so much is connected with it? In one word Let it be done *conscientiously*. Let every one who undertakes that office know fully his work & count the cost. 2. Let him faithfully dedicate his time to it. 3rd. Let Him use the time dedicated in the best manner he can. Perhaps one of the greatest Hindrances to a proper discharge of this (& many other) labours amongst upright Men is a mismanagement of time. Class Leaders frequently persuade themselves that they only have Time to do a part of their work. For want of Time—they cannot visit with their people tho' long absent—or attend the Leaders Meeting—& sometimes their class. By this means members are neglected & scattered. The hands of their Brethern (Leaders & Preachers) hang down—discipline hindered—Temporal matters embarrassed—a spirit of Zeal and Unity damped & all for want of time. Those who have the charge of Business & Families cannot in every instance command the leisre they in general Expect. Unforeseen & unavoidable hinderances will occur. But are these more to Class Leaders than others? Have not Travelling & Local preachers the same causes? But is it not obvious that it is neither *unforeseen*—nor *unavoidable* hinderances which prevent Leaders from visiting the Houses of their Members, attending Leaders & Society Meetings. Is it not rather a want of a thoro' conviction how much is connected with it. How many truly pious men are there amongst the Leaders thro these kingdoms who never lay it to Heart that their omission of attendance at a Leaders Meeting may eventually prove an Hinderance to some great & good work, by which the prosperity of that Society may be affected for Years. The non attendance of Leaders in these Society Meetings probably wounds the mind of some zealous & holy Preacher—who can do little more than mourn in secret before God—for the Lukewarmness of the Men he is amongst. His plans of good to that Society are broken by this Means. He has none to strengthen his hands. He carries this spirit into the pulpit—& Society with Him. He addresses a "dead-hearted & fallen people." This promotes the very spirit. The People are discouraged. Their Hands hang down. The Conference takes place. The Preacher is removed. Those who are named in succession receive the impression of the last—& the same Cause produces the same Effects. Whilst much of this has arisen not really from any lawful Hinderance, but from a want of conviction in the Breast of 2 or 3 men, perhaps of unblemished Character, that every one who undertakes any office in the Lord's House should be faithful—keeping his place whether or not he has any other work.

I have suffered myself to dwell longer on this point because it seems to me nowhere sufficiently laid to Heart. Humanly speaking everything depends on the proper union of our Leaders & preachers & it is to be feared many Leaders consider their work nearly finished when they have met their Class. They imagine they have not Time for other things. If they really have not they ought not to remain in the Office—or they should have an Helper. But perhaps tis not an improper Calculation to state that *three Hours* [per] week, will in general enable every Leader to do his work faithfully, as far as time is requisite—visiting 1 or 2 Absent members each week & allowing 3/4 Hour for Leaders Meeting. I would observe here by the way that Leader's Meetings are oft unnecessarily prolonged for want of a little more Resolution & Prudence in the Preacher present, to keep his Brethern to the point in Hand. By this Means Subjects of Moment are left undetermined. It is of much Consequence (if Time be valuable), that all our Meetings on business should be done with Order & dispatch. On the whole you will rightly conclude from these Reflections that I consider NonAttendance at Leaders Meetings as one Cause of a want of Prosperity in our Societies—& diligence in that as a Means of its removal. My next will enter upon another part of a Leaders duty.

My dr. Sr.

If the Class Leader stedfastly dedicates a part of his time to discharge the office he undertakes. If He understands the work he is appointed to—he can only discharge it to the best in his power. My last particularly considered the evil consquences of Omission in Leaders, esp. at a Leaders Meeting. Nor need I at present enter particularly upon his duty when there. I would only observe in general terms—that it is not merely to request a Preacher to visit an afflicted Member—or reprove a disorderly walker—or pay in weekly Contributions to Stewards, but it is to unite with the preachers & Leaders in every thing which affects the Interests of conveying Subjects thought necessary by Leaders & preachers to the Individuals in his Class. This Sentiment I may more fully illustrate hereafter. This is certainly an additional Reason for constant Attendance—but before I enter upon this—Let me notice what appears naturally to precede & introduce it . . .

How may a Class Leader employ the season of Class Meeting to the greatest advantage? Doubtless by keeping his Eye first upon the End proposed—& by using all his Understanding—& all his strength in Attaining that End—our different Constitutions, dispositions, Capacities & Talents will produce an indescribable Variety of Methods in Conversing with our people. Leaders, as well as preachers, should avoid affectation—they should not be anxious to *imitate*, what may appear most excellent in the method of others. Whilst they keep a single Eye—& in simplicity & godly Sincerity converse with their people, they should act according to the best of their own Judgment in the choice of Subjects—& application of them. Yet no concessions on this side of the Question Must be admitted as a Reason for neglecting the Express purpose for which these Meetings are held.

The purpose of these meetings is—to enquire after the soul's Prosperity to see that each Member walk by the rules of the Society to receive such contributions as are necessary. I shall not at present enlarge on the most profitable manner of enquiring into the State of Mind of those who are met in Class. A Leader ought to know how to discriminate between common place Expressions & the genuine language of a Heart devoted to God. Whilst he has all the Bowels of a Father towards his people, every sentence he utters, eether [sic] in prayer or Counsel, Reproof, or Exhortation, should have a tendency to draw his people to a present Sense of the divine Presence—an immediate Application of

Soul to the Father thro' the Son—& an entire dedication of their all to Him.

He should know how to bind up the broken hearted—to comfort the Mourner—as well as alarm those who are at ease in Zion—Constantly Recollecting at the same time that He is not an infallible Judge of his fellow Creatures altho he must watch over them, as one that must give an account. This 2fold conviction will tend to render him at once pitiful & affectionate. It will produces [sic] that charity in his Spirits & Language which hopeth all things—behaveth not itself unseemly—& yet searches to the bottom every wound that may thro neglect prove deadly.

You my frd. know so well how to apply these general Remarks—that I purposely decline adding more on this head—especially as there is another point which I suspect is too much overlooked amongst us. I know not that I can express myself with sufficient Clearness upon it. Yet as I do not recollect ever seeing or hearing [it] treated as a Subject of that Consequence it appears to me, I will be as explicit as I can, consistent with the brevity I attempt in these Letters.

It is an indisputable Maxim "The tree is known by its fruits" Hence our Lord says "If ye Love me keep my Commandments" In these principles the Rules of the Methodist Societies are formed—we are united "professing to desire to flee from the wrath to come" This desire to be manifested by "doing no Harm, doing all the good in our own Power, diligently attending the Ordinances of God" in other words "Living righteously soberly & godly" The duty of a Class Leader is to observe if his People walk by these Rules. Hence it appears that a Leader ought not only diligently to enquire into the State of his People's Mind, but whether or not they walk by the Rules of the Society—that he ought to do the one as faithfully as the other. It is extremely difficult to form a true Judgement respecting large communities—Yet I cannot help imagining that this part of Class Meeting is not only not generally practised, but very generally omitted—& that this omission is one principal Cause of Relaxation in our discipline, & decay of divine life in our societies. It will be necessary to explain what is meant by this part of Class Meeting—& assign some Reasons for these Conclusions. These will be the Subject of my next.

Dr. Sir.

By enquiring whether our people walk by the Rules of the Society—
in Class Meeting is not meant a constant catechizing as it were, the
Members by the Letter of the Rules as they stand—this would soon
become formal & obsolete.

Neither is it meant that the ensuing plan should be exactly followed
by all Leaders—but as it contains in the simplest form I can at present
suggest the purport of what is intended You will permit me to notice a
Method which has been already tried & which points at the whole the
writer has in view in this part of the subject.

1st When a person first visits a Class on trial they are asked "Do you
know the design of our meeting together?" The Rules of the Society are
given to them with some such Remarks as these "If you continue to
meet with us, you will observe these Rules describe both End you ought
to have in veiw [sic] & the Conduct you are expected to manifest. Take
them Home with You—consider them alone, as in the Sight of God.
Consider with much Prayer what you are about to do, & if you do not
sincerely intend, with divine help, to forsake your Sins, to take up your
cross & follow Jesus Christ, do not increase your Guilt by professing to
belong to his followers. But if you do indeed feel the Burden of Sin &
want to be saved *from* it, However weak you feel, be not afraid. Give up
yourself in sincerity to God—this Cause—Whatever your determination be—Be sincere in it. Consider it throly [sic] in Solitude with much
prayer & if you conclude that Your union will help you, & are sincerely
purposing to walk by these Rules we shall rejoice to receive you.

An Exhortation to this purpose being given with the Rules, if that
person returns, some Questions similar to what follows are proposed
them. Have you seriously considered these Rules? Are you conscious
that yr. Sins have Exposed you to the wrath to come & is it your chief
concern to flee from it?

Do you conclude that it is yr. duty to walk by these Rules, & will you
esteem it a Priviledge to meet here? Do you understand that it is the
duty of yr. Leader to speak with the utmost plainness to you?

In some Instances our friends particularly notice to new Members the
Expence they may be liable to.

With respect to the old Members & the Method pursued in enforcing the Rules of the Society upon them, I shall simply relate what was substantially a fact.

"A Class Leader whose Class was not very well attended—took an opportunity at a Season when there was more than usual, to Explain the Nature of Class Meetings. He urged that it ought to be conscientiously attended—or forsaken—after an affectionate address to the people. He then put these 2 Questions to each person individually. Do you consider it a priviledge to attend here? Will you seriously engage not to permit trifles to hinder you?

At that or an ensuing Meeting He addressed to them to this purpose. Whilst seriously reflecting on my duty as yr. Leader, & the best means to fulfill it I am convinced of a serious Omission—if it has been attended to at all—it has been very partially—Some of us have met together several years, during which period we have had frequent displays of the Lords presence & many of our companions have gone to rest. We do not meet in vain. We often feel our Hearts burn within us whilst we converse, sing & weep & pray together. Yet this does not prove that all have been done that might in reading the Rules of our Society lately. I was convinced that my Enquiries in this place had been nearly confined to the State of yr. Souls. This is certainly our great End—but the duty of a Leader is also to see that "his people walk by the Rules of the Society."

In this place I have been very defective—not that I can particularly blame myself for continuing Members *openly convicted* of Sin—but there appears more to be my duty. Many of our Rules, prudently used may afford us Matter for very serious Enquiry in this Meeting. It is your Leaders place to use the utmost of his Judgement in selecting & applying these subjects from time to time. At our next Meeting, if the Lord will, I will read over in the Class the Rules—& spend some little time in remarks on them—After which, at certain periods I will endeavour to form Questions on some or most of our Rules—which if Your replies are given in Simplicity & godly Sincerity will enable me to form some clearer Judgement than other Means can have for your profession affects your general Temper & Conduct.

At an ensuing Meeting, the Rules were read with some general observation & Prayer. At certain periods afterwards a Question founded on some Rule of the Society was the subject of conversation instead of a particular Enquiry into the state of their Minds.

These sort of Questions are not too frequently introduce[d] perhaps—once in 4 or 6 weeks—neither have the Members any previous Notice but the Judgement of Leader is used—both as to the Question, the Season & Manners.

They are formed so as obtain—as far as their own profession goes/ the attention paid by every Member to the whole Rules. You will forgive me sending You one or two as far as I can recollect, not having access at present to any written Memo.

"Leader. After the profession we make of seeking or rejoicing in God, of fleeing the Appearance of Evil I cannot allow myself to suppose one Member in this class "prophanely blasphemes the Name of God." Nor do I know just cause to think you can mention it in a trifling & irreverent Manner. You know one of our Rules is "not to take the Name of God in vain" I do not ask you if you do this—most of you profess to love God. You know if you heard the name of yr. Husband, Wife, Parent, Child, Brother &c treated with contempt by your fellow Creatures, what your feelings would be—yr. Esteem, yr. Love to yr. Relatives would produce a sincere Compunction of Mind when they were, in yr. Sight, so unworthly [sic] treated. Let me ask you do you feel any thing of this nature when you hear the Name of God yr. Maker & Redeemer not only blasphemed, but irreverently used.

Questions, respecting Prayer—Family Worship. Searching Scriptures. Bearing Insults &c &c &c, naturally follow.

But these may suffice to shew the Method in which the Rules of our Society are used—at once to discover the State of Mind & regulate the conduct. You will see what is meant by this part of Class Meeting.

The Reasons which appear to warrant the conclusion, that it is much neglected, & is one cause of decay in Societies are—

In many Classes there are numerous Members who do not appear to make any Progress in their Experience—these are inattentive to our discipline, & careless about relative Religion, others who can speak strong words in these meetings, whose zeal is an uneven flame. They can bear little contradiction or Insult. In a word, we are not so pure a Body as we ought to be. Many Preachers, both travelling & local, as well as private members, see & mourn over—yet Scandals & offences are frequently arising—Corrupt Branches are breaking off—Wild fruit discovering itself. Members have been continued long in Classes after repeated Accusations of Scandalous Offences, for want of sufficient proof. It is impossible that Leaders or Preachers can help it, but is there none of this to be attributed to the formal, superficial manner in which some classes are met, from years End to years End. You will recollect that nothing is said in these letters as to the most excellent method of obtaining Information from each Member concerning their State of Mind—any particular set of Questions soon may become formal. Our present Subject is to suggest that the Rules of our Society should be used, at Seasons, as a matter of Examination by every Leader. Were this judiciously & faithfully done, would it not tend 1st To *inform* every Member respecting the chief parts of the christian temper & conduct, hence the people would not long remain so ignarant [*sic*] as some are tho' they have met class & heard Sermons for Years. 2nd. Would it not afford a Leader many Opportunities for pointing out the spirits & temper his people should manifest in a great variety of circumstances—consequently the operations of the human heart—devices of Satan—assistance of the holy Ghost—the precepts—promises—threatenings of the Gospel—the Offices & grace of J. Xt. would all be brought Home as it were in these Conversations. 3rd. Would it not afford many opportunities for searching his People to the *very Soul*. He would learn whether their Joys & Sorrows, their Peace & distress, was attended with tenderness of conscience—a scrupulous attention to known duty—whether they were persons of a strict, selfdenying diligent frame of mind—whether they were much in Prayer—in Searching Scriptures, &c &c. In short, He would instead of dealing in general, come at particulars & frame his advice not on a few customary Expressions which he may have heard, scores of times, but on facts & would hereby be much better qualified to deal personally in private, when necessary with any individual.

Need I say more to prove that Class Meeting of this sort tends to purify a Society, whilst an opposite method must produce a contrary effect—for if a Leader always judges of his People by the state of their Affections or propriety of their Expressions at a Class Meeting, he may oft "make the Religious sad whilst He strengthens the hands of the wicked." But if He does his utmost to discern the habitual temper &

conduct of his people, He will speak consolation to the Mourner & reproof to the trifler with much greater confidence. Yet after all He will often have to rest his thoughts concerning his people with the great shepherd & Bishop of souls who cannot err. I shall more briefly notice the remaining hints on the office of a Leader.

The duty of a leader *in his class* does not close with faithful Enquiries & advice—but he ought to consider himself placed at the Head of that little company to render them & theirs every possible Help he can (consistent with more important duteis [sic] this side the grace. He is certainly as a Pastor, a Father to them. Hence his thoughts ought frequently & seriously to be employed how he can most effectually serve them, esp. by provoking them to Love & good works. Yet there is one part of this duty more distinguished than others. A Leader is the great means of uniting his people with the other members of the Society in supporting the Gospel. This peculiar work of faith & Labour of Love on which, if I may so speak, the support of a Gospel Ministry & relief of distressed Saints depends, belongs to the office of Leader & according to the sphere he fills, he is either doing much good or Harm continually in this Respect. I am afraid many of our Leaders have not sufficiently considered this.

The support of a Gospel ministry & relief of poor Saints & many Labours of Love are helped or hendered [sic] in Methodist religious Societies by the temper & conduct of Leaders. And they will most assuredly have much Honour or Blame from Jesus Christ at the last day on this ground. I feel the subject whilst I write. You must bear with me if I err. You know I receive nothing [of] any contribution, having neither necessities nor claim. Sorry extremely sorry should I be to write a line, to grieve an upright Mind unnecessarily—much more to oppress the poor members of our Societies, in order to load Preachers with Superfluities, but There may be improper traveling Preachers, a waste of public monies, &c &c as all human systems are imperfect, so defects may be in every part—this & more may be admitted. Yet "Men professing Godliness" should act consistently. Methodists are fully persuaded that they ought to unite for the Support of their preachers, that their preachers ought not to suffer real wants. Yet they also know that great Embarrassments have taken place. Are there not many Circuits whose Preachers suffer real Hardships? Is this owing to the Poverty of the body at large? Few will assert that. There are many causes. Amongst others this is not the Least—Leaders not interesting themselves with their people in raising temporal supplies. Prudence is necessary to do this. For that very Reason, who so competent as a Leader. He knows—or ought to know—the Circumstances, disposition &c &c of every member of his class. He ought to be able to say "The Body of Leaders in this Society, for such & such reasons consider it necessary to raise such a sum, for such a purpose. I have considered what part of our Class can bear & believe you can without Inconvenience produce—part. He should be able in simplicity & love to say "Brother or sister I believe if you fully understood the case, you would do a little more than this" or My brother or sister, I am unwilling to receive this from you because I am persuaded you must take it from something more important."

This parental Union should subsist between a Leader & his people, & in some such manner should it be exercised in Temporal Matters. 1st Because tis the avowed office of Leader to receive what each Member will give towards the support of the work. & 2nd Because He is especially set over his people to provoke them to Love & good works. If all Leaders were to be faithful & prudent in this part of their work, not only how comfortable would our preachers be! What provision might be made for the spread of the Gospel in foreign countries. But what poor children might be educated! What sick visited & relieved! What Books circulated! Much is done, yet surely much more might.

In page 5 it was said "a Leader in a certain Sense, may be the immediate Instrument of conveying to the Individuals of his class, every Subject Preachers & Leaders deem important. You have in these last lines one Instance which may serve to illustrate that sentence. Were I not afraid of being tedious, I would go further on this point, but forbear with saying in a similar manner "Every subject which a Meeting of preachers & Leaders may see necessary to inculcate on the Members of a Society, a Leader if he fills his Office faithfully has the opportunity of inculcating as a Father amongst his children. What a Body might we be, if this Union was fully used! We cannot be sufficiently thankful that it exists & produces blessed effects. May it be daily increased & purified!

Appendix K

The following extracts are from the biography of John Braithwaite (1770-1822), who joined a Methodist society in 1788, and was appointed by the Methodist Conference as an itinerant preacher in 1790. It is a classic of early Methodist spirituality, written by his close friend and band-fellow, Robert Dickinson.

The first is a fragment of a personal covenant with God found, undated, among his private papers.

I most firmly believe,

I. That things eternal are of far greater importance than things temporal.

II. That things not seen, but revealed in the Scriptures, are as certain as the things that are seen. And,

III. That upon my present *choice* depends my endless state!
Fully persuaded of the very great moment, and unshaken veracity, of what I have above professed to believe; and deeply sensible of my manifold failings, in my duty towards God and man; as also earnestly desiring to be more faithful for the future; I here solemnly engage, in the presence of the great tri-une Jehovah, to enter into a firm and lasting covenant with Himself.

O thou most holy, pure, mighty, and merciful Jehovah, suffer a feeble, helpless, and unworthy worm to approach thy awful Majesty, through the merit and intercession of thy dear Son Jesus Christ, with whom 'thou art ever well-pleased.' I acknowledge, O Lord, my many offences! I especially bewail my past indolence and effeminacy, my sloth and idleness, my pride and self-will, my cowardice and shame. I see, O Lord, and would sensibly feel too, that all those sins are much heightened by the consideration of my being accounted a minister and preacher of the Gospel. (But O how unworthy the name!) I mourn also, O my God, (for such I wish from this time to call thee,) I mourn on account of my past lightness, and vain, unprofitable conversation; particularly as hundreds are under my immediate care, and thousands looking up to me for instruction, to be taught the wiles and devices of Satan, the deceitfulness of the human heart, and the treachery of an alluring world! But nothing grieves me more, O Lord, (as I hope thou now seest,) than a consciousness of my base and vile ingratitude towards thee. Many and great have been thy favours conferred upon me: But, O! I have been an unthankful creature! I have too often, alas!, rebelled against that kind parent who has hitherto 'nourished and brought me up.' Neither would I wish to conceal from thee, O Lord, the sinful gratification I find in being praised, and the uneasiness occasioned by hearing an equal or superior extolled above myself. I will not forget my base backwardness and carelessness in the discharge of my ministerial and sacred office. I own my neglect of prayer, my dulness therein, my sin in hastening it over, and in often entirely omitting it. I acknowledge also, that, instead of denying myself by fasting or abstinence, I have indulged myself, especially in unnecessary sleep and pleasant meat and drink.

There are many examples in the biography of the closeness between those who attended class meetings together, and the deep spiritual kinship of those who shared in band. The following letter, dated January 8, 1792, was written to Dickinson by Braithwaite in the second year of his appointment as an itinerant Methodist preacher.

My Kind and Dear Brother,

I heartily agree with you, in holding the *first* part of our letters sacred to Christian experience; in appropriating the *second*, to ask advice; the *third*, to an account of the work of God amongst us, and around us; and the *fourth*, to things of a miscellaneous and spiritual nature. And with these I the more readily acquiesce, as I see, and have before been convinced of, the justice of your remark, 'that our letters of last year were not so strictly spiritual and experimental, as they might have been.'

First, then, (and here I purpose being very plain, and simply honest,) I will give account of my experience. In preaching, in general, I find something to say; and frequently I have very much liberty, freedom, comfort, and a hope that good will be done. At some other times, my experience in this respect has been reversed. I frequently have found much of SELF in preaching; a desire to be thought a great, good, or correct preacher: And when another preacher has been praised in my hearing, sometimes I have been a little envious, and have wished I might be spoken well of. Now, I clearly see, this is from the bottomless pit; and

I resist it, in general, with my might; and when any one would speak well of me, it has been very painful. What is very wonderful, I, for a short moment, have been troubled sometimes with atheistical, sometimes with deistical, and sometimes with blasphemous thoughts! I have also frequently been made to doubt of the whole progress of the work of God in my soul. At other times, I have wondered how I could ever doubt. To-day, I have been made to think, that I was the vilest wretch breathing, and consequently have been thrown into a state of despondency. Perhaps to-morrow, again, I have thought myself in a high state of grace, and one of the most happy mortals living. Surely I have waded through deep waters, and have had no confidant; nor yet durst I keep any, lest my follies and weaknesses should hinder me from being useful in a public character. Notwithstanding all this, to see me move from place to place, and to have heard me converse with Christian friends, you would have thought all was calm and peaceable within. Sometimes I have thought, *I am all sanctified*; again, *I am and ever was an unbeliever*. I believe, the devil has frequently played upon my weak (and perhaps too scrupulous) conscience; and when I could not believe in one thing, he has frequently wrested the shield of faith from me in every other respect. Now I know my failing here. I should have held fast what I had, and not foolishly given up *all* on account of one particular circumstance. Of late I have been pretty comfortable, and have taken up, (in some things at least,) my cross cheerfully and profitably. I see the necessity of faith always, and the comfort of having a single eye. My desire appears to be, to please God, and all men for their good to edification. In general, the Lord gives me favor in the eyes of the people amongst whom I labour.

I have said so much of myself, (and I was afraid of it when I began,) that I cannot, in this letter, follow on in our newly-adopted method; especially as I appear to have as much more to say of myself. I would just observe, that I have been at four Love-feasts, since I came into this circuit; at the last of them were ten preachers, — five itinerant, and five local! I partook of the sacrament on Christmas-day. All these were profitable ordinances.

I am, dear Robert,
Your unworthy
J. BRAITHWAITE.

Excerpted from *The Life of the Rev. John Braithwaite, Wesleyan Methodist Preacher, Late of Mountpleasant, Whitehaven, Cumberland. Containing An Account of his Travels,*

Labours in the Ministry, and Writings; with a short Memoir of his Wife, Mrs. Mary Braithwaite. Compiled from his Letters and other Authentic Documents, by Robert Dickinson, Late Managing Partner at Seaton Iron Works (London: J. Kershaw, 1825), pp. 154-55, 114-16.

Appendix L

A

Description

OF

CLASS-MEETINGS

IN AN EPISTLE

FROM

A YOUNG LADY

OF THE METHODIST CONNEXION,

TO A

Female Acquaintance.

—»»◉‹‹—

WHITBY:

PRINTED AND SOLD BY CLARK AND MEDD, SOLD ALSO BY T. AND
H. EELES, STOCKTON, GARBUTT, SUNDERLAND, WHITING,
SCARBRO', TOPPING AND DAWSON, HULL, BLANSHARD,
LONDON, AND BY THE METHODIST PREACHERS
THROUGHOUT ENGLAND.

1817.

ADDRESS

The original of the following short production was written by a young lady, and sent to a Relation of the Editor, who, at her request, and for her private satisfaction, revised it, and arranged it in its present form. With deference to the young Lady's abilities, he begs to remark, that the ideas of the original were good, and sometimes new, but the style was such that it could not with propriety have appeared in print. Whilst it was in manuscript, of course few copies could be circulated; but thinking it might be of some little service to those who are unacquainted with the nature of the Methodist Class Meetings, he has now, though without her knowledge, taken the liberty of presenting it to the public.

A DESCRIPTION OF CLASS MEETINGS

When to our sev'ral classes we repair,
We strive to banish every earthly care;
With fervour strive that each rebellious thought
Into a due subjection may be brought:
And on our ent'ring, humbly kneeling, pray
That God would guide and lead us on our way,
Would, by his grace divine, fresh light impart,
And point the path of duty to each heart.
Yet conscious that no blessings we can claim,
We rest our hopes in our Emmanuel's name,
And whilst we bow contrited at his feet,
We find our intercourse both free and sweet.

At length sedate, our Leader takes his stand,
With pious Wesley's hymn-book in his hand;
Of an appropriate hymn he thence makes choice,
Inviting all to join with heart and voice
In praising God, for his abundant grace
So richly show'r'd upon the human race: —
And those whose voices are not tun'd to sing
May yet a tributary off'ring bring,
For, inwardly retir'd, the pious mind

Sweet seasons of refreshment oft will find:
Since God, who every secret thought descries,
Does not demand an outward sacrifice; —
He judges by the heart, from whence proceed
Fervent desires, and counts the will the deed.
Hence a soft tear, a soul emitted sigh,
Will sometimes call down blessings from the sky,
With strongly pleading accents will prevail,
When loud, though less sincere petitions fail.

The hymn concluded, we return to pray'r: —
And each, in this, becomes the Leader's care.
For whilst at Mercy's throne, he, suppliant, bends,
He craves divine assistance for his friends,
Prays that through grace they may be sanctified,
That Christ may enter in their hearts, and there abide!
And from the lips of those who are sincere,
A soft "Amen!" will gently echo here.
(Amen! when feelingly pronounc'd, implies
We breathe with him our wishes to the skies.)
Nor is this pray'r to us alone confin'd.
No! — it includes the wants of all mankind.
And charity, whose wide diffusive band
Embraces ev'ry kindred, ev'ry land,
Acknowledges with joy the pious strain,
And bids our tongues responsive cry, "Amen.!"

Finish'd the pray'r, each one resumes his seat
With silent order, and devotion meet.
Then in a strain all artless and sincere,
(No pompous diction is demanded here,)
Our leader first his simple tale relates,
His mental troubles, conflicts, and debates;
Tells how he struggles hard to conquer sin,
Assur'd that he must fight, if he would win.
A Christian must maintain a vig'rous strife,
But then it is for everlasting life;
A battle this with care and danger fraught,
For which he finds full exercise of thought: —
And far more worthy an immortal soul
To curb passions, and the will controul,

Than, arm'd in terrors, with a ruthless hand,
To spread destruction round a ruin'd land!
Thus, of th' importance of this strife aware,
He doubles ev'ry effort, ev'ry care;
And though his tribulations may increase
His Maker and his Conscience, whisper peace!
For oft the Sun of Righteousness will rise
And shine resplendent through the low'ring skies,
Disperse the clouds by Sin and Satan spread,
And calm the storm just bursting on his head.
Serenely mild, he feels his God impart
Inward support divine to cheer his heart;
His purest joys, that from religion flow
Have no dependance on this world below;
The world's vain pleasures leave behind a sting,
But these nor sorrow nor remorse will bring:
Pure as the bliss of the celestial bands;
Firm as the rock on which Heav'n's Altar stands!

Th' attentive hearers silently admire
The wond'rous goodness of their Heav'nly Sire,
And in their Leader's bless'd experience find
Instruction seal'd upon each serious mind;
They learn from his example how to bear
Of griefs, their portion, — of distress, their share.
And since ev'n to the favourites of Heav'n
Unnumber'd tribulations still are giv'n,
They learn to kiss the gently chast'ning rod,
And bow, submissive, to the will of God.

Our Leader then with meek persuasive strain,
Bids us without reserve our states explain;
What are our sev'ral views, — our hopes, — our fears? —
Is peace our portion, or repentant tears?
Have we from duty's dictates gone astray?
Or closely kept the rugged narrow way?
If admonition or reproof we need
The cause of truth his tongue will mildly plead,
Will place our errors in their proper light,
Warn us when wrong, encourage us when right,
Cheer the desponding self-abhorring soul

And bid the streams of comfort round it roll: —
And whilst the path of duty he pursues,
The blessed Gospel as his guide he views,
Acts by its laws, adores its saving plan,
And shows its influence on the heart of man.

Then is not Class a precious means of grace?
May we not sometimes thence our blessings trace?
For when we have our testimony giv'n,
We really often feel a little heav'n.
Bound in the chain of our Redeemer's love,
Our mounting spirits soar the world above:
The sacred leaven spreads throughout the whole
Till all th' assembly seems one mutual soul,
And a rich stream of grace pour'd from the skies
Each true Believer's thirsting breast supplies.

Those who have talents, and a gift of pray'r,
Are here invited to perform their share
Of that essential duty. — Should they shrink
And shun the cross, and into silence sink,
Our watchful Leader counsel will impart
To animate afresh the flagging heart.

Thus join'd in social fellowship, we find
We have an int'rest in th' Eternal Mind;
An int'rest bought by our Redeemer's blood,
When from his side it stream'd a purple flood!
He lives a sacred pledge God's word is true,
And all the promises through him we view;
Faith's piercing eye pervades the heav'nly shore,
And sees those promises reserv'd in store, —
For whom? — For us! — For all who will believe!
This rich inheritance they shall receive.
We cannot plead our Saviour's death in vain,
The Holy Spirit owns the pow'rful strain,
With pleasure hears the tender moving plea,
And gives the purchas'd blessing, — full and free.
The fountain of Salvation ne'er is dry;
Its flowing streams can ev'ry want supply;
And the sole passport requisite to bring

Is faith in him who owns the healing spring.
The seeking spirit, ardent and sincere,
Need no repulse, no harsh refusal fear,
For 'tis affirm'd that all who seek shall gain,
And all who knock an entrance shall obtain.
Peace, plac'd beyond the world's fugacious pow'r,
Cheers and supports us in each trying hour.
The stimulating fervour of pure love
Makes duty on the wings of pleasure move.
Receiv'd at first by faith, through faith we hold
A treasure,—richer far than burnish'd gold!
A treasure,—which no worldly wealth can buy!
A treasure,—which can time and death defy!
The sure and certain hope of that reward
Prepar'd for all true servants of the Lord!

In the pure bonds of love I now impart
Without reserve the feelings of my heart,
And soon, I trust, in fellowship you'll find
In this respect we all have but one mind!
All simple Methodists!—but mark me here,
All are not Methodists who such appear.
Religion's sacred garb some will assume,
To give their evil passions greater room;
Self int'rest oft will recommend deceit,
Nor is it easy to detect the cheat.

But here, my friend, let us forbear to roam,
And inward turn our eyes, and look at home;
If carefully explor'd, that soil will yield
For mental exercise an ample field.
'Tis not a mere profession or a name,
That will substantiate an eternal claim;
There needs a something more to win the prize,—
Couch'd in three words the sole condition lies,—
"Follow thou me!" This one command obey.
Thine is the crown, and thine the realms of day.

Though low my state, and small my stock of grace
I am acquainted with that heav'nly place
Whence an abundant stream of love divine

At times o'erflows this rebel heart of mine.
Mary, she chose the spot and better part,
And worshipp'd with an undivided heart,
Whilst Martha, cumber'd with the world's affairs,
Paid more attention to her household cares.
Could we attain that precious humble state,
Regardless if the world, or love, or hate,
Its frowns we might despise, its praise reject,
And calmly bear derision and neglect;
For Jesus' sake with patience all endure,
And thus a rich inheritance secure.

    The world, so prone to judge by outward show,
Of heart-felt piety can little know,
And hence no unregenerated man
Can comprehend the Methodist plan.
For those to whom its influence is not known,
Who reason but from theory alone,
Morality with faith will still confound,
And on their works their future hopes they ground.

    But here such prospects open on my view,
My Muse no longer must this theme pursue,
Lest launching forth into a space too wide
Her fault'ring footsteps fail without a guide.

    Then let me turn, and in a brief survey
Our various priviledges here display;
The consolations and the hopes unfold,
Resulting from the tenets that we hold.
In Jesus' wounds we find a pow'rful balm
That can our fears allay, our foes disarm.
The wretch who liv'd to sin a willing slave,
Feels his strong fetters burst at Jesus' grave.
The sick find comfort in their deep distress.
The heavy-laden feel their burdens less.
The weak are strengthen'd, and the naked clad.
The hungry fed, the mourning soul made glad.
Our great Physician gives to ev'ry state,
A remedy completely adequate.

The sensual world can never comprehend
The rich resources that we have, my friend:
Yet these are not exclusively confin'd
To Methodists: — they reach to all mankind
Who live according to the gospel Law,
And of their Lord's commandments stand in awe.

Yet, I confess, your name I wish to see
Upon the list of our fraternity,
As one more vot'ry in the cause of God,
Treading the path our pious founder trod.
But lest, deceiv'd; you should suppose the road
To truth, with blooming flow'rs alone is strew'd,
With friendly zeal I'll act a candid part
And 'gainst the flatt'ring vision guard your heart;
My own experience frankly I'll declare
That for the strife your soul you may prepare.

And first, false reas'nings, near allied to sin,
Harrass'd my mind, and crept unwelcome in,
With groundless doubts and fears my steps assail'd,
And sometimes even o'er my faith prevail'd;
The bursting flames of eager zeal repress'd,
And damp'd the pious ardour of my breast;
But as my name was written on the cross,
I found I ought to count all things as dross
That would obstract my path, when call'd to meet
My class: — yet thither oft I dragg'd my feet,
Reluctant dragg'd, — My duty then became
An irksome task, not an inspiring flame.
When there arriv'd and 'twas my turn to speak,
The silence oft I had no pow'r to break;
Mute consternation seiz'd my trembling tongue
And on my lips th' unwilling accents hung.
But whilst I totter'd on perdition's brink
And felt my fainting soul within me sink,
My gracious Saviour, near in time of need,
Bade me still hope, and on my way proceed:
Pow'rful to help, and merciful to save,
Fresh strength and courage to my heart he gave;
He wip'd the streaming tears that dimm'd mine eye,

And from my heaving bosom chas'd the sigh.
And though self-love, dire enemy to good,
My spiritual progress oft withstood,
With subtle arguments oppos'd my course,
And undermin'd my soul with winning force,
Yet Jesus, in his fear whilst I abode,
Divine assistance graciously bestow'd,
Enabling me to quell this inbred foe,
And at his feet to lay the rebel low.
He taught me ev'ry moment to deny
Myself, and all my lusts to crucify,
That he alone might reign within my breast,
Of all my wishes, all my love possess'd.

    With you, my friend, O may this be the case,
This lively spiritual growth in grace,
That will your carnal appetites subdue,
And teach you what to shun, and what pursue!
Devote yourself to God,—and you will prove
The height, and depth, and breadth of pard'ning love.
Devote yourself to God,—in Him believe,
And ev'ry blessing from his hand receive.
But self must be subdued ere we can find
Free intercourse with the Eternal Mind;
Yet vainly all exertions will be made
To subjugate our wills without his aid,
For our own unassisted strength and pow'r
Will prove too feeble in temptation's hour.
But he, in whom alone we place our trust
Knows that we are but animated dust;
He knows the frailties of our mortal state,
Unable to oppose infernal hate,
And hence has promis'd his right arm to bare,
Whene'er his people need his guardian care.
With confidence these promises we claim
Through faith in Jesus' blood, in Jesus' name,
Nor will our God the claims of those deny,
For whom a Saviour left his Heav'n to die!

    But Time, that urges on his course amain,
Now presses hard and would my pen restrain,

Yet ere my verse I close and drop the lyre,
Just let me add how fervent my desire
That Christ may pour his spirit in your breast,
And lead you to his everlasting rest!
When you peruse these harsh unpolish'd lines
Where no persuasive wit nor beauty shines,
O may he work upon your yielding heart,
And all my meaning to your soul impart!
And should it be his gracious will to bless
These efforts, and to crown them with success,
Soon shall the Methodists with joy behold
Your name amongst their thick'ning ranks enroll'd,
With them one Triune God t'adore, and raise
To Father, Son, and Spirit, hymns of praise!

As for myself, I humbly bless the day
When first my wand'ring feet, so prone to stray,
Warn'd by free grace to shun impending wrath,
With trembling fervour sought the heav'nward path.
Then, joining with the Methodists, I found
Pure were their principles, their doctrines sound,
And, as their tenets more and more I knew,
Stronger attachment in my bosom grew,
Till in their ordinances now I feel
Constant alacrity, and eager zeal.

But yet, my friend, do not mistake me here.
My Mother Church I piously revere;
Her long-established rites I still commend,
And at her Altars with devotion bend.
My pen no wild schismatick frenzy guides,
No party spirit o'er my breast presides;
But having found at length sweet peace of mind,
I wish'd my friend that treasure too might find.
Accept then this small tribute of my love,
With pray'rs that it may beneficial prove.
Pardon defects: its various faults excuse:
For sure the theme is far above my Muse.
Farewell, dear Maid! in Christian love, farewell!
In the best bonds believe me yours.

Appendix M

"MY CLASS LEADER"

When first I joined Zion's band,
Who kindly took me by the hand,
And prayed that I might faithful stand?
                    My Class Leader!

Who bade me flee from Satan's wile,
And shun the world's alluring smile,
Nor let its charms my soul beguile?
                    My Class Leader!

When peace and love my soul possesst,
And holy triumph fill'd my breast,
Who did rejoice to see me blest?
                    My Class Leader!

In fierce temptation's trying hour,
When clouds and darkness round me lour,
Who bids me trust God's mighty power?
                    My Class Leader!

When keen affliction's pointed dart,
And grief and anguish wound my heart,
Who consolation doth impart?
                    My Class Leader!

When worldly vanity and care
Have in my heart too great a share,
Who warns me of the fatal snare?
                    My Class Leader!

When'er my wandering footsteps stray
From wisdom's sweet and pleasant way,
Who over me doth weep and pray?
                    My Class Leader!

How grateful, then, I ought to be,
And bless that mercy rich and free,
Which ever granted unto me
     A Class Leader!

But faintly language doth express
The feelings which my soul possess;
O may a God of mercy bless
     My Class Leader!

May thy sojourning days below
In quiet peace and pleasure flow, —
Free from all sorrow, pain, and woe,
     My Class Leader!

And in thy last, thy closing scene,
May Jesu's glory round thee beam,
Without a cloud to intervene,
     My Class Leader!

And when with me life's dream is o'er,
And I shall weep and sigh no more,
O may we meet on Canaan's shore,
     My Class Leader!

Reproduced from *The Wesleyan Methodist Association Magazine*, 4 (1841): 126-27.

BIBLIOGRAPHY

PRIMARY SOURCES
(including later editions)

Alleine, Joseph. *An Alarm to Unconverted Sinners*. London: Printed by Nevil Simmons, 1672; Nashville: Publishing House of the M.E. Church, South, 1920.

Alleine, Richard. *Vindiciae Pietatis: or, A Vindication of Godlinesse, In the greatest Strictness and Spirituality of it, from the Imputations of Folly and Fancy. Together with Several Directions for the Attaining and Maintaining of a Godly Life*. London: Printed for Peter Parker, 1663.

Ames, William. *The Marrow of Theology* (1623). Translated and edited by John D. Eusden. Boston: Pilgrim Press, 1968.

Andrewes, Lancelot. *The Works of Lancelot Andrewes*. Edited by J.P. Wilson and J. Bliss. 11 vols. Oxford: J.H. Parker, 1841-54.

Arminian Magazine, Consisting of Extracts and Original Treatises on Universal Redemption. 1778 &ff.

Atkinson, John. *The Class Leader: his work and how to do it*. New York: Phillips and Hunt, 1882.

Bancroft, Richard. *Daungerous Positions and Proceedings, published and practised within this Iland of Brytaine and under pretence of Reformation, and for the Presbyteriall Discipline*. London: Imprinted for John Wolfe, 1593.

Barnes, Robert. *The Whole Workes of W. Tyndall, John Frith and Doct. Barnes*. London: John Daye, 1573.

Baxter, Richard. *Aphorisms of Justification*. London: printed for Francis Tyton, 1649.

_____. *Gildas Salvianus: The Reformed Pastor: shewing the nature of the pastoral work: especially in private instruction and catechising: with an open confession of our too open sins*. London, 1656.

_____. *A Treatise of Episcopacy; confuting by Scripture, Reason, and the Churches Testimony, that sort of Diocesan Churches, Prelacy, and Government, Which casteth out The Primitive Church-Species, Episcopacy, Ministry and Discipline, and confoundeth the*

Christian World by Corruption, Usurpation, Schism, and Persecution. London: printed for Nevil Simmons, 1681.

————. *Reliquiae Baxterianae: Or, Mr. Richard Baxter's Narrative of The Most Memorable Passages of his Life and Times.* Faithfully Publish'd from his own Original Manuscript, by Matthew Sylvester. London, 1696.

————. *The Practical Works of The Rev. Richard Baxter: with a life of the author and a critical examination of his writings, by the Rev. William Orme.* 23 vols. London: James Duncan, 1830.

Benham, Daniel. *Memoirs of James Hutton; Comprising the Annals of His Life and Connection with the United Brethren.* London: Hamilton, Adams, and Co., 1856.

Bettenson, Henry, ed. *Documents of the Christian Church.* 2d ed. London: Oxford University Press, 1963.

Bucer, Martin. *Common Places.* Translated and edited by D.F. Wright. The Courtenay Library of Reformation Classics: 4. Appleford, Berkshire: The Sutton Courtenay Press, 1972.

Bull, George. *Harmonia Apostolica: Or Two Dissertations; in the Forms of which the Doctrine of St. James on Justification by Works is Explained and Defended: in the latter the Agreement of St. Paul with St. James is clearly shown.* 2d ed. Library of Anglo-Catholic Theology. Volume 24. Oxford: John Henry Parker, 1844.

Calvin, Jean. *Institutes of the Christian Religion.* Edited by John T. McNeill, translated by Ford Lewis Battles. Library of Christian Classics. Volumes 20 & 21. Philadelphia: Westminster Press, 1960.

Carvosso, William. *A Memoir of Mr. William Carvosso, Sixty Years a Class Leader in the Wesleyan Methodist Connection.* From the 10th edition. New York: Lane & Scott, 1849.

Class Book, A; containing Directions to Class-Leaders, Ruled Forms for Leaders' Weekly Accounts, and The Rules of the Methodist Societies. London: Printed by T. Cordeux for T. Blanchard, 1820.

Cranmer, Thomas. *Writings and Disputations.* Edited for The Parker Society by John Edmund Cox. Cambridge: at the University Press, 1844.

————. *Miscellaneous Writings and Letters.* Edited for The Parker Society by John Edmund Cox. Cambridge: at the University Press, 1846.

Cranz, David. *The Ancient and Modern History of the Brethren, or, a Succinct Narrative of the Protestant Church of the United Brethren, or Unitas Fratrum, In the remoter Ages, and particularly in the present Century.* Translated by Benjamin La Trobe. London: W. and A. Strahan, 1780.

Crowther, Jonathan. *A True and Complete Portraiture of Methodism; or the History of the Wesleyan Methodists: including their Rise, Progress, and Present State &c.* New York: James Eastburn, 1813.

Coulson, John E. *The Peasant Preacher: Memorials of Mr. Charles Richardson, A Wesleyan Evangelist, commonly known as the "Lincolnshire Thrasher"; with Sermon Notes and an Itinerary.* London: Hamilton, Adams, and Co., 1865.

Dickinson, Robert. *The Life of the Rev. John Braithwaite, Wesleyan Methodist Preacher, Late of Mountpleasant, Whitehaven, Cumberland. Containing An Account of his Travels, Labours in the Ministry, and Writings; with a short Memoir of his Wife, Mrs. Mary Braithwaite. Compiled from his Letters and other Authentic Documents.* London: J. Kershaw, 1825.

Drew, Jacob Halls. *The Life, Character, and Literary Labours of Samuel Drew, A.M.* By his elder son. London: Longman, Rees, Orme, Brown, Green & Longman, 1934.

Entwhistle, Joseph. *Memoir of The Rev. Joseph Entwhistle, Fifty-four Years a Wesleyan Minister.* By his son. Bristol, 1848.

Fletcher, John. *The Works of.* 9 vols. London: John Mason, 1859.

Garner, William. *The Life of The Rev. and Venerable William Clowes, one of the patriarchs of the Primitive Methodist Connexion.* London: William Lister, 1868.

Goodell, Charles L. *The Drillmaster of Methodism; principles and methods for the class leader and pastor.* New York: Eaton & Mains, 1902.

Graham, J.J. *A History of Wesleyan Methodism in Sheffield Park, Sheffield.* Sheffield: Sir W.C. Leng & Co., 1914.

Grindal, Edmund. *The Remains of Edmund Grindal, D.D., Successively Bishop of London, and Archbishop of York and Canterbury.* Edited for The Parker Society by William Nicholson. Cambridge: at the University Press, 1843.

Halévy, Elie. *A History of the English People in the Nineteenth Century. Volume 1: England in 1815.* Translated and edited by E.I. Watkin and D.A. Barker. Introduction by R.B. McCallum. New York: Barnes & Noble, 1961.

――――――. *The Birth of Methodism in England.* Translated and with an introduction by Bernard Semmel. Chicago: University of Chicago Press, 1971.

Harrison, Robert, and Browne, Robert. *The Writings of.* Edited by
    Leland H. Carlson. Elizabethan Nonconformist Texts. Volume 2.
    Published for The Sir Halley Stewart Trust. London: George Allen
    and Unwin, Ltd., 1953.

Hone, Richard B. *Lives of Eminent Christians.* 3 vols. London: J.W.
    Parker, 1837-39.

Hooker, Richard. *The Ecclesiastical Polity and other Works of Richard
    Hooker; with His Life by Izaak Walton, and Strype's Interpolations,
    &c.* Edited and with an introduction by Benjamin Hanbury. 3 vols.
    London: Holdsworth and Ball, 1830.

Homilies. *Certain Sermons or Homilies appointed to be read in
    Churches in the time of Queen Elizabeth.* London: SPCK, 1899.

Horneck, Anthony. *Several Sermons upon the Fifth of St. Matthew;
    being part of Christ's Sermon on the Mount.* 2 vols. 3d ed.
    London: Jer. Batley, 1717.

Hymns. *A Collection of Hymns, for the Use of the People called
    Methodists.* Preface by John Wesley, London, Oct. 20, 1779.
    London: Paramore, 1780. See also Wesley, *Oxford Edition.*

*Independent Methodist Magazine; or, Repository of Religious Knowl-
    edge, &c.* 1826 & ff.

Jackson, Thomas, ed. *The Lives of Early Methodist Preachers. Chiefly
    Written by Themselves.* 6 vols. 4th ed. London: Wesleyan Con-
    ference Office, 1876.

King, Lord Peter. *An Enquiry into the Constitution, Discipline, Unity
    and Worship, of the Primitive Church, That Flourish'd within the
    first Three Hundred Years after Christ. Faithfully Collected out of
    the Extant Writings of those Ages. By an Impartial Hand.* London:
    Printed for J. Wyat, 1713.

Laud, William. *The Works of the Most Reverend Father in God, William
    Laud, D.D., Sometime Archbishop of Canterbury.* Edited by W.
    Scott and J. Bliss. 7 vols. in 9. Oxford: J.H. Parker, 1847-60.

Law, William. *A Serious Call to a Devout and Holy Life.* London:
    Printed for William Innys, 1729.

Leslie, James. *An Address to the Weslean [sic] Methodist Preachers and
    Leaders of Edinburgh. By two members of the Society.* Edinburgh,
    1826.

Lloyd, Charles, ed., *Formularies of Faith put forth by Authority during
    the reign of Henry VIII.* Oxford: at the Clarendon Press, 1825.

Martin, Thomas. *Thoughts on the Nature and Advantages of Class-
    Meeting, (As Adopted in the Methodist Societies:) Including an
    Account of the Origin, Authority, and General Oeconomy of that*

*Institution: Intended to Explain and Recommend it, to whom-
soever it may concern.* London: Printed at the Conference Office
by Thomas Cordeux, 1813.

*Methodist Magazine, being a Continuation of the Arminian Magazine,
consisting chiefly of Extracts and Original Treatises on General
Redemption.* 1798 & ff.

Miley, John. *A Treatise on Class Meetings.* Cincinnati: The Methodist
Book Concern, 1851.

*Minutes of the Methodist Conferences, from the first, held in London,
by the late Rev. John Wesley, A.M., in the year 1744. Volume 1.*
London: at the Conference Office, 1812.

———. *John Bennet's Copy of the Minutes of the Conferences of
1744, 1745, 1747 and 1748; with Wesley's Copy of those for 1746.*
Publications of The Wesley Historical Society. No. 1. London:
Wesley Historical Society, 1896.

Murray, Gilbert [Richard Newman Wycherley]. *The Methodist Class
Meeting.* London: Robert Cully, n.d.

Myles, William. *A Chronological History of the People called Methodists; from their rise in the year 1729, to their last Conference in
1802.* 3d ed., enl. London, 1803.

Nelson, John. *Journal of; being an account of God's dealing with his
soul from his youth to the forty-second year of his age, and his
working by him: Likewise the Oppressions he met with from
People of different Denominations, Written by Himself.* Introduction by William Reed. London: W. Reed, United Methodist Free
Churches' Book Room, 1870.

Nightingale, Joseph. *A Portraiture of Methodism: being An Impartial
View of the Rise, Progress, Doctrines, Discipline, and Manners of
the Wesleyan Methodists. In a Series of Letters, Addressed to a
Lady.* London: Longman, Hurst, Rees, and Orme, 1807.

Owen, John. *Of the Divine Originall, Authority, self-evidencing Light,
and Power of the Scriptures.* London: 1659.

Peirce, William. *The Ecclesiastical Principles and Polity of the Wesleyan
Methodists.* 3d ed. Revised by Frederick J. Jobson. London:
Wesleyan Conference Office, 1873.

Preston, John. *The New Covenant, or The Saints Portion. A Treatise
unfolding the All-sufficiencie of God, and Mans uprightnes, and the
Covenant of Grace.* London: Printed by I.D. for Nicolas Bourne,
1629.

———. *The Breast-plate of Faith and Love. A Treatise Wherein ground and exercise of Faith and Love, as they are set upon*

Christ their Object, and as they are expressed in Good Workes, es explained. London: Printed by W.I. for Nicholas Bourne, 1630.

Rimius, Henry. *A Candid Narrative of the Rise and Progress of the Hermhuters, commonly called Moravians, or, Unitas Fratrum; with a short Account of their Doctrines, drawn from their own Writings.* London: Printed for A. Linde, 1753.

Rosser, James. *The History of Wesleyan Methodism in the Isle of Man.* London: J. Mason, 1849.

_____. *Class Meetings: Embracing their Origin, Nature, Obligation and Benefits.* Richmond: published by the Author, 1855.

Rule,William H. *Wesleyan Methodism regarded as the system of a Christian Church.* London: Aylott & Jones, 1846.

Rutherford, Samuel. *The Covenant of Life Opened: Or, a Treatise of the Covenant of Grace.* London: Printed for Andrew Crook, 1655.

Savoy Declaration of Faith and Order, 1658. Edited by Albert Peel. London: Independent Press, 1939.

Schaff, Philip. *Creeds of Christendom.* 3 vols., 4th ed., rev. & enl. New York: Harper & Brothers, 1877; reprint ed., Grand Rapids, Michigan: Baker Book House, 1983.

Scougal, Henry. *The Life of God in the Soul of Man.* London: Printed for J. Downing, 1726.

Southey, Robert. *The Life of Wesley; and the Rise and Progress of Methodism.* 2 vols. 2d ed. London: Longman, Hurst, Rees, Orme, and Brown, 1820.

Spener, Philip Jakob. *Pia Desideria.* Translated, edited and with an introduction by Theodore G. Tappert. Philadelphia: Fortress Press, 1964.

Stamp, William W. *Historical Notices of Wesleyan Methodism, in Bradford and its vicinity.* London: Mason, 1841.

_____. *The Orphan-House of Wesley; with notices of early Methodism in Newcastle-upon-Tyne, and its vicinity.* London: John Mason, 1863.

Stevenson, George J. *City Road Chapel, London, and its Associations Historical, Biographical, and Memorial.* London, George J. Stevenson [1872].

Stillingfleet, Edward. *Irenicum; a Weapon Salve for the Church's Wounds.* 2d. ed. London: Mortlock, 1662.

Strype, John. *Annals of the Reformation and Establishment of Religion, and other various occurrences in the Church of England, during*

Queen Elizabeth's happy reign; &c. 4 vols. in 7. Oxford: at the Clarendon Press, 1824.

Sunman, W.R. *The History of Free Methodism in and about Newcastle-on-Tyne.* Newcastle-on-Tyne: A. Dickson, 1902.

Taylor, Jeremy. *The Whole Works of the Right Reverend Jeremy Taylor.* Edited by Reginald Heber. Revised and corrected by Charles Page Eden. 10 vols. London: 1862.

Theologia Germanica of Martin Luther. New York: Paulist Press, 1980.

Thirty-nine Articles, The, of the Church of England. Explained with an Introduction by Edgar C.S. Gibson. 2 vols. London: Methuen & Co. Ltd., 1897.

Two Elizabethan Puritan Diaries; by Richard Rogers and Samuel Ward. Edited by M.M. Knappen. Chicago: The American Society of Church History, 1933.

Two Liturgies, The, A.D. 1549 and A.D. 1552: with other Documents set forth by authority in the reign of King Edward VI. Edited for The Parker Society by Joseph Ketley. Cambridge: at the University Press, 1844.

Tyndale, William. *Doctrinal Treatises and Introductions to Different Portions of the Holy Scriptures.* Edited for The Park Society by Henry Walter. Cambridge: at the University Press, 1848.

Wesley, John, ed. *The Doctrine of Salvation, Faith, and Good Works. Extracted from the Homilies of the Church of England.* London: [Strahan] for James Hutton, 1739.

————, *The Nature, Design, and General Rules of the United Societies in London, Bristol, King's-wood, and Newcastle upon Tyne.* Newcastle upon Tyne: John Gooding, 1743.

————, ed. *An Extract of Mr. Richard Baxter's Aphorisms of Justification. Publish'd by John Wesley . . .* Newcastle upon Tyne: John Gooding, 1745.

————, ed. *A Christian Library. Consisting of Extracts from and Abridgments of the Choicest Pieces of Practical Divinity, Which Have Been Published in the English Tongue.* 50 vols. Bristol: W. Pine, 1749-55.

————. *Explanatory Notes upon the New Testament.* London: Bowyer, 1755.

————. *The Journal of the Rev. John Wesley, A.M.* Edited by Nehemiah Curnock. Standard Edition, 8 vols. London: The Epworth Press, 1909-16.

————. *The Letters of Rev. John Wesley, A.M.* Edited by John Telford.

Standard Edition, 8 vols. London: The Epworth Press, 1931.

_____. *The Bicentennial Edition of The Works of John Wesley.* Editor-in-chief Frank Baker. Volume 1: Sermons I: 1-33. Edited by Albert C. Outler. Nashville: Abingdon Press, 1984.

_____. *The Oxford Edition of The Works of John Wesley.* Editor-in-chief Frank Baker. Oxford: at the Clarendon Press.

Vol. 7: *A Collection of Hymns for the Use of the People called Methodists.* Edited by Franz Hildebrandt & Oliver Beckerlegge with the assistance of James Dale. 1983.

Vol. 11: *The Appeals to Men of Reason and Religion and Certain Related Open Letters.* Edited by Gerald R. Cragg. 1975.

Vol. 25: *Letters I: 1725-1739.* Edited by Frank Baker. 1980.

Vol. 26: *Letters II: 1740-1755.* Edited by Frank Baker. 1982.

_____. *The Standard Sermons of John Wesley.* Edited by Edward H. Sugden. 2 vols. London: Epworth Press, 1921.

_____. *The Works of John Wesley.* 14 vols. London: Wesleyan Conference Office, 1872. Reprint ed., Grand Rapids, Michigan: Baker Book House, 1979.

_____. *John Wesley.* Edited by Albert C. Outler. Library of Protestant Thought. New York: Oxford University Press, 1964.

_____. *Letter to a Roman Catholic.* Edited by Michael Hurley, S.J. Nashville: Abingdon Press, 1968.

Wesley, Samuel. *The Pious Communicant Rightly Prepar'd.* London: Printed for Charles Harper, 1700.

Wesleyan Methodist Association Magazine. 1838 & ff.

Whitefield, George. *Journals of; A new edition containing fuller material than any hitherto published.* London: The Banner of Truth Trust, 1960.

Whitgift, John. *The Works of.* Edited for The Parker Society by John Ayre. 3 vols. Cambridge: at the University Press, 1853.

Woodward, Josiah. *An Account of the Rise and Progress of the Religious Societies in the City of London, &c., and of their Endeavours for the Reformation of Manners,* 1698. 5th ed. London: J. Downing, 1724.

[_____.] *An Account of the Societies for Reformation of Manners, in London and Westminster, And other Parts of the Kingdom. With A Persuasive to Persons of all Ranks, to be Zealous and Diligent in Promoting the Execution of the Laws against Prophaneness and Debauchery, For the Effecting a National Reformation.* London: Printed for B. Aylmer, 1699.

SECONDARY SOURCES

Addison, William George. *The Renewed Church of the United Brethren, 1722-1930.* London: S.P.C.K., 1932.

Agnew, Theodore L. "Methodism on the Frontier," in *The History of American Methodism.* Edited by Emory Stevens Bucke. 3 vols. Nashville: Abingdon Press, 1964.

Allen, W.O., and McClure, Edmund. *Two Hundred Years: The History of the Society for Promoting Christian Knowledge, 1698-1898.* London: S.P.C.K., 1898.

Allison, C.F. *The Rise of Moralism: The Proclamation of the Gospel from Hooker to Baxter.* New York: The Seabury Press, 1966.

Arias, Mortimer. *Announcing the Reign of God: Evangelization and the Subversive Memory of Jesus.* Philadelphia: Fortress Press, 1984.

Back, Kurt W. "Influence through Social Communication." *Journal of Abnormal and Social Psychology* 46 (1951):9-23.

_____. *Beyond Words: The Story of Sensitivity Training and the Encounter Movement.* Baltimore, Md.: Penguin Books Inc., 1973.

Baker, Frank. "John Wesley and the 'Imitatio Christi'." *The London Quarterly and Holborn Review* 166 (1941):74-87.

_____. "The Beginnings of the Methodist Covenant Service." *The London Quarterly and Holborn Review* 180.3 (July 1955):216.

_____. *Methodism and the Lovefeast* (London: Epworth Press, 1957).

_____. "John Wesley's Churchmanship." *London Holborn and Quarterly Review* 185 (1960): 210-15, 269-74.

_____. "Wesley's Puritan Ancestry." *London Quarterly and Holborn Review* 187 (1962):180-86.

_____. "The People Called Methodists. 3: Polity." In *A History of the Methodist Church in Great Britain.* Edited by R.E. Davies and E.G. Rupp. Volume 1. London: The Epworth Press, 1965.

_____. *A Union Catalogue of the Publications of John and Charles Wesley.* Durham, N.C.: Duke University, 1966.

_____. *John Wesley and the Church of England.* Nashville: Abingdon Press, 1970.

_____. *From Wesley to Asbury: Studies in Early American Methodism.* Durham, N.C.: Duke University Press, 1976.

Barreiro, Alvaro. *Basic Ecclesial Communities: The Evangelization of the Poor.* Maryknoll: Orbis Books, 1982.

Barrett, C.K. *A Commentary on The Second Epistle to the Corinthians.* New York: Harper & Row, 1973.

Bavarel, Michel. *New Communities, New Ministries: The Church Resurgent in Africa, Asia and Latin America.* Orbis Books, 1983.

Bennis, Schein, Berlew, and Steele. *Interpersonal Dynamics: Essays and Readings on Human Interaction.* 2d ed. Holmewood, Illinois: The Dorsey Press, 1968.

Bishop, John. *Methodist Worship in Relation to Free Church Worship.* Scholar Studies Press, Inc., 1975.

Bowmer, John C. *Pastor and People: A Study of Church and ministry in Wesleyan Methodism from the death of John Wesley (1791) to the death of Jabez Bunting (1858).* London: Epworth Press, 1975.

Brauer, Jerald C. "Reflections on the Nature of English Puritanism." *Church History* 23.2 (June 1954):99-108.

Bromiley, G. W. *Thomas Cranmer, Theologian.* London: Lutterworth Press, 1956.

Burrage, Champlin. *The Early English Dissenters in the light of recent research.* 2 vols., 1912. Reprint ed., New York: Russell & Russell, 1967.

Butterfield, Herbert. "England in the Eighteenth Century," in *A History of the Methodist Church in Great Britain, Vol. 1.* Edited by R.E. Davies and E.G. Rupp. London: Epworth Press, 1965. pp. 1-33.

Cardenal, Ernesto. *The Gospel in Solentiname.* 4 vols. Maryknoll: Orbis Books, 1976-82.

Carré, Meyrick H. *Phases of Thought in England.* Oxford: at the Clarendon Press, 1949.

Chambers, J.D. *Population, Economy, and Society in Pre-Industrial England.* Edited by W.A. Armstrong. London: Oxford University Press, 1972.

Chiles, Robert E. *Theological Transition in American Methodism, 1790-1935.* New York: Abingdon Press, 1965.

Church, Leslie F. *The Early Methodist People.* London: S.P.C.K., 1948.

_____. *More About the Early Methodist People.* London: Epworth Press, 1949.

Clarke, W. Lowther. *A History of the S.P.C.K.* London: S.P.C.K., 1959.

Clebsch, William A. *Christianity in European History.* New York: Oxford University Press, 1979.

Cohn, Norman. *The Pursuit of the Millenium: Revolutionary Millenarians and Mystical Anarchists of the Middle Ages.* New York: Oxford University Press, 1970.

Collinson, Patrick. *The Elizabethan Puritan Movement.* London: Jonathan Cape, 1967.

Cook, William. "Historic Patterns in Protestant Grass Roots Communities." *Occasional Essays.* San José, Costa Rica: Latin American Evangelical Center for Pastoral Studies 9.1 (June 1982):3-40.

Cragg, Gerald R. *Puritanism in the Period of the Great Persecution 1660-1688.* Cambridge: at the University Press, 1957.

_____. *The Church and the Age of Reason, 1648-1789.* Baltimore, Md.: Penguin Books, 1960.

_____. *Reason and Authority in the Eighteenth Century.* Cambridge: at the University Press, 1964.

Currie, Robert. *Methodism Divided: A Study in the Sociology of Ecumenicalism.* London: Faber & Faber, 1968.

Cushman, Robert E. *Faith Seeking Understanding: Essays Theological and Critical.* Durham, North Carolina: Duke University Press, 1981.

Davies, Horton. *Worship and Theology in England.* Vol. 2: *From Andrewes to Baxter and Fox, 1603-1690.* Princeton: Princeton University Press, 1975.

Dayton, Donald W. *Discovering an Evangelical Heritage.* New York: Harper & Row, 1976.

Dean, William W. "The Methodist Class Meeting: The Significance of its Decline." *Proceedings of the Wesley Historical Society* 53:3 (December 1981):41-48.

Dearing, Trevor. *Wesleyan and Tractarian Worship.* London: Epworth Press, 1966.

Deschner, John. "Methodism," in *A Handbook of Christian Theology.* Edited by M. Halverson and A.A. Cohen. New York: Living Age Books, 1958.

Dickens, A.G. *The English Reformation.* New York: Schocken Books, 1964.

Dillenberger, John and Welch, Claude. *Protestant Christianity interpreted through its development.* New York: Charles Scribner's Sons, 1958.

Dring, Tom. "The World Family in History." *London Quarterly and Holborn Review* 177 (1952): 111-17, 206-12.

Edwards, Maldwyn. *Family Circle: A Study of the Epworth Household in Relation to John and Charles Wesley.* London: Epworth Press, 1949.

Emerick, Samuel, ed. *Spiritual Renewal for Methodism: A Discussion of the Early Methodist Class Meeting and the Values Inherent in Personal Groups Today.* Nashville: Methodist Evangelistic Materials, 1958.

Estes, James M. "Johannes Brenz and the Problem of Ecclesiastical Discipline." *Church History* 41.4 (December 1972):464-79.

Ferguson, Charles W. *Methodists and the Making of America: Organizing to Beat the Devil.* 2d edition. Austin, Texas: Eakin Press, 1983.

Festinger, Leon, and Aaronson, Elliot. "Arousal and Reduction of Dissonance in Social Contexts." In *Group Dynamics: Research and Theory.* 3d ed. Edited by Dorwin Cartwright and Alvin Zander. Evanston, Illinois: Row, Peterson & Company, 1968.

Festinger, Leon. *A Theory of Cognitive Dissonance.* Evanston, Illinois: Row, Peterson and Company, 1957.

Flew, R. Newton. "Methodism and Catholic Tradition." In *Northern Catholicism: Centenary Studies in the Oxford and Parallel Movements.* Edited by N.P. Williams and Charles Harris. London: S.P.C.K., 1933.

_____. *The Idea of Perfection in Christian Theology. An Historical Study of the Christian Ideal for the Present Life.* London: Oxford University Press, 1934.

Fowler, James W. *Stages of Faith: The Psychology of Human Development and the Quest for Meaning.* San Francisco: Harper & Row, 1981.

Gollin, Gillian Lindt. *Moravians in Two Worlds.* New York: Columbia University Press, 1967.

Gordon, Alexander, ed. *Freedom After Ejection: A Review (1690-1692) of Presbyterian and Congregational Nonconformity in England and Wales.* Manchester: at the University Press, 1917.

Green V.H.H. *The Young Mr. Wesley: A Study of John Wesley and Oxford.* New York: St. Martin's Press, 1961.

Griffith, G. Talbot. *Problems of the Age of Malthus.* 2d ed. London: Frank Cass & Company, 1967.

Hamilton, Kenneth G. "The Office of the Bishop in the Renewed Moravian Church." *Transactions of the Moravian Historical Society* 16.1 (1953):30-58.

Hamilton, J. Taylor, and Hamilton, Kenneth G. *History of the Moravian Church: The Renewed Unitas Fratrum.* Bethlehem, Pa.: Interprovincial Board of Christian Education, Moravian Church in America, 1967.

Hammond, J.L. and Barbara. *The Village Labourer.* London: Longmans, Green & Co. Ltd., 1911. Reprint ed., Guild Books, 2 vols., 1948.

_____. *The Town Labourer (1760-1832)*. London: Longmans, Green and Co. Ltd., 1917. Reprint ed., Guild Books, 2 vols., 1949.

Harrison, A.W. "The Church," in *Methodism in the Modern World*. Edited by J. Scott Lidgett and Bryan H. Reed. London: The Epworth Press, 1929.

Healey, Joseph G. *A Fifth Gospel: The Experience of Black Christian Values*. Maryknoll: Orbis Books, 1981.

Heitzenrater, Richard P. "John Wesley and the Oxford Methodists, 1725-35." Ph.D. Dissertation, Duke University, 1972.

_____. *The Elusive Mr. Wesley: John Wesley His Own Biographer.* 2 vols. Nashville: Abingdon Press, 1984.

Henderson, D. Michael. "Christian Education: Instructional Theology." In *A Contemporary Wesleyan Theology: Biblical, Systematic and Practical.* 2 vols. Edited by Charles W. Carter, R. Duane Thompson and Charles R. Wilson. Grand Rapids, Michigan: Francis Asbury Press, 1983.

Hill, Christopher. *The World Turned Upside Down: Radical Ideas during the English Revolution*. New York: Schocken Books, 1964.

Hill, Michael, and Turner, Bryan. "John Wesley and the Origin and Decline of Ascetic Devotion." In *A Sociology Yearbook of Religion in Britain—4*. Edited by Michael Hill. London: SCM Press, 1971.

Hillerbrand, Hans J. "Anabaptism and the Reformation: Another Look." *Church History* 29.4 (December 1960):404-23.

Hobsbawm, E.J. *Labouring Men: Studies in the History of Labour.* New York: Basic Books, Inc., 1964.

_____. *Identity and Empire: The Making of Modern English Society. Volume 2: 1750 to the Present Day.* New York: Pantheon Books, 1968.

Hutton, J.E. *A Short History of the Moravian Church.* London: Moravian Publication Office, 1895.

Jones, R. Tudur. *Congregationalism in England, 1662-1962.* London: Independent Press, 1962.

Källstadt, Thorvald. *John Wesley and the Bible: A Psychological Study.* Stockholm: Nya Bokförlags Aktiebolaget, 1974.

Kent, John H.S. *The Age of Disunity.* London: The Epworth Press, 1966.

Kirkham, Donald H. "Pamphlet Opposition to the Rise of Methodism." Duke University PhD. Dissertation, 1973.

Kirkpatrick, Dow, ed. *The Doctrine of the Church.* New York: Abingdon Press, 1960.

Kissack, Reginald. *Church or No Church: A Study of the development of the concept of Church in British Methodism.* London: Epworth Press, 1964.

Knappen, M.M. *Tudor Puritanism: A Chapter in the History of Idealism.* Chicago: The University of Chicago Press, 1939.

Knight, John Allan. "Aspects of Wesley's Theology after 1770." *Methodist History* 6.3 (April 1968):33-42.

Krass, Alfred C. *Evangelizing Neo-Pagan North America.* Scottdale, Pa.: Herald Press, 1982.

Laslett, Peter. *The World We Have Lost: England Before the Industrial Age.* New York: Charles Scribner's Sons, 1965.

Lee, Umphrey. *The Historical Backgrounds of Early Methodist Enthusiasm.* New York: Columbia University Press, 1931.

Lewin, Kurt. *Field Theory in Social Science.* New York: Harper, 1951.

Lewis, A.J. *Zinzendorf, The Ecumenical Pioneer: A Study in the Moravian Contribution to Christian Mission and Unity.* Philadephia: Westminster Press, 1962.

Lindström, Harald. *Wesley and Sanctification: A Study in the Doctrine of Salvation.* Stockholm: Nya Bokförlags Aktiebolaget, 1946; reprint ed., Wilmore, Kentucky: Francis Asbury Publishing Company, Inc. [1980].

Lyles, Albert M. *Methodism Mocked: The Satiric Reaction to Methodism in the Eighteenth Century.* London: The Epworth Press, 1960.

Martin, Hugh. *Puritanism and Richard Baxter.* London: SCM Press, 1954.

Matthias, Peter. *The First Industrial Nation: An Economic History of Britain 1700-1914.* 2d ed. New York: Methuen, 1983.

McAdoo, H.R. *The Structure of Caroline Moral Theology.* London: Longmans, Green and Co., 1949.

————. *The Spirit of Anglicanism: A Survey of Anglican Theological Method in the Seventeenth Century.* New York: Charles Scribner's Sons, 1965.

Meeks, Wayne A. *The First Urban Christians: The Social World of the Apostle Paul.* New Haven: Yale University Press, 1983.

Miller, Perry. *The New England Mind: The Seventeenth Century.* New York: The Macmillan Company, 1939.

Monk, Robert C. *John Wesley: His Puritan Heritage.* New York: Abingdon Press, 1966.

Moore, Robert. *Pit-Men, Preachers & Politics: The effects of Methodism in a Durham Mining Community.* Cambridge: Cambridge University Press, 1974.

Morgan, Edmund. *Visible Saints: The History of a Puritan Idea.* Ithaca: Cornell University Press, 1963.

Newton, John A. *Susanna Wesley and the Puritan Tradition in Methodism.* London: Epworth Press, 1968.

Nuttall, Geoffrey F. *The Holy Spirit in the Puritan Faith and Experience.* Oxford: Basil Blackwell, 1946.

————. ed. *Philip Doddridge 1702-51: His contribution to English Religion.* London: Independent Press Ltd., 1951.

————. *Richard Baxter and Philip Doddridge: A Study in a Tradition.* London: Oxford University Press, 1951.

————. *Visible Saints: The Congregational Way 1640-1660.* Oxford: Basil Blackwell, 1957.

Oden, Thomas C. *The Intensive Group Experience: The New Pietism.* Philadelphia: Westminster Press, 1972.

O'Halloran, James G. *Living Cells: Developing Small Christian Community.* Maryknoll: Orbis Books, 1984.

Other Side, the. Edited by Mark Olson and John F. Alexander. Published monthly by *Jubilee, Inc.*, 300 West Apsley Street, Philadelphia, Pennsylvania 19144.

Outler, Albert C., ed. *John Wesley.* Library of Protestant Thought. New York: Oxford University Press, 1964.

————. "Do Methodists have a Doctrine of the Church?" In *The Doctrine of the Church.* Edited by Dow Kirkpatrick. Nashville: Abingdon Press, 1964.

————. "The Place of Wesley in the Christian Tradition." In *The Place of Wesley in the Christian Tradition: Essays Delivered at Drew University in celebration of the commencement of the publication of the Oxford Edition of the Works of John Wesley.* Edited by Kenneth E. Rowe. Metuchen, N.Y.: The Scarecrow Press, Inc., 1976.

Packer, John W. *The Transformation of Anglicanism 1643-1660, with special reference to Henry Hammond.* Manchester: Manchester University Press, 1969.

Passmore, John. *The Perfectibility of Man.* New York: Scribner's Sons, 1970.

Pearson, A. F. Scott. *Thomas Cartwright and Elizabethan Puritanism.* Cambridge: at the University Press, 1925.

————. *Church and State: Political Aspects of Sixteenth Century Puritanism.* Cambridge: at the University Press, 1928.

Peters, Robert. "John Hales and the Synod of Dort." In *Studies in Church History*. Volume 7. Edited by G.J. Cuming and Derek Baker. Cambridge: at the University Press, 1971.

Piette, Maximin. *John Wesley in the Evolution of Protestantism*. New York: Sheed & Ward, 1937.

Pike, David. "The Religious Societies in the Church of England (1678-1723) and their influence on Early Methodism." *Proceedings of the Wesley Historical Society* 35 (1965-66):15-20, 32-38.

Porter, H.C. *Reformation and Reaction in Tudor Cambridge*. Cambridge: at the University Press, 1958.

Portus, Garnet V. *Caritas Anglicana; or, An Historical Inquiry into those Religious and Philanthropical Societies that flourished in England between the Years 1678 and 1740*. London: A.R. Mowbray & Co. Ltd., 1912.

Rack, Henry. "The Decline of the Class-Meeting and the Problems of Church-Membership in Nineteenth-Century Wesleyanism." *Proceedings of the Wesley Historical Society* 39 (1973-74):12-21.

Rigg, James H. *The Churchmanship of John Wesley, and the Relations of Wesleyan Methodism to the Church of England*. London: Wesleyan-Methodist Book-Room, 1886.

Rohr, John von. "Covenant and Assurance in Early English Puritanism." *Church History* 34.2 (June 1965):195-203.

Rogers, Carl R. *Carl Rogers on Encounter Groups*. New York: Harper & Row, 1970.

Rogers, Charles. "The Concept of Prevenient Grace in the Theology of John Wesley." Ph.D. Dissertation, Duke University, 1967.

Rudé, George. *The Crowd in History, 1730-1848*. New York: John Wiley and Sons, 1964.

_____. *Paris and London in the Eighteenth Century: Studies in Popular Protest*. New York: The Viking Press, 1973.

Ruether, Rosemary. " 'Basic Communities': Renewal at the Roots." *Christianity and Crisis* 41.14 (September 21, 1981).

Runyon, Theodore. "Wesley and the Theologies of Liberation." In *Sanctification and Liberation: Liberation Theologies in Light of the Wesleyan Tradition*. Edited by Theodore Runyon. Nashville: Abingdon Press, 1981.

Schmidt, Martin. *John Wesley: A Theological Biography*. 2 vols. Nashville: Abingdon Press, vol. 1, n.d.; vol. 2, pt.1, 1972; vol.2, pt.2, 1973.

Schutz, W.C. *FIRO: A Three-Dimensional Theory of Interpersonal Behavior*. New York: Holt, Rinehart and Winston, 1958.

Semmel, Bernard. *The Methodist Revolution* (New York: Basic Books, 1973).

Simon, John S. *John Wesley and the Religious Societies.* London: Epworth Press, 1921.

Smith, Thornley. *Memoir of the Rev. John Wesley Etheridge.* London: Hodder & Stoughton, 1871.

Snyder, Howard A. *The Radical Wesley & Patterns for Church Renewal.* Downers Grove, Illinois: InterVarsity Press, 1980.

Sojourners Magazine. Edited by Jim Wallis. Published monthly by *Sojourners,* 1321 Otis Street N.E., Washington D.C. 20017.

Spinka, Matthew. *John Amos Comenius, That Incomparable Moravian.* Chicago, Illinois: University of Chicago Press, 1943.

————. *John Hus' Concept of the Church.* Princeton, N.J.: Princeton University Press, 1966.

Strohl, Henry. *La Pensée de la Réforme.* Manuels et Précis de Théologies, vol. 32. Neuchatel: Delachaux et Niestlé S.E., 1951.

Tate, W.E. *The English Village Community and the Enclosure Movements.* London: Gollancz, 1967.

Taylor, E.R. *Methodism and Politics 1791-1851.* Cambridge: at the University Press, 1935.

Thompson, Edgar W. *Wesley: Apostolic Man. Some Reflections on Wesley's Consecration of Dr. Thomas Coke.* London: The Epworth Press, 1957.

Thompson, E.P. *The Making of the English Working Class.* New York: Vintage Books, 1966.

Tjernagel, Neelak S. *The Reformation Essays of Dr. Robert Barnes.* St. Louis: Concordia Publishing House, 1963.

————. *Henry VIII and the Lutherans: A Study in Anglo-Lutheran Relations from 1521-1547.* St. Louis: Concordia Publishing House, 1965.

Toon, Peter. *The Emergence of Hyper-Calvinism in English Nonconformity 1689-1765.* London: The Olive Tree, 1967.

Torres, Sergio, and Eagleson, John, ed. *The Challenge of Basic Christian Communities.* Papers from the International Ecumenical Congress of Theology, February 20-March 2, 1980, Sao Paulo, Brazil. Maryknoll: Orbis Books, 1981.

Towlson, Clifford W. *Moravian and Methodist: Relationships and Influences in the Eighteenth Century.* London: Epworth Press, 1957.

Townsend, Workman, and Eayrs, eds. *A New History of Methodism.* 2 vols. London: Hodder and Stoughton, 1909.

Tripp, David. *The Renewal of the Covenant in the Methodist Tradition.* London: Epworth Press, 1969.

Trinterud, Leonard. *Elizabethan Puritanism.* Library of Protestant Thought. New York: Oxford University Press, 1971.

Troeltsch, Ernst. *The Social Teaching of the Christian Churches.* 2 vols. Reprint ed., Chicago: University of Chicago Press, 1976.

Turner, Victor. *The Ritual Process: Structure and Anti-Structure.* Chicago: Aldine Publishing Co., 1969. Reprint ed., Ithaca, N.Y.: Cornell University Press, 1977.

Tuttle, Robert G., Jr. *John Wesley: His Life and Theology.* Grand Rapids, MI: Zondervan Publishing House, 1978.

Tyerman, Luke. *The Life and Times of the Rev. Samuel Wesley, M.A., Rector of Epworth, and the father of the Revs. John and Charles Wesley, the founders of the Methodists.* London: Simpkin, Marshall & Co., 1866.

Udy, Gloster S. *Key to Change.* Sydney, Australia: 1962.

Usher, Roland G. *The Presbyterian Movement in the reign of Queen Elizabeth, as illustrated by the Minute Book of the Dedham Classis.* London: Camden Society. 3d series, Volume 8, 1905.

————. *The Reconstruction of the English Church.* 2 vols. New York: Appleton and Company, 1910.

Wakefield, Gordon S. *Puritan Devotion: its place in the development of Christian Piety.* London: Epworth Press, 1957.

Wallis, Jim. *The Call to Conversion: Recovering the Gospel for These Times.* San Francisco: Harper & Row, 1981.

Walsh, John. "Origins of the Evangelical Revival." In *Essays in Modern Church History; in Memory of Norman Sykes.* Edited by G.V. Bennett & J.D. Walsh. London: Adam & Charles Black [1966].

Walsh, J.D. "Elie Halévy and the Birth of Methodism." *Transactions of the Royal Historical Society.* Fifth Series 25 (1975):20.

Ward, W.R. *Religion and Society in England 1790-1850.* New York: Schocken Books, 1973.

————. *Early Victorian Methodism: The Correspondence of Jabez Bunting 1830-1858.* University of Durham Publications. Oxford: Oxford University Press, 1976.

Warner, Wellman J. *The Wesleyan Movement in the Industrial Revolution.* London: Longmans, Green and Co., 1930.

Watkins, Owen C. *The Puritan Experience: Studies in Spiritual Autobiography.* New York: Schocken Books, 1972.

Watson, David Lowes. "Professing the Call to Serve: Vocation, Competence, and Identity in the Ministerial Office." *Quarterly Review* 2.1 (Spring 1982):27-42.

_____. "Christ Our Righteousness: The Center of Wesley's Evangelistic Message." *Perkins Journal* 37.3 (Spring 1984).

Wearmouth, Robert F. *Methodism and the Working-Class Movements of England 1800-1850.* London: Epworth Press, 1937.

_____. *Methodism and the Common People of the Eighteenth Century.* London: Epworth Press, 1945.

Wedgwood, Julia. *John Wesley and the Evangelical Reaction of the Eighteenth Century.* London: Macmillan and Co., 1870.

_____. *Wesley Historical Society, Proceedings.* 1897 & ff.

Wilks, Michael. "Reformatio Regni: Wyclif and Hus as Leaders of Religious Protest Movements." In *Schism, Heresy and Religious Protest.* Studies in Church History, Volume 9. Edited by Derek Baker. Cambridge: at the University Press, 1972.

Willey, Basil. *The Eighteenth Century Background: Studies on the Idea of Nature in the Thought of the Period.* London: Chatto & Windus, 1946.

Williams, C.H. *William Tyndale.* London: Thomas Nelson & Son, 1969.

Williams, Colin. *John Wesley's Theology Today.* Nashville, Abingdon Press, 1960.

Wilson, Bryan R. *Religion in a Secular Society.* Baltimore, Md.: Penguin Books, 1966.

_____. "Analysis of Sect Development." In *Patterns of Sectarianism: Organization and Ideology in Social and Religious Movements.* Edited by Bryan R. Wilson. London: Heinemann, 1967. pp. 24-45.

Wood, A. Harold. *Church Unity without Uniformity: A Study of Seventeenth-century English Church Movements and of Richard Baxter's Proposals for a Comprehensive Church.* London: Epworth Press, 1963.

Zuck, Lowell H., ed. *Christianity and Revolution: Radical Christian Testimonies 1520-1650.* Philadelphia: Temple University Press, 1975.

INDEX OF NAMES, PLACES AND SUBJECTS

INDEX OF AUTHORS CITED